My Cookbook PASSION

*"A room without books is like
a body without a soul"*

CICERO

Pamela Kure Grogan

My Cookbook PASSION

Culinary History and Recipe Adventure in Exploring My Personal Collection

Editor: S.P. Grogan

Photography: Barrett A. Adams

GAUDIUM

Gaudium Publishing
Las Vegas • Oxford • Palm Beach

Published in the United States of America by

Histria Books

7181 N. Hualapai Way, Ste. 130-86

Las Vegas, NV 89166 USA

HistriaBooks.com

Gaudium Publishing is an imprint of Histria Books. Titles published under the imprints of Histria Books are distributed worldwide.

All rights reserved. No part of this book may be reprinted or reproduced or utilized in any form or by any electronic, mechanical or other means, now known or hereafter invented, including photocopying and recording, or in any information storage, QMyst, or a retrieval system, without the permission in writing from the Publisher.

First Edition, First Printing

Library of Congress Control Number: 2021947864

ISBN 978-1-59211-117-6 (hardcover)

Copyright © 2021 by Pamela Kure Grogan and S.P. Grogan

CONTENTS

CHAPTER ONE
Basic Ingredients — **10**

CHAPTER TWO
Reach for the Stars... — **18**

CHAPTER THREE
Publishing Houses: Barrows — **32**

CHAPTER FOUR
More Barrows Mixed Drinks — **50**

CHAPTER FIVE
International — **62**

CHAPTER SIX
Men at Work — **70**

CHAPTER SEVEN
Inns & Farms — **84**

CHAPTER EIGHT
Publishers: Farm Journal — **104**

CHAPTER NINE
Reservations Preferred — **118**

CHAPTER TEN
Jovial Ghosts of Dining — **130**

CHAPTER ELEVEN
Super American Chefs — **150**

CHAPTER TWELVE
Bottoms Up — **162**

CHAPTER THIRTEEN
Entertainment is Fun! — **188**

CHAPTER FOURTEEN
Social Studies — **206**

CHAPTER FIFTEEN
Tradition — **222**

CHAPTER SIXTEEN
Return to the Stars — **234**

CHAPTER SEVENTEEN
Final Musings Parts One, Two & Three — **246**

Recipe Index — **270**

DEDICATION

To the ancestry of family which led me to the kitchen and taught me the tastes of the Old World; to the branches of Kure, Nemanic, Nemeth, Klobucar, Muhic, Taskay, Benco, Szedlyak-Skolka, Kovács —brave travelers seeking better futures, bringing with them their mosaic-colorful culture, especially proud of their generational heritage recipes.

To the late Chuck Williams of Williams-Sonoma who led me to my first official cookbook purchase, which led to the next, and next.

To my husband, Stephen, my special sous-chef in my personal as well as my baking life who saw my library creating not as an obsession but a work of art and who oversaw the research and editing of this book.

A special word of prayers and support to the thousands upon thousands of restaurant workers and restaurant management and food service industry employees who have borne the economic brunt of this international pandemic. My wish is for a healthy recovery where we again enter a restaurant to have that special meal.

PKG

1981
My first apartment, Willowbrook, Illinois and my first book case and first cookbooks, which included 28 instructional volumes of the Time-Life Good Cook series, published between 1978-1980 overseen by Chief Series Consultant, American cookbook author Richard Olney

Pamela Kure Grogan

CHAPTER ONE

BASIC INGREDIENTS

MY COOKBOOK PASSION

CHAPTER ONE
Basic Ingredients

Every once in a while I find myself purging cookbooks which no longer excite me, those that lost their flair. Or as they say, 'fine tuning' my collection. One such tuning occurred many years ago when I moved from the Chicago area to Las Vegas. In the move I probably sold or gave away nearly 200 cookbooks. To me, any collection must express vitality, a life force of its own. When I walk into my library I want these books to draw me in, make my fingers run across their bindings, where a title or a name ensnares me, forces me to pull out a selection and thumb through the pages.

Memories. My first serious, interactive toy. Yes, you could bake with the help of the electric light bulb inside the stove. Like a meticulous collector I held on to original box and contents, replacing what went missing over time.

MY COOKBOOK PASSION

CHAPTER ONE
Basic Ingredients

This passion came to me over time, evolving, educating. Passion, it is. Our great culinary prophet, Julia Child, once said: **"Find something your passionate about and keep tremendously interested in it."**

Two personality traits give edge to my passion: I am industrious and as a baby a gypsy, so my grandmother swore, put a curse on me, a reverse curse, that whatever happened, I would always smile, and with those ingredients my life followed.

My first memories of cooking: 4 or 5 years old and I told the babysitter I would be making Jell-O for a snack. Surprise, years later I would have a binder full of colorful collectible Jell-O advertising pamphlets.

I can recall that in the 1st Grade for my birthday my Mother offered me one of two choices, a birthday party or an Ez-Bake Oven. I chose the oven, my starting point of exploring baking. Somewhere in the storage closet is that same oven.

My first cookbook, a birthday gift, the **Better Homes & Gardens Junior Cookbook.** Out of that book my favorite recipe, fudge. Yes, that book, a little soiled from use, sits proud in my collection.

Being industrious, or because family tradition required it, I was a full time employee by the time I was 14 years old working in one of my Father's several businesses; in the summer working retail at the swimming pool store and in

the winter selling Christmas trees and decorations. In 1986 I began working as a sales associate for Williams-Sonoma store in Oakbrook, Illinois. When I first started working there my apartment held two book shelves with the entire **Time-Life Good Cook Series** (28 volumes) and several other assorted cookbooks. With Williams-Sonoma, I was a kid in the candy [kitchen equipment] store, my eyes opened wide and eager. I found the job enthusiastic because I wanted to know everything about food, amazed at all the kitchen goodies, enjoying the small talk with customers, who loved to cook & bake. Here I could converse in the same culinary language, getting to meet the restaurant people and those in the food industry who arrived at the store for book signings and cooking demonstrations: Jeremiah Towers of Star Restaurants; Lee Bailey; and Nicholas Malgieri, just to name a few.

PAMELA KURE GROGAN

CHAPTER ONE
Basic Ingredients

Helping the customers provided part of my education. As example, when a customer wanted the recipe for *Red Velvet Cake*, telling me his Mom made that cake I searched out that recipe, mailed it to him, receiving his eternal gratitude. That sort of job satisfaction kept me enthused in the work place, and must have rubbed off, since between 1986 and 1996, I trudged up the retail ladder from sales associate to lead sales to store manager.

Chuck Williams, founder of Williams-Sonoma, introduced me to collecting vintage cookbooks. I'm standing next to him second from right.

I first met Chuck Williams at a Managers Conference in Scottsdale, Arizona. At the luncheon breaks I would sit at his table and listen to his personal reminiscences in the company of James Beard or Julia Child. He knew of my novice interest in cookbooks. Shortly thereafter, Chuck Williams started me on collecting older cookbooks. The book he suggested I acquire was **Clementine in the Kitchen** by Phinneas Beck (Hastings House, 1943). With that book my interest piqued. I started searching, preferring older to new, but not passing up any chance to acquire interesting titles and recipes.

The cookbook search flourished. I would seek out book stores and many times went to antique and craft shows like those held at the Chicago O'Hare Expo Center. One time while I was there I picked up an old-time advertising pamphlet and -- voilà! – so began a sub-collection. I didn't try to make recipes from these advertising hand-outs but collected them for their colorful artistry.

Another focus occurred because of heritage. We should all look back to establish our historic family ties, understand the cultural ties that brought us to this modern time, made us what we are, how we act within civilization. Uniquely, as in my case, I think in times past, back in the Old Country, genetic turmoil mixed my bloodline as a smorgasbord of Hungarian, Slovakian, Slovenian, and with good measure, Croatian. The family name, in the mist of history, became clan 'Kure'. And today, I am an online ancestry-heritage family tree enthusiast with over 1,000 confirmed close and distant relatives.

Cooking from that heritage, with my grandparents from the Old World, I remember during Lent we would have cabbage and potato soup made with a roux with butter and flour. The browning butter smells drifted from grandma's cast iron skillet. Best part of the meal, we called it cottage cheese

CHAPTER ONE
Basic Ingredients

potica, but made with a strudel dough. That's why my family loves eating, and I can see the term 'foodie' liberally applied to us: my late parents: John and Elsie and my siblings being Debbie, Kathy, John, Randy & Bryan. I can recall that when we left the supper table we immediately started talking about the next meal in the near future.

From my recipe box

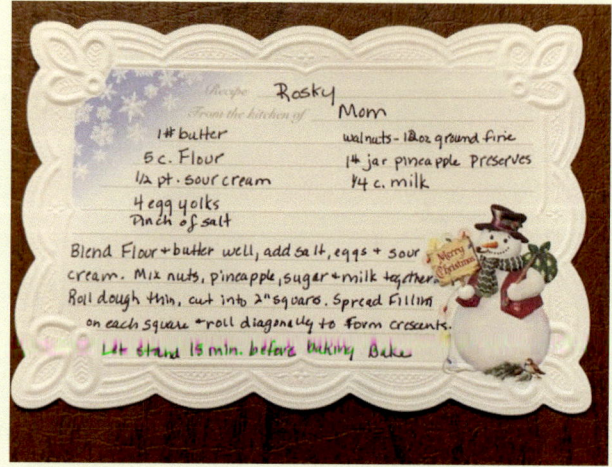

Bake 350° for 25 minutes. Dust with powdered sugar

These cookies are Old World Eastern European. My Mom wrote down what she heard—'Rosky'. Probably the reason so many Old World names were by the ear, Americanized.

Retail is not an easy business. Many retail years of unpacking shipping boxes and stacking shelves took a toll on my legs and back. By the end of 1997 I had quit work to recuperate from knee surgery. Before Williams-Sonoma I

Grandma Taskay in her kitchen

PAMELA KURE GROGAN

CHAPTER ONE
Basic Ingredients

had been enrolled at Ray Vogue School of Design, Michigan Ave, Chicago believing I would be forever designing children's clothes. To generate income I thus employed my seamstress skills and started working designing and creating christening gowns, bridesmaid and flower girl dresses. Fate fortunately intervened. My best friends, the Hopewells, asked if I wanted to move out with them to Las Vegas. Talk about lightening out of the blue sky. I had no desire to go to Las Vegas. None of my family ever ventured beyond their homestead city of Lockport, Illinois. At that time 95% of Kure families lived within a three mile radius of each other. What the heck. Facing a milestone by turning 40, I'd be adventuresome, go check it out. The Hopewells moved into an upscale suburb community called Lake Las Vegas. Not too shabby.

Making life changes is difficult. I spent Christmas in Las Vegas, my first ever away from my family. In January I made the hard decision: time to achieve something from my own talent. The best decision of my life. If you don't take the risk, unknown regret will always nag you.

My start included dress design and seamstress work with party catering on the side, looking for a full time job. While adjusting to this new world I met my future husband, Stephen. As he tells it, I was the catch for him: no baggage of previous marriages (he had a few!). I enjoyed working, no game plan for children (he showed up with two great--thankfully, grown--children), and best of all I came equipped (like a dowry) with a full pantry of cooking utensils and dishes and bookcases filled with cookbooks. (He was a catch too, but don't tell him).

One Sunday morning while at the kitchen table reading the newspaper's Help Wanted ads, I jumped, "Oh my gosh, Sur La Table is hiring'. I absolutely loved Sur La Table, the kitchen store. I never thought I'd get back into retail but I missed the people-to-people contact, talking cooking and kitchenware. Within a year I found myself the store manager—in a city with the most fabulous chefs and amazing dining experiences! Back to being that kid in the candy store! Okay, enough, let's talk cookbooks.

Diva Moment. That's me (second from the right), hard-working store manager, with master chef Julia Child. I haven't tried to collect all her books, and rather focus on ones I actually cook from. Several are signed. It's always a treat at special appearances when an author personalizes a message for you when signing their cookbook.

MY COOKBOOK PASSION

CHAPTER ONE
Basic Ingredients

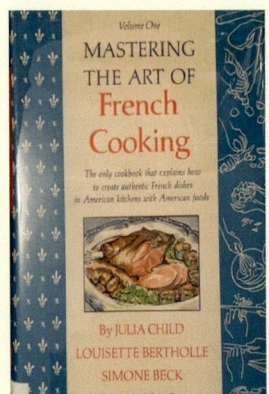
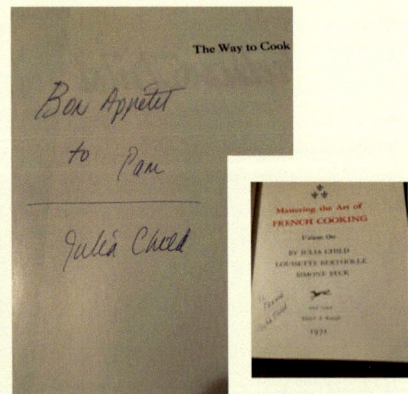

Signed Julia Child

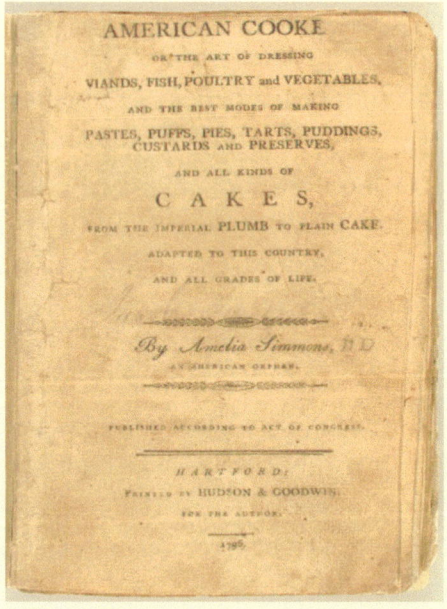

Library of Congress calls 1795 'American Cookery' one of the 'Books that shaped America'

My Criteria. Being totally honest, I don't care for the really old ones, say like, **American Cookery** by Amelia Simmons, 1796, 'an American orphan', the first genuine American cookbook (only four copies of first edition known to exist). Couldn't afford it anyway, and one should not go into debt, even if smote by passion. As I see it, for books before 1900, you need to be a history buff as well as have the extra funds to repair anticipated shabby and worn book conditions. Further, you'd need to be excited by reading 'receipts' (recipes) in stilted early American colonial language posting unintelligible ingredients. Fine, if that's your passion, go for it.

I like to cook from the books I own so basic 20th – 21st century dogma must apply. Certain cases, I might make a choice in acquisition because I like the book's cover art. My favorites are between the 1930's into the 1960's. To my way of thinking this is when a major shift in the culinary tastes of Americans was brought about by urbanization, a world at war, modern technology, and specifically women trying to define their role as co-breadwinner, struggling for self-satisfaction, yet still seeking quality and style in anything they sought to accomplish. In these three decades, as traced through a pile of past cookbooks, sociologists and anthropologists will find a treasure trove of humanistic philosophies applicable today. As we will. Yes, in old recipe books.

Sidenote: The recipes you find in these pages have been written exactly as they appear in the cookbook as first published. They have not been modernized. Try them; time will not alter great meals.

PAMELA KURE GROGAN

CHAPTER ONE
Basic Ingredients

Art of the Culinary. In the course of acquiring books for my library it is no surprise that over time art work with a culinary theme found its way into our home. Throughout this book I will draw attention to some of my favorite artistic pieces hanging in our house. Each has its own background tale to tell.

"Bon Appétit" by Ralph Cahoon (1910-1982). I spent many summers on Cape Cod in the ambiance of sea spray and smells of chowder dishes. While visiting, the art of Ralph Cahoon caught my fancy for his whimsical portrayal of mermaids. This art theme (mermaids in the kitchen painted by Cahoon in 1966) hangs in my library. Another Cahoon artwork resides in what we call our Nantucket guest room. As you'll discover, I'm going to feature several New England and seafaring recipes, for my own benefit, a little spice of nostalgia.

MY COOKBOOK PASSION

CHAPTER TWO
Reach for the Stars...

CHAPTER
TWO

REACH
FOR THE STARS

PAMELA KURE GROGAN

CHAPTER TWO
Reach for the Stars...

In our pop culture, achieving fame means a cookbook is soon to follow. For any hit television show or theatre box office smash the bookstores will soon be promoting the related glossy insider look at the stars and their so-called kitchen expertise. Usually celebrity cookbooks are ghost written and created by the Publicity Department, heavy on photos less on creative taste as they try to ride the crest of ratings popularity.

There are a few notable exceptions, those true epicure who come home from a hard day working on stage or location filming and unwind by dabbling with their own recipes. Their book and recipes reflect this sincere excitement.

To me, one of the hidden gems of celebrity cookbooks, is "Candy Hits" by actress ZaSu Pitts (1894?-1963). Compiled by Edi Horton [93 pages, Meredith Publishing Company, published in the year ZaSu died].

Candy Hits is lightly autobiographical as it gets right to the point of confectionary recipes. The opening of her book sums it up: "Many people have asked me how I happened to choose candymaking for a hobby. It really began in my childhood, and if I close my eyes, I can still see the kitchen in our Santa Cruz home, smell the fragrant odor of spice cookies baking in our old iron stove and molasses candy bubbling in the iron frying pan we called a spider." Now, that's passion.

Zasu Pitts embodied the era of early films, not a major star but always the recognizable ingénue. I like her because her talent adapted as the medium changed, from silent films to television. And every time she appeared on set location her fellow stars and the set crew were asking if she had brought them any sweet treats. Chocolate seemed to be her specialty. She wrote, "Chocolate is the devil incarnate. It not only must be treated with respect—it must be catered to and cajoled into acceptable behavior." I believe this is one of her four basic recipes she would want new found fans to appreciate:

MY COOKBOOK PASSION

CHAPTER TWO
Reach for the Stars…

Chocolate Fudge

2 cups sugar
2 one-ounce squares unsweetened chocolate
Dash of salt
1 teaspoon corn syrup
2 tablespoons butter or margarine
1 teaspoon vanilla
1/2 cup coarsely chopped nuts

ZaSu: I use a heavy two-or three-quart saucepan for this amount. It is ridiculous to use a kettle that is too small. An absent-minded candymaker can find her syrup boiling all over the range if the telephone rings or if she starts reciting the last act of The Bat. Butter the sides of the saucepan. In it combine the sugar, milk, chocolate, salt, and corn syrup. Heat and stir over medium heat till sugar dissolves and mixture comes to a boil. Clip on candy thermometer if you have one. Cook till thermometer registers 238° F. Do not stir while mixture is cooking unless necessary to keep it from sticking.

If you do not have a thermometer, you must rely on the softball test: Remove pan from heat; drop a few drops of fudge into cold water; you should be able to form the drops into a soft ball that flattens when removed from the water.

Add butter and let cool to lukewarm (110° F.) without stirring. The kettle should be cool to touch. Now add vanilla and start beating vigorously. Soon the mixture will become very thick and will start to lose its gloss. Toss in the nuts—I like toasted almonds, but walnuts are delicious, too.

You must gamble on that precise moment when your candy is about to "set up" and pour it out into a buttered shallow pan just before that critical split second arrives. You will then achieve a sheet of smooth fudge that can be cut in beautiful squares when cool.

My special variation on this method is that I pour the mixture out onto a marble slab or buttered board and knead it like dough, instead of pouring it into a pan. Then I roll it into logs, wrap it in waxed paper, and chill it. I slice it like ice-box cookies, and it is always fresh and creamy.

CHAPTER TWO
Reach for the Stars...

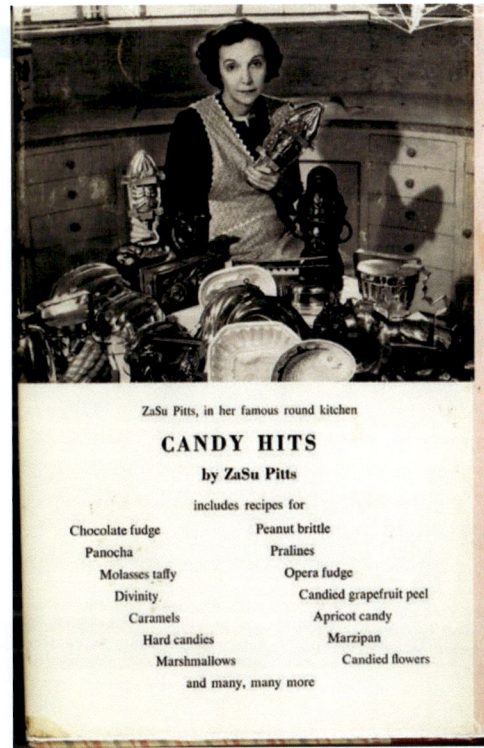

"Did you know?"
ZaSu's name is derived from two relatives, "Eliza" and "Susan". Discovered by screenwriter Frances Marion, her first film in 1917 was with screen legend Mary Pickford. Director Erich von Stroheim called her "the greatest dramatic actress" for her role in his film "Greed" but when a silly short comedy she was in preceded the release of the major silent film, "All Quiet on the Western Front", the screening audience laughed at her serious role and all her scenes were cut. Director Hal Roach saved her career by saying she was a natural born comedienne. She appeared in over 200 films and television shows. Her last film was "It's a Mad Mad Mad World" (1963), playing Gertie the switchboard operator. In 1994 she was honored with her image on a U.S. postage stamp designed by caricaturist Al Hirschfeld.

The character "Olive Oyl" in the animated cartoons of "Popeye" is based of ZaSu Pitt's voice and fidgety mannerisms.

ZaSu Pitts collected odd-shaped and antique cooking moulds. About her passion, she wrote: "All I wanted to do was to make the best candy I possibly could."

Liberace Cooks!
There was only one Liberace.
(**Liberace Cooks!** Doubleday & Company, 1970. 225 pages)

I like the book's subtitle: *"Hundreds of delicious recipes for you from his seven dining rooms"*. Only Mr. Showmanship can boast the extravagance of multiple eating rooms. Whoever cleaned them was a saint. Also, stated: "As told to Carol Truax". Here's one co-author deserving of praise. I have two of Liberace's books both signed and I'm showing here the one book that is framed on my library wall with autograph photo, circa 1985.

"Why don't I slip out and get into something more spectacular."

Liberace once taught cooking. "It was the Depression in those days. Mom was a great cook, but she had to go to work, and who was there to make the meals but me." He

MY COOKBOOK PASSION

CHAPTER TWO
Reach for the Stars...

taught cooking in high school to the football team! When they first asked him to do a television show, according to his own anecdote, he showed up thinking they wanted him to host a cooking show. Within **"Liberace Cooks!"** one can read between the lines to see that he chose dishes his Mother cooked and enjoyed, those that showed well in his Hollywood house. Color photos include a meal with Mom and Brother George and the performer proud of his TV dining room. For the passion I chose Carol Truax's words:
Most of us call it lunch, Liberace calls it breakfast. His working hours are late, from 8 p.m. to midnight, and usually even later because his audiences have a way of refusing to go home...When Liberace takes over his own kitchen, he likes to prepare for himself what he calls his "fifteen minute breakfast."

"You break two eggs into a baking dish," says Liberace, almost cover them with half-and-half, dot with butter, sprinkle with salt and pepper, and top with grated Parmesan cheese. Bake it in a moderate oven for about 8 minutes. Eat it right away," warns Liberace, "don't let it sit around and get hard."

Who wouldn't eat it right away? Add toasted English muffins and hot coffee, and it makes a breakfast fit for the king of the keyboard. Perhaps that's why so many people seem to drop in about the noon hour. In their honor, Liberace christened it brunch, adding supernumerary goodies like chopped salami, diced Swiss cheese, or a julienne of ham, tongue, or chicken.

PAMELA KURE GROGAN

CHAPTER TWO
Reach for the Stars...

Co-Author star: Carol Truax
She moved in 1920 to Colorado for her health but that never slowed her down. An active independent woman she had a career as an outstanding fine arts administrator and educator both in Colorado and New York. Even a stint as a concert promoter at the renowned Broadmoor Hotel resort in Colorado Springs. To her own credit she wrote over 20 cookbooks including **The 60 Minute Chef** (1947) [I have this book signed], **The Ladies Home Journal Cookbook** (1970), a series of *Woman's Day* cookbooks, and **All About Steam Cooking** (Doubleday, 1981). **Liberace Cooks!** by far was her most successful. And dear to my browsing heart, for many years, she operated a book store.

Liberace Cooks by Carol Truax © 1970. Book cover and excerpts used by permission of Doubleday, a division of Random House, Inc.

> "Nobody will believe in you unless you believe in yourself."

Rock 'n roll singer Little Richard wanted to be known as the Bronze Liberace.

TV Show Host and Singer Michael Douglas reminiscing on Liberace: *"Working with him was incredible. I learned so much. I was a kid starting out in -- it was 1948, and I played the first important date of my life. I was opening the show at the Empire Room of the Palmer House in Chicago, and Liberace was the star, and in between there was an act called Gower and Belle, who later became Marge and Gower Champion. Well, I have to tell you, that was quite a show. We went in for four weeks and we stayed 12. And I had two -- my two twin daughters were infants, and I remember walking with Jen to the room one night and I heard the maid say, "Somebody's cooking on this floor." And we were heating bottles and I thought it was our burner. And later on Liberace called and said, "Can you -- have you had dinner?" We said no. He said, "Come over, have dinner." He was cooking out of this double burner in the Palmer House. It was great -- the food was great, by the way."* --[From a Douglas interview on Larry King TV show. Mike Douglas produced his own cookbook.]

Many celebrity cookbooks for fans are a compilation of all-star photos and supposedly suspending reality for the moment that what you read are star favorite dishes from cherished heirloom recipes. Here are a few more:

MY COOKBOOK PASSION

CHAPTER TWO
Reach for the Stars...

I enjoy glancing at these photo-recipe pages for the nostalgia, my husband and I playing guessing games, trying to place name and face to an old time movie or early era television show, wondering where they stood in their careers that singled them out for this particular culinary honor. Fun books to play trivia.

I like the star photos within since most faces you would recognize. Ronald Reagan shows up to offer his "Corned Beef Hash in Bell Peppers". Was there a romantic recipe swap? His future first wife, Jane Wyman (they would marry in 1940 a year after this book's publication) shows off her "Frosted Cup Cakes". That probably started it all, especially any recipe that begins: 'take ¾ cup bacon fat'.

Famous Recipes by Famous People
compiled & edited by Lane Publishing (1940)

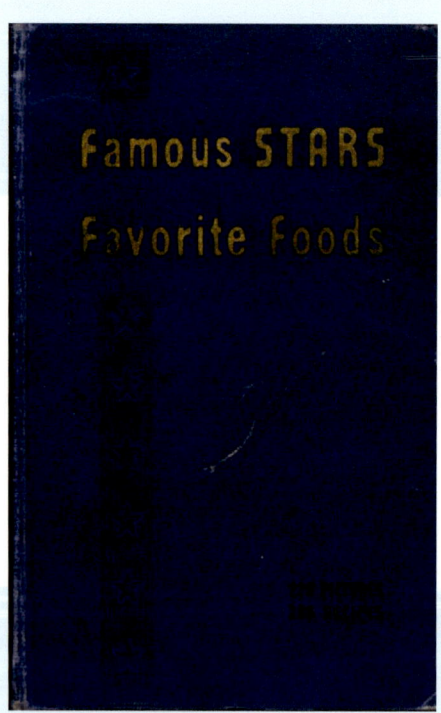

Famous Stars, Favorite Foods;
by Fannie Sniff (1938)

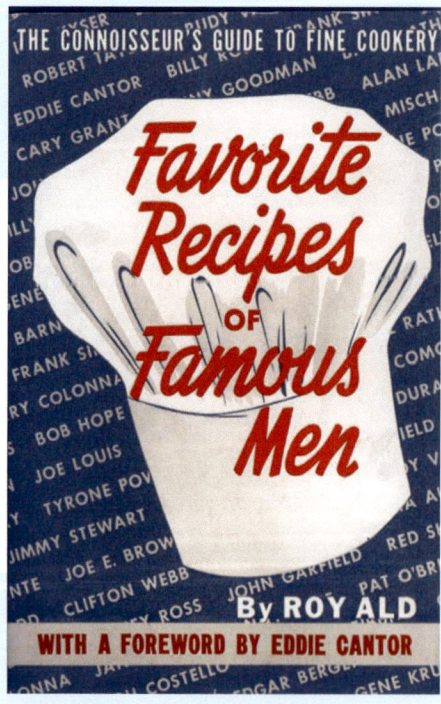

Favorite Recipes of Famous Men by Roy Ald
(foreword by Eddie Cantor) Ziff- Davis Publishing (1949)

CHAPTER TWO
Reach for the Stars...

Try one of these: Actor Robert Young offers us his *Eels in Aspic;* there's Lamb Chops *a la Danny Kaye;* Bob Hope's *Dove and Mushroom Stew;* how about Theda Bara's *Snails a La Mouquin.* Lionel Atwell starts off his *Mock Turtle,* saying, "Get a calf 's head and soak it well in cold water..."At least I'm safe with Olivia De Havilland's Baked *Carrot Ring Filled with* Peas and John Wayne tells us how he makes his old fashion rolled hamburger

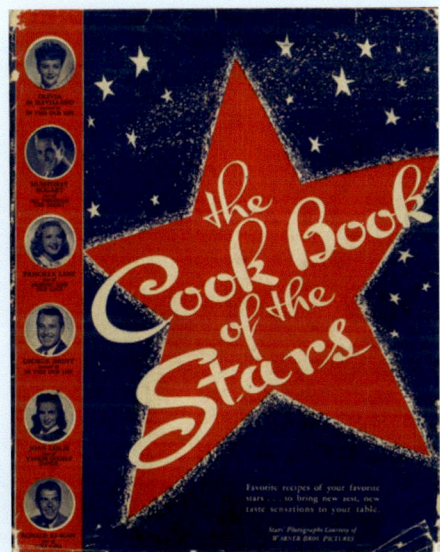

The Cook Book of the Stars
['1195 Modern Recipes'] by Helena Renaud, Windsor Editions/Grosset & Dunlap, (1939, 1941) 393 pages.

Celebrated Actor-Folk's Cookeries;
published by Mabel Rowland, Inc. (1916)

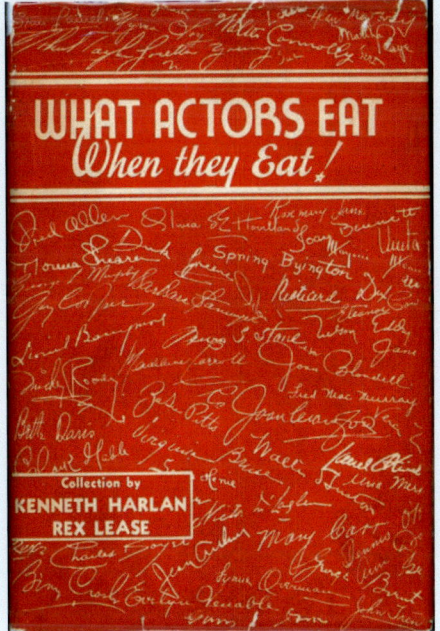

What Actors Eat--When they eat!
by Kenneth Harlan, Rex Lease Lymanhouse Publishers (1939) © by Ken-Rex Enterprises 241 pages.

MY COOKBOOK PASSION

CHAPTER TWO
Reach for the Stars...

LIONEL BARRYMORE
Metro-Goldwyn-Mayer

Born in Philadelphia, Pennsylvania, on April 28, 1878, son of Maurice and Georgia Drew Barrymore, and brother of Ethel and John. Educated at New York and Seton Hall, East Orange, N. J. Started his career in stock companies and road shows then went to Paris to study art. Returned to New York and became an illustrator for a year, then yielded to the family persuasion and returned to the stage, scoring many New York hits including "The Copperhead" and "Peter Ibetson". First appeared in pictures for D. W. Griffith in 1909, alternating this and scenario writing with stage work. Won the Academy Award in 1931 for best acting performance of year in "A Free Soul". 6 ft. tall, steel blue eyes. Weight 180 lbs. Talented pianist, composer and well known for his etchings and is a member of the Society of American Etchers. Under contract to Metro-Goldwyn-Mayer Studios.

This dish won for Alfredo, its creator, a title. I first tasted it in Alfredo's little restaurant in Rome. There its quality is improved by showmanship. A platter of what looks like very plain noodles is brought to the table. Then, while a violinist plays softly, Alfredo manipulates his golden spoon, and the clammy looking noodles change to a dish of delicate thoughtfulness. When the king tasted it, he knighted Alfredo. The house-wife can make it with Italian spaghetti or obtain the flat noodles from which fettucini is concocted, at an Italian store.

FETTUCINI ALFREDO

Boil noodles, un-broken, in as much boiling water as your largest pot will hold for twenty minutes, adding the salt when the water first starts to boil, then immersing the noodles. Have a hot platter ready. Cut butter in chunks, place hot noodles over it, bring to table, and stir in the cheese, mingling noodles, butter thoroughly. Then serve.

1½ lbs. noodles
1 teaspoon salt
½ lb. butter
3 handfuls Parmesan cheese (grated)

Of course, the housewife hasn't Alfredo's golden spoon or the violinist. But if desired, she can turn on the radio.

Lionel Barrymore

[19]

The Cook Book of the Stars is coordinated with the Warner Brothers publicity. Book actually lacks a book full of stars but offsets it with in-depth how-to prep and menu planning. Ronald Reagan touting 'Baked Peaches' and promoting "Juke Girl". Doesn't sound like that film will help his resumé if he wants to go places.

What motivation is behind a celebrity cookbook? Author Roy Ald of **Famous Men** operated a New York fitness gym and massage salon and sees his book from a health standpoint laced with humorous illustrations. **Celebrated Actor-Folks Cookeries** supports the Red Cross and The Actors Fund at the onset of World War I (artsy with powerful vaudeville, theatre and early silent film stars); Fannie Sniff, editor of **Famous Stars** is hoping the book's success will "accomplish the purposes of providing an education for my fatherless daughter, a lively hood for the two of us..." In **What Actors Eat-When they eat!** the opening titles credit twenty-two publicity studio reps, the true worker bees behind the project, behind the making of the stars, or covering up their indiscretions.

[Barrymore in **What Actors Eat,** and Bogart in **Cook Book of the Stars**]

PAMELA KURE GROGAN

CHAPTER TWO
Reach for the Stars...

Bogie's Manhattan Clam Chowder

Sauté 2 onions, minced, 1/4 cup chopped celery and 1/2 green pepper, minced, in 2 tablespoons butter. Add 2 cups diced potatoes, 3 cups boiling water and cook 15 minutes or until potatoes are soft. Heat to boiling 1 pint fresh clams with their liquor, 2 cups canned tomatoes and a dash of thyme. Add to potato mixture seasoning to taste. Serve with hard crackers. Approximate yield: 6 portions.

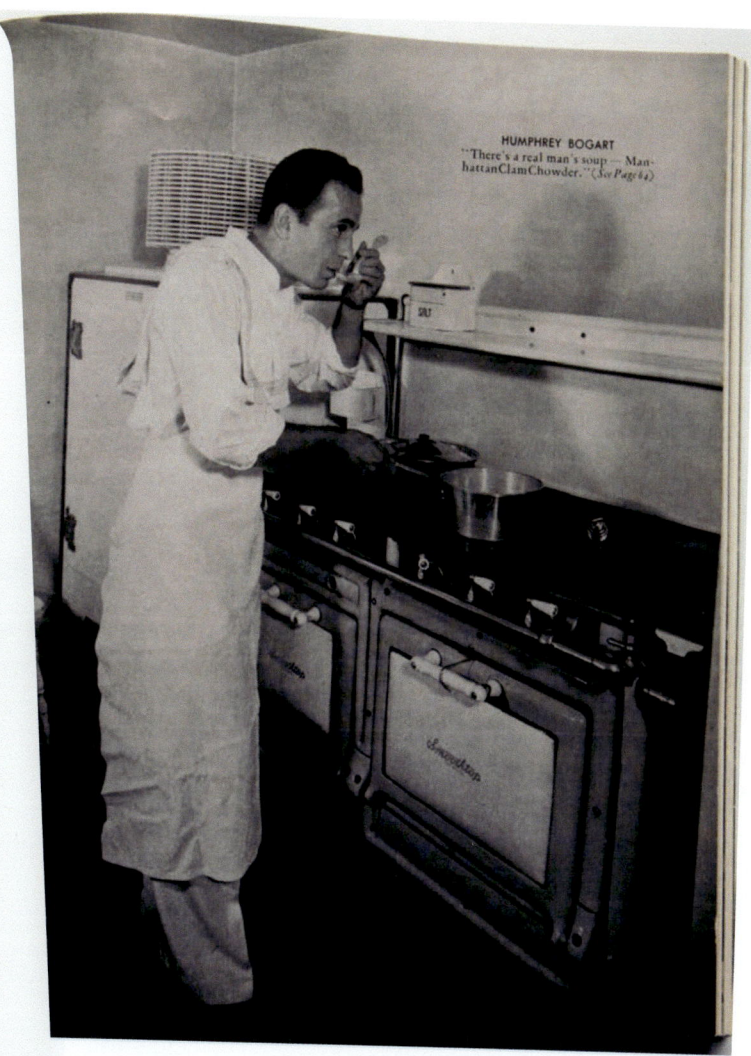

Actor Humphrey Bogart-- 'Bogey' (1899-1957) Won Academy Award for "African Queen". In 1999, American Film Institute selected Bogart as the top of 25 male film legends of classic American cinema

MY COOKBOOK PASSION

CHAPTER TWO
Reach for the Stars...

When a Star is a Galaxy

Why haven't they made a movie about this woman?! Corinne Griffith (1895- 1979): Her *passion* was not a word but a life style. What can you say about a woman that was considered the most beautiful woman on the silent screen, who acted as director on many of her own films; where her voice was insured for $1 million and yet her voice, when talkies arrived, spelled the end of her career; that when she went into court for divorce from her fourth husband, she denied who she was, saying she was Corinne's sister, that Corinne had died (against several friends testimony to the contrary). A smart businesswoman in real estate reputed to be worth over $150 million at the time of her death.

And finally, whose cookbooks are a good society read: she admits she can't cook but "I love to eat". In **I Can't Boil Water** we got the inside scoops of the era's restaurants (Trader Vic's, The Colony, The Senate Dining Room, even The Betty Crocker Dining Room) with tidbit stories about her culinary travels, meeting along the way the who's who of her rolodex. I read with surprise her journey to *The Red Fox Tavern*, Middleburg, Virginia where she met at lunch a direct descendent of Robert E. Lee who gave her a 19th century oil painting of Thomas Jefferson. "Mrs. Jacqueline Kennedy, in riding clothes, was just leaving." Talk about coincidence of mutual passions: just last summer Stephen and I had lunch at the Red Fox Tavern while he was in pursuit of one his famous authors for his own first edition collection, best seller and ex-jockey, Dick Francis, who was visiting the National Sporting Library (a must-see visit). I distinctly recall lunch: Red Fox Tavern's Peanut Soup, Baked Brie in

Corinne Griffith

Puff Pastry, Shrimp and Asparagus Salad, and their house specialty, Crab Cakes.

CHAPTER TWO
Reach for the Stars...

Lily of the Cookery Field

So, here's Corinne's 1963 recipe (Red Fox Tavern's) for:

Virginia Fruit Muffins

5 dried figs, chopped
1 tbsp. honey
1 tsp. grated orange rind
1/3 cup peanut butter
1 tbsp. orange juice
English muffins, split
sliced almonds

Add figs, orange rind, juice to peanut butter, mixing well. Spread over cut sides of muffins. Sprinkle with almonds. Broil until bubbly.

I Can't Boil Water by Corinne Griffith. Published by Julian Messner, New York. 1963. 140 pages. Signed.

MY COOKBOOK PASSION

CHAPTER TWO
Reach for the Stars...

Almond Marron Mousse

1 1/2 cups blanched almonds
1 teaspoon vanilla
1/4 cup sugar
1 1/2 pints whipping cream
2 bottles marrons [chestnuts]

Chop almonds. Caramelize sugar in a heavy skillet. Add almonds and brown. Pour into mold while hot. Whip cream and sweeten to taste. Add vanilla.

Cut marrons fine. Add to cream. Pour into mold over caramelized almonds. Place in deep freeze or pack in ice and salt for 4 hours. Very good.

[Today, versions of this are known as Marrons Glacé (candied chestnuts). Recipe from Corrine's Eggs I Have Known]

"Eggs I Have Known", Corinne's first travel book with recipes, sets out her culinary goal: 'to gather recipes wherever I go..." How can you not want to read the start of each chapter, when one begins, *"One day, late in spring, I was driven through the woods of the Bois at the outskirts of Paris to the edge of Versailles and the chateau of Sir Charles and Lady Mendl—Elsie de Wolf."* Where on her travels she asks recipes of every famous person she dines with; including a recipe from Cole Porter, that's the night she's partying with him and Elsa Maxwell, and Cole asks 'what is that dance?' 'This is the Beguine' Elsa explains and fascinated he has the first line of music written by the end of the evening, "When you be- gin the Beg- uine." Name dropping a few of those who sweep through her book: Mrs. Evalyn Walsh McLean (the Hope Diamond owner supplying her caviar omelette recipe), the Prince of Wales (with Mrs. Wallace Simpson in the background), picnic lunch with William Randolph Hearst and Marion Davies at San Simeon. What more can you ask for: elegant dining 'of fine and unusual food' with interesting people.

CHAPTER TWO
Reach for the Stars...

Did you know?

Less than ten of Corinne's sixty-six films survive today. She wrote eleven books. Her third marriage, 1936-1958, was to George Preston Marshall, the owner of the Washington Redskins football team. She wrote the best selling book, **"My Life With the Redskins"** (1947). At the end of that marriage, in **"Eggs I Have Known"** she referred to him as "Marshall without a plan". The joke: the Marshall Plan, being a billion-dollar foreign aid package for post-war Europe. Her successful book, **"Papa's Delicate Condition",** turned into a film vehicle for actor Jackie Gleason. Come on, Hollywood, why doesn't someone make a movie about this fascinating lady.

Eggs I Have Known by Corinne Griffith. Published by Farrar Strauss & Cudahy, New York, 1955.

CHAPTER THREE
Publishing Houses: Barrows

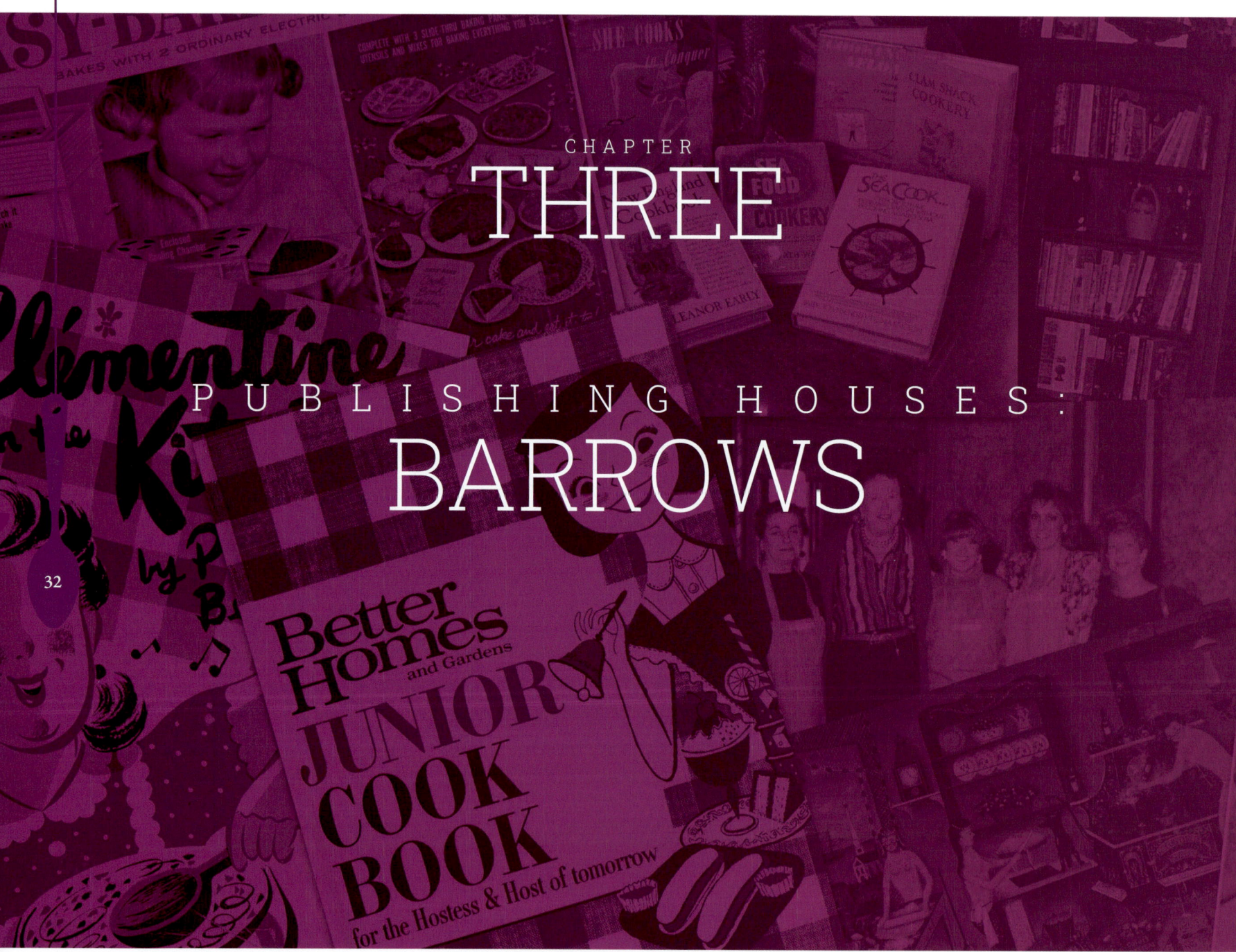

PAMELA KURE GROGAN

CHAPTER THREE
Publishing Houses: Barrows

"Cook-books have always intrigued and seduced me. When I was still a dilettante in the kitchen they held my attention, even the dull ones, from cover to cover, the way crime and murder stories did."
The Alice B. Toklas Cook Book (1954)

Funny how one thing leads to another. Several years back I'm in a bookstore in Burbank, Illinois that specialized in cookbooks and I fall in love with this little book, **"Macaroni Manual"**. What attracts me is the simplicity of the cover and the novelty of the subject matter covered in those times (1947), not pasta, but as macaroni. Some time later I am browsing Toad Hall Books and Records in Rockford, Illinois when I stumbled across **"Pies -a Plenty"** and noticed that the publisher, M. Barrows & Company, New York, is the same for the "Macaroni Manual". On the back cover is a list of other books published by Barrows, all interesting titles, and several of which I had purchased earlier not realizing the publisher the same. Never allow a passionate collector a list to check off.

Now when I entered a bookstore or looked on- line I held my wish list in hand and after the years all titles were scratched off except one book. Once again, husband Stephen surprised me with a holiday gift, **"Soups, Stews & Chowder"**, and my list completed to my satisfaction, with over 85 Barrows books on the shelves. M. Barrows & Company, New York, went into business in 1904 and disappeared from the scene in the late 1960's. I don't know what happened. I sense their styling of books did not 'modernize' to today's color gloss. In the time period I focused on, the 1930's and 1940's, their books dealt with specific niche topics. I could not envision many copies sold and am guessing marginal sales did them in.

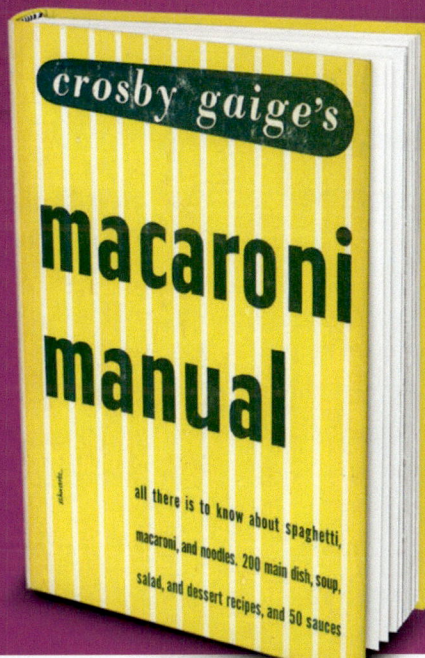

One of the more interesting authors of the bon vivant was Crosby Gaige who enjoyed life as a theatrical producer, a private publisher to many literary intelligentsia of the day. Crosby served as President of the New York Wine & Food Society (a founder of the International society), and owned a massive cookbook collection in his own right. A regular to the swank nightclubs and elegant lounges, one of his books deserves a special read: **Dining with My Friends: Adventures with Epicures** (Crown, NY, 1949). See pages 51, 53, 75.

CHAPTER THREE
Publishing Houses: Barrows

Further on, we'll run across a few more of the books he authored. From Crosby Gaige's Manual:

Macaroni À La Chef Lugot
This recipe is a classic and will please everyone.
8 ounces macaroni, 3 ounces freshly grated Parmesan cheese, 1/4 pound good fresh butter, 3 ounces freshly grated Gruyére cheese, 1/8 teaspoon grated nutmeg

Cook the macaroni in rapidly boiling salted water until tender. Drain and rinse. Put the macaroni in a chafing dish or hot casserole, and bring to the table. Then add the butter, grated nutmeg, Parmesan and Gruyère cheese, and mix well. Serves six.

Better known for her 1936 semi-autobiographical, **The Country Kitchen**, about rural life in Michigan, Della Lute's earlier book of **Bridge Food for Bridge Fans** (shown here) revealed marketing savvy catching the fad of bridge playing then in vogue. A lot of her chapters start like "Odd Tricks...for After bridge Tea".

Della Lutes (1872-1942) launched her career in writing for and editing various magazines that were marketed to women, and in 1924 she started writing about food. The Great Depression caused the magazine she worked for to go bankrupt and she shifted into freelance as a food writer. She frequently published in magazines such as *Reader's Digest*, *the Atlantic Monthly*, *American Mercury*, and *Woman's Day*. Her columns were often compiled in book form and her writing often lyrical and whimsical. From "**Bridge Food**":

The "Opening Hand" is the theme song for the menus on this page. Properly interpreted, this means that you are leading through weakness...

New Shrimp Wiggle on Toast Points Sweet Pickle Olives, Orange Cream Sherbet, Rolled Sugar Cookies Coffee

- This doesn't mean a new wiggle. It simply means "fresh" shrimps to use in the wiggle, and goodness knows why we didn't say so, except that it sort of goes against one to think of a "fresh shrimp." Shrimps we have known have been rather modest and retiring.

- This means that, (a) you roll out the dough for the cookies; (b) you roll the cookies in sugar; (c) that instead of passing the cookies you roll them. This causes what is known as divertissement.

PAMELA KURE GROGAN

CHAPTER THREE
Publishing Houses: Barrows

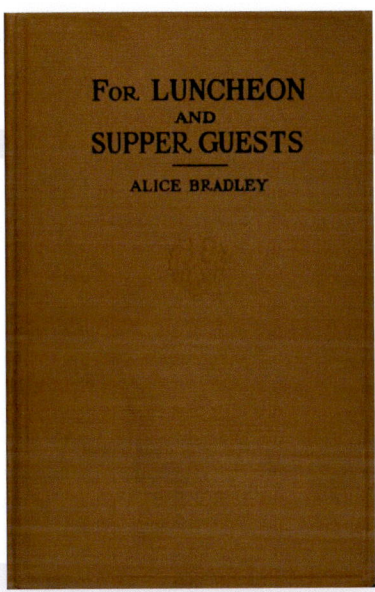

For Luncheon and Supper Guests
by Alice Bradley Copyright 1922, 1933 edition

Ms. Bradley lists herself as "Principal of Miss Farmer's School of Cookery, Author of **'Desserts'**, **'The Candy Cook Book'** and **'Cooking For Profit: Catering and Food Service Management'**." Another book, **Electric Refrigerator Menus and Recipes-- Recipes Prepared Especially for the General Electric Refrigerator** (1927) commissioned by General Electric as the first 'how-to' use your electric refrigerator.

Stina, the Story of a Cook – Kitchens, Near and Far
by Herman Smith (1942) and (1944)

Both are nostalgic remembrances, one of childhood **(Stina)**, the other **(Kitchens)** of childhood and world travel, each with compelling narrative and recipes to match. Here, two cookbooks achieve literary prose worthy of great literature but are mislabeled into oblivion. Cookbooks can be inspiring and like these, they can be quite moving.

"A relative of 'the lady who did the wash', Stina had come to our house in the late 'seventies—long before I was born. Where she came from exactly I never knew, save that it was from *un beau village* in Alsace-Lorraine. Her mother was French, her father German, and she had lost a husband and son in the Franco-Prussian War. She had starved through the siege of Paris, where she had been a refugee, and this gave her, I am sure, her extraordinarily deep and reverent attitude toward food... A despot she was—not always amiable—but a cook whom I know now to have been deserving of *cordon bleu*. She slept in a small cold immaculate chamber not far from mine, but all her waking hours were spent in the kitchen which was her pride."

MY COOKBOOK PASSION

CHAPTER THREE
Publishing Houses: Barrows

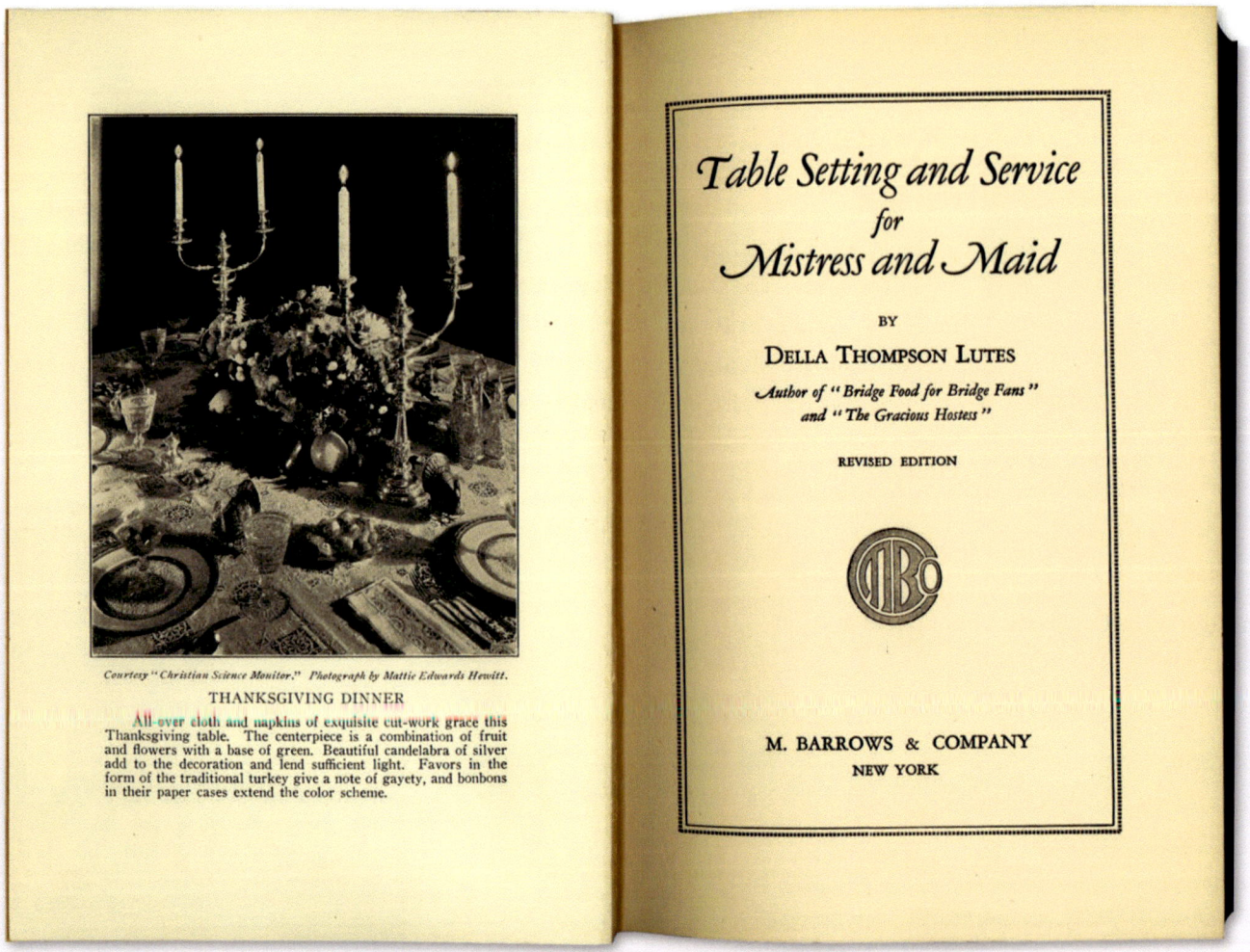

Copyright 1928, Revised 1934. Another book by the prolific magazine writer Della Thompson Lutes. She wrote " **Gracious Hostess**" (1923), and "**A Book of Menus & Recipes**" (1936) not to be confused with the soft cover, "**The Presto Book of Menus and Recipes**" (early 1920's), a how-to on home canning when she was Housekeeping Editor of *Modern Priscilla Magazine*.

CHAPTER THREE
Publishing Houses: Barrows

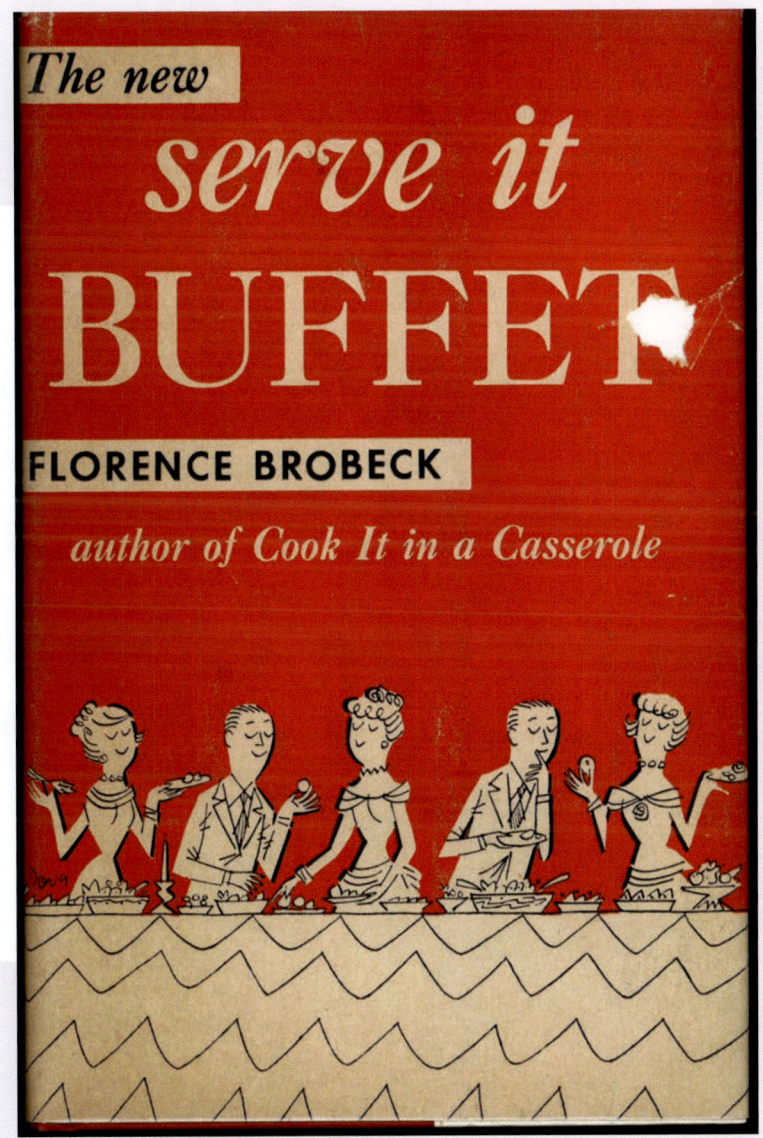

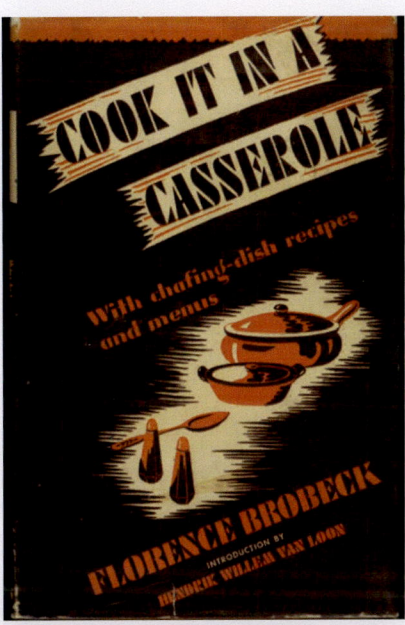

Go With The Flo

All these Barrows published books were authored by Florence Brobeck (1895-1979). She edited the women's pages of *The New York Herald Tribune* during the 1940's and prior to that wrote a weekly column, 1936 and 1937, for the *New York Times Magazine*. She wrote for *McCall's* magazine as an associate editor, and as a free lance writer contributed to *Good Housekeeping*, *Town and Country* and the *New Yorker*. In 1948 after living for a time in Sweden she published **"Scandinavian Cookery for Americans**." During her career she penned, not counting magazine articles, approximately twenty cooking and entertaining books. We'll see more of her works on the next page and later.

CHAPTER THREE
Publishing Houses: Barrows

It was typical stereotyping that, pre mass social media, before the world of television, the public of yesteryear envisioned cooking personalities of the day where men were the gracious bon vivants of wine and epicurean delights who followed dinner with brandy and cigars, wherein women, if very talented, became graduates of 'domestic science'. We sometimes look down on that vocation as being old fashioned, even a prepubescent required school class. Hardly the real truth behind the-scenes. From the 1900's to the beginning of the 1950's women in the industrial and educational kitchens were at the forefront of experimenting with food preparation to make meals easy and simple for the housewife as women moved into the work place and became more independent, yet maintaining the feminine touch when entertaining.

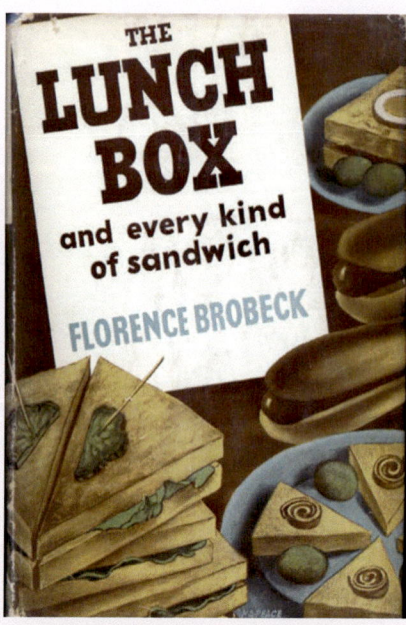
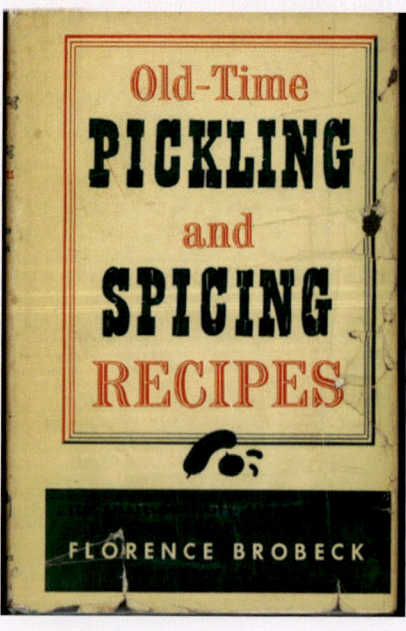

PAMELA KURE GROGAN

CHAPTER THREE
Publishing Houses: Barrows

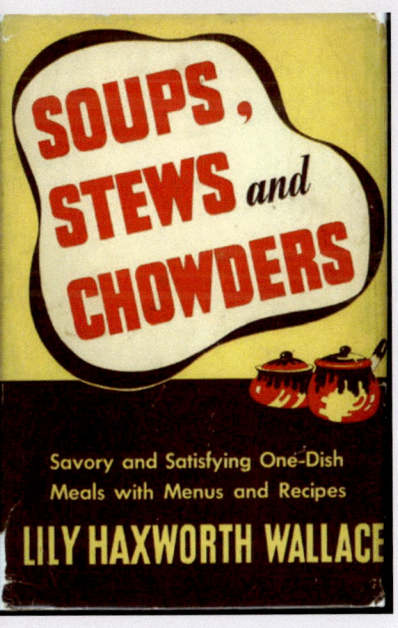

Lily of the Cookery Field

Here is one such author. Lily Haxworth Wallace (1870-1953) was born in England and graduated from the National Training College of Cookery of London. She was national president of the Associated Clubs of Domestic Science and Chairman of Homemaking in the Department of the American Home of the New York City Federation of Women's Clubs. Whew! For sixteen years she was homemaking editor of "Woman's World" and worked with the Household Arts Department of the Ballard School. Sounds like paid- your-dues credentials. All Lily's books seen above demonstrate a wide range of true scope of culinary knowledge. No mere kitchen domestic!

CHAPTER THREE
Publishing Houses: Barrows

Beginning Beard

One of the crazes of the post Depression late 1930's was the cocktail party circuit. When he did not succeed as an actor on his arrival in New York in 1937 James Beard (1903- 1985) opened a catering company known as Hors D'Oeuvre, Inc. Rationing in World War II (see 'War Years' next) ended this business but he bounced back in 1946 when a fledgling television network NBC asked him to host a weekly show called "I Love To Eat" and from then on until his death he gained the reputation and accolades to be considered

the 'Father of American Gastronomy'. What I point out is his first (1940) and his second (1941) cookbooks were published by Barrows. Also known as 'Dean of American Cookery', after his death and led by a call from Julia Child, fostered by cooking school founder Peter Krump, led to the establishment in 1986 of the James Beard Foundation 'to provide a center for the culinary arts and to continue to foster the interests James Beard inspired in all aspects of food, its preparation, and of course, enjoyment'.

CHAPTER THREE
Publishing Houses: Barrows

War Years

Here are examples on how Barrows Publishers contributed to the World War II effort. For the culinary trade during these 'save democracy' years the key words for shoppers and food preparers were 'self sacrifice'. It is important to gain the feeling of this era when violent history directly affected our parents and grandparents with valid concerns for the future.

This tribulation felt by all arrived right after Americans were surviving the Great Depression. Talk about daunting challenges we barely face today.

Both books were printed in 1942 during months the war went badly against the Allies. Author Harriet Hester of **"300 Sugar Savings Recipes"** sets the tone: *"This book is joyfully dedicated to every American housewife who is all out for victory on her own home front. We have a double problem now that America is at war: we must guard and build the health of our families; at the same time we must do our part to conserve those foodstuffs and materials of which there may be a scarcity, or which are needed for our armed forces."*

The Great Oscar Dinner
Excerpt from "Gourmet Dinners"

"In the Grand Ballroom of the Waldorf-Astoria Hotel, more than eleven hundred guests gathered on October 7, 1937, to pay tribute to Oscar Tschirky—better known as Oscar of the Waldorf—and to Mrs. Tschirky, on the occasion of their golden wedding anniversary.

"The affair was as impressive as any dinner which it has been my good fortune to attend, ever since the launching of my daily newspaper column made of me somewhat of a professional banquet chairman... Members of the dinner judges included: Major Edward Bowes, Messmore Kendall, Crosby Gaige [remember him?], Richardson Wright; two chefs of outstanding ability, Gabriel Lugo and Charles Scotto...

"The wedding cake [conceived by Joseph Fleuriot, one of the world's greatest pastry chefs] weighed one hundred pounds and was fifty inches high. It was surmounted by a golden bell, made of sugar, and was decorated with gold leaves and ribbons." Next page, here is the menu for that dinner with paired wines:

MY COOKBOOK PASSION

CHAPTER THREE
Publishing Houses: Barrows

The Menu for Buffet russe

Dubonnet London Club Amontillado
Fino Imperial Amontillado

Clear Turtle Soup
Imperial Amontillado

Olives Pecans Celery

Brook Trout Gourmet
Cucumbers, Sour Cream Dressing
Wurzburger Slyvaner Riesling 1935
Kirsch Sherbet

Gray Legged Partridge Roasted Wild Rice
Currant Jelly Original Waldorf Salad
Musigny, Estate, Comte Georges de Vogue 1930

Golden Anniversary Cake Fruit
Champagne (choice of 12 brands)

Courvoisier, 50 years old

CHAPTER THREE
Publishing Houses: Barrows

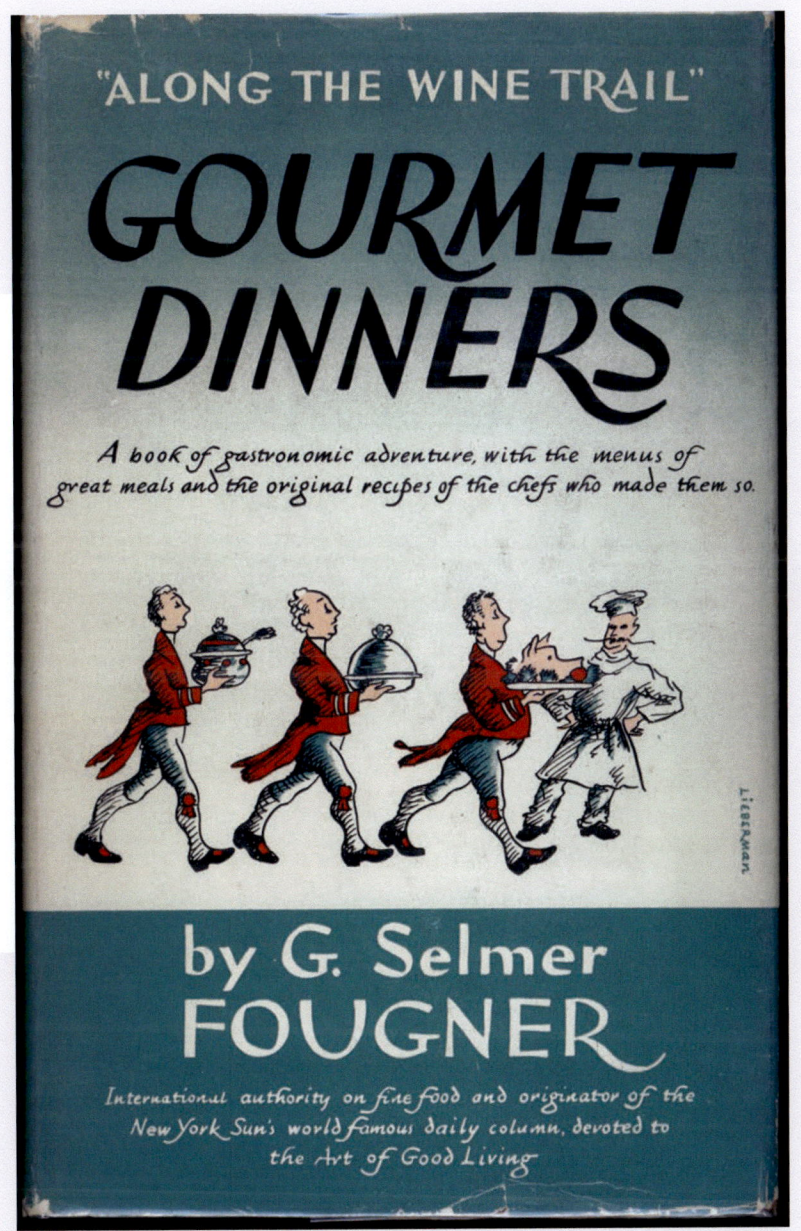

Brook Trout Gourmet
Colorado brook trout of one-half pound each, well cleaned and boned entirely, stuffed with a combination of chopped spinach, little shallots, a little well cooked rice, all passed in hot butter and well seasoned. Roll the brook trout in light cream and a little flour, fry slowly in hot butter on both sides. Remove, put two slices of lemon on top, season, add chopped parsley and finish with light browned sweet butter having an addition of anchovy. —One of my favorites from Fougner's book.

[See preceding page] G. Selmer Fougner wrote "Along the Wine Trail" column in the *New York Sun*. In the 1930's he would ask readers for a 'cocktail call' to send him their variations of cocktails of the day and would receive hundreds of responses. He founded no less than 14 epicurean societies, notably the famed "Les Amis d'Escoffier." (See Menu next page) This book, **Gourmet Dinners** published in 1941, the year of his death at 56.

Collector's Corner
In writing this book I reviewed in more detail what I had acquired over time and realized that years ago I bought a book because I liked its styling or perhaps for the recipes inside, not with any long-term economic plan to someday have my catalogued collection dispersed in a spectacular affair at Sotheby's or Christie's auction houses. Back then I did not buy with my Collector Criteria in mind, that is, in part to hold for appreciative value. Books thus acquired might be the 25th printing or with a dust jacket torn. Putting the book into my hands remains the primary goal.

CHAPTER THREE
Publishing Houses: Barrows

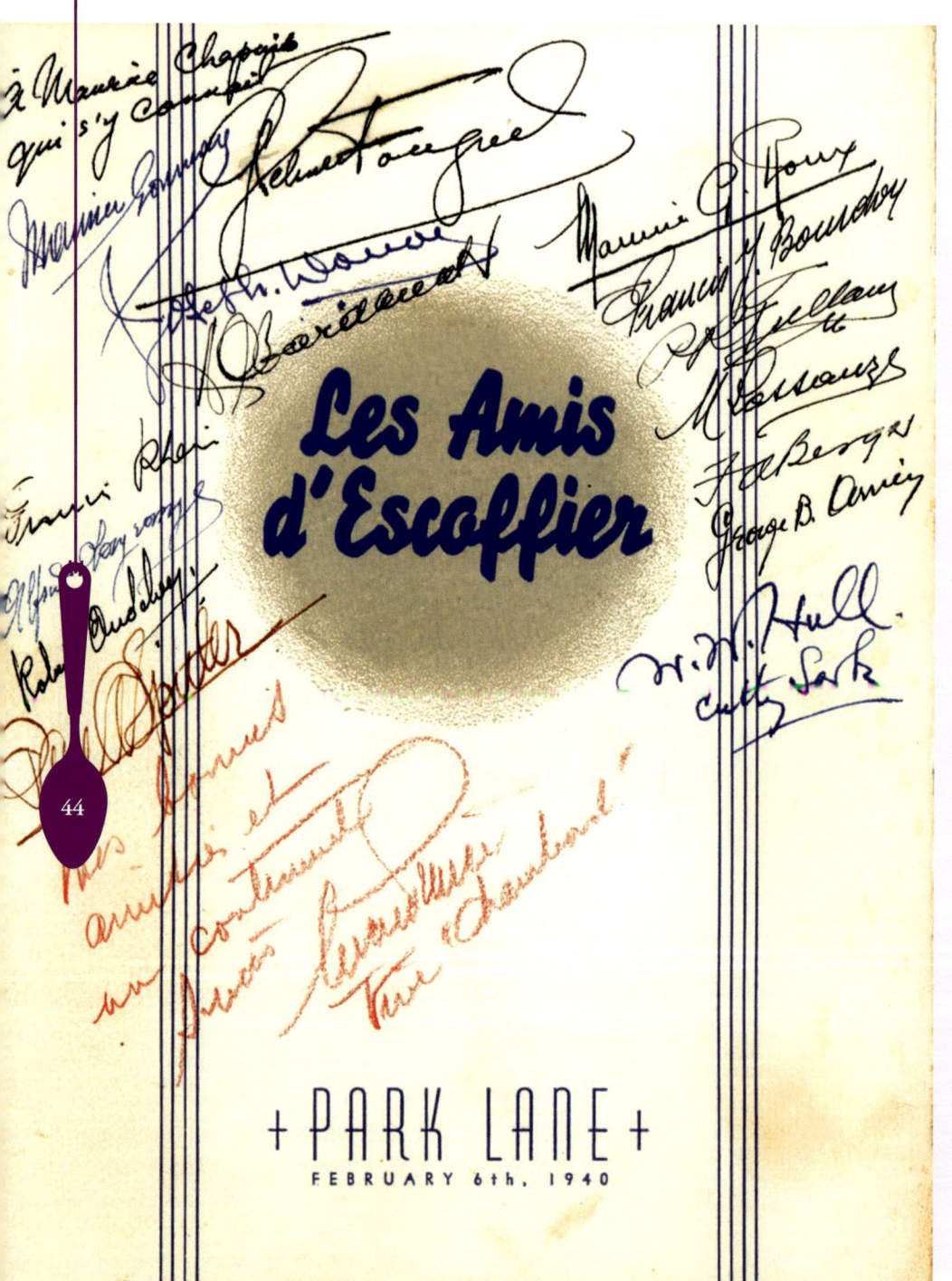

Nowadays, whenever possible I seek quality upgrades. In recent months I've been surprised these older books can be discovered, many at reasonable prices, though dust jackets in good condition are more elusive. Book club editions abound (don't collect). Pages in time face yellowing and go brittle. To always achieve the best the search is never-ending; that's what makes the hunt fun. If you just want to simply enjoy the book in hand, going for the tasting of untried recipes that is totally acceptable. Forget buy-sell values and be satisfied with a 25th edition. After all, the recipes are the same and possibly in later published editions the language of preparation might be modernized.

In 1936 the American Culinary Federation gathered at the Waldorf Astoria to form an epicurean society based 'to bring together members of the culinary profession and loyal friends who appreciate good food and good wines…who believe the adage, 'Live and let live'. The society named The Friends of Escoffier," as a tribute to Auguste Escoffier (1846-1935), who had recently passed away and was considered at the time as the 'King of Chefs'. Les Amis d'Escoffier Society Foundation, is still active today with city chapters around the country.

"Les Amis D'Escoffier" Dinner at the New York Park Lane, February 6th, 1940. Signed Menu by many of the participants.

PAMELA KURE GROGAN

CHAPTER THREE
Publishing Houses: Barrows

MAURICE GONNEAU Chef des Cuisines

The "Les Amis d'Escoffier" Society is not merely a society of "bon vivants" and epicures, but also a meeting of kindred spirits. Members must cultivate true good-fellowship, the tradition of witty repartees without fear of ridiculous aloofness...
Examples of the 'Rules':

- Persons under the influence of liquor will not be permitted to sit at the table.

- The napkin MUST be worn tucked in the collar.

- Needless to say, smoking will be absolutely forbidden up to the time dessert is served. A person who smokes while eating does not deserve the title of "gourmet".

- There will be no speeches.

Byrrh *** Vermouth *** Dubonnet *** Sherry

Le Menu

Moselle — La Délice Park Lane

Le Homard à la Française
Le Potage Renaissance

Bordeaux
Le Coeur de Pintadon Fougner
Les Pommes de Terre Olivette
Le Céleri Braisé Colbert

Les Fromages
La Salade du Chef

Champagne
La Bombe Nougatine
Le Panier de Friandises

Cognac — Le Café — Cigares

MY COOKBOOK PASSION

CHAPTER THREE
Publishing Houses: Barrows

From my collection here are a few more titles from **Barrows Publishers** demonstrating a range targeting the then reader interest, from cocktail suppers to table setting tips to feeding invalids. Not the best-selling subject matter of today. Publishers in these times must take major economic risks to what the reading public will find worthy to purchase. That is why you see publishers leaning towards the tried and true safety of cookbooks penned (supposedly) by recognized celebrities and/or food television stars with established fan followers. I own a sizable number of present day cookbooks and make my purchase leaning towards the joy of trying new dishes, while full page color succulent food photos may be enough of a teaser for many. My selections of what I consider the best of today's cookbooks may appear in a future 'Cookbook Passion' review presentation. Meanwhile, what I am attempting to emphasize here is: 'the Past is Prologue'.

Spaghetti Ring

8 ounces spaghetti
1 cup milk or cream,
1 cup soft bread crumbs
1 cup cheese, grated
1/4 cup melted butter
1 pimiento, chopped scalded
1 onion, chopped
3 eggs
Salt and pepper

Break spaghetti in small pieces, cook about eight minutes, and drain. Soak bread crumbs in milk. Stir in well-beaten eggs and remaining ingredients. Season to taste. Turn into buttered ring mold and set in pan of hot water and bake at 350° F. for thirty minutes, or until mixture is solid like custard.
Charlotte Adams

CHAPTER THREE
Publishing Houses: Barrows

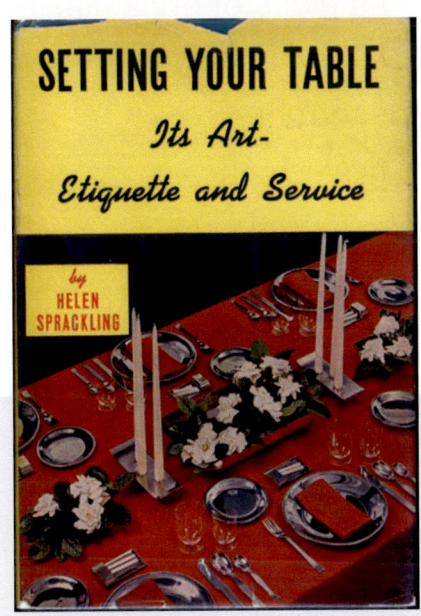

MY COOKBOOK PASSION

CHAPTER THREE
Publishing Houses: Barrows

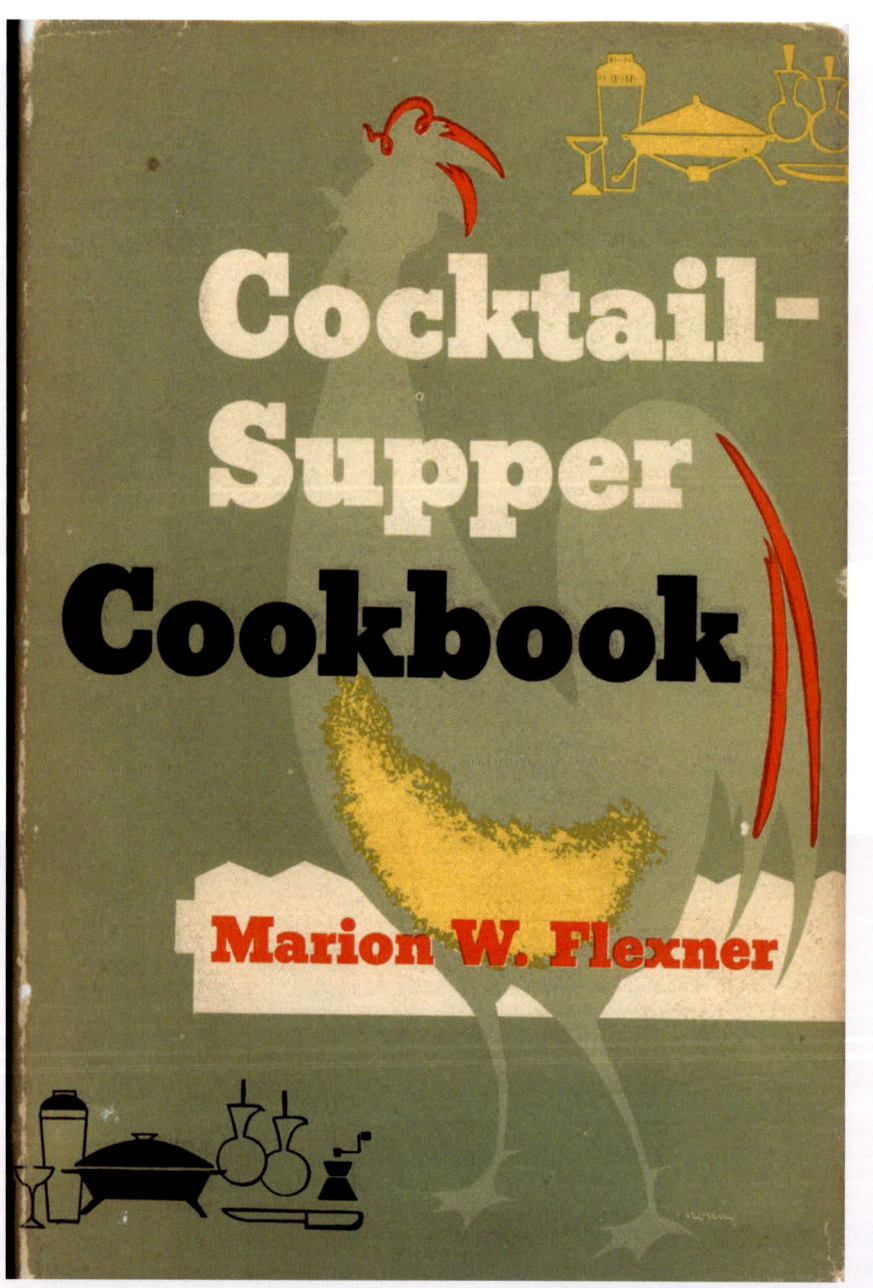

Signed by Author

Hawaiian Pineapple Pickle (6 servings)

In Hawaii, where I first tasted this wonderful relish, it was sometimes colored green, sometimes red. But always thoroughly chilled and delicious. My thanks to Patricia Collier of Dole Pineapple for letting me include this recipe.

No. 2 or 2 1/2 can pineapple Chunks in heavy syrup
3/4 cup cider vinegar
1 to 1 1/4 cups sugar
6 whole allspice berries
6 whole cloves
6-inch piece of stick cinnamon
1/2 teaspoon powdered coriander seeds (optional)
Few grains salt
Green or red vegetable coloring

Drain pineapple, reserving ¾ cup syrup. Put all ingredients (except pineapple chunks and coloring). In a saucepan and cook 10 minutes. Add drained pineapple, bring to hard boil. Skim if necessary.

Remove from heat, add coloring to your liking. Cool, place in a jar, cover and refrigerate. Do not serve for at least 24 hours—it's even better after several days. Marion W. Flexner

CHAPTER THREE
Publishing Houses: Barrows

MY COOKBOOK PASSION

CHAPTER FOUR
More Barrows -- Mixed Drinks

CHAPTER FOUR

MORE BARROWS
MIXED DRINKS & TASTE BUDDIES

MY COOKBOOK PASSION

CHAPTER FOUR
More Barrows -- Mixed Drinks

"All I want is the best of everything and there's very little of that left."
Lucius Beebe

So here again is bon vivant Crosby Gaige with two of his cocktail books, one of them with the Forward written by Lucius Beebe, the famed journalist and raconteur, and I'll let Mr. Beebe put us in the right frame of mind: *"It is only fitting that the subject of cocktails should be approached with levity slightly tinctured with contempt because, for every good compound arrangement, or synthesis of liquors, wines, and their adjacent or opposite fruits and flavors chilled and served in a variety of glasses, there are approximately a million foul, terrifying, and horrendous similar excitements to stupefaction, cuspidor-hurling, and nausea. Some of the most maligned cocktails, exist in superior redactions which would cause their detractors to stand happily corrected, and later fall on their faces in the same state of mind."*

Copyright, 1944. As you can see both Gaige book covers not in great shape but book itself in good condition.

MY COOKBOOK PASSION

CHAPTER FOUR
More Recipes -- Mixed Drinks

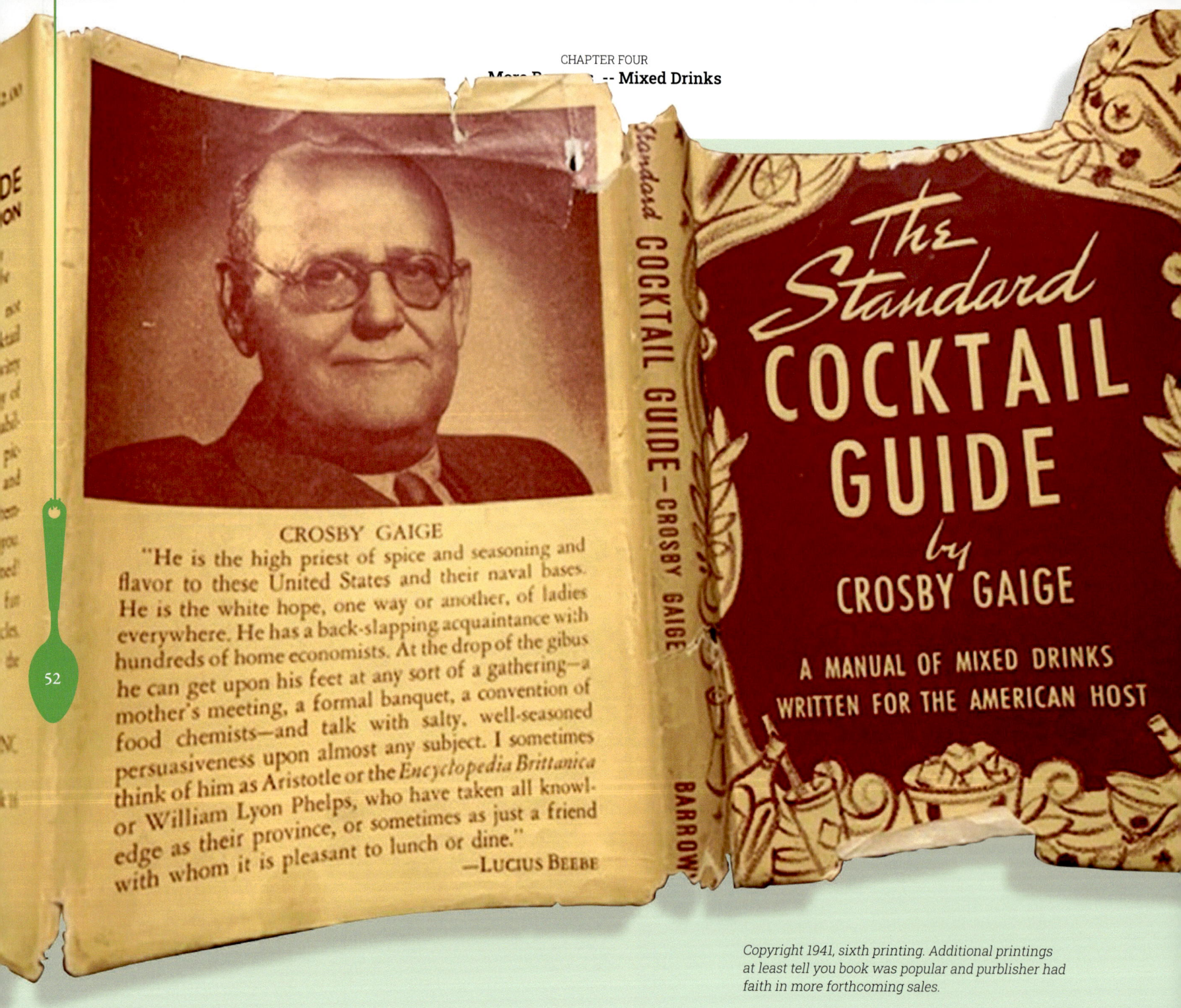

Copyright 1941, sixth printing. Additional printings at least tell you book was popular and purblisher had faith in more forthcoming sales.

CHAPTER FOUR
More Barrows -- Mixed Drinks

1 oz. Tropical heavy Bodied Rum, 2 oz. Gold Label Rum, 1 oz. White Label Rum, 2 teaspoonfuls Apricot Brandy, ¾ oz. unsweetened Pineapple Juice, ¾ oz. Papaya Juice, 1 teaspoon fine granulated Sugar, juice of 1 Lime. Shake well with plenty of cracked ice and pour into a 14-ounce Zombie glass. Float splash of 151 proof Tropical Heavy Bodied Rum on top. Spike on a toothpick, in the order named, 1 green Cherry, 1/2 inch Pineapple stick, 1 red Cherry. Decorate with this and a sprig of Mint. Sprinkle powdered Sugar over all and serve. *[One of those for me and it's siesta time in the hammock]*

Champagne Punch (20 persons)

2 boxes fresh or defrosted frozen Strawberries
1 pound Powdered Sugar
1 bottle Moselle
1 bottle Champagne
1/2 bottle Claret

Put the Strawberries in a large glass bowl packed in ice and sprinkle with the Sugar. Pour in Moselle and let stand from 2 to 6 hours. When ready to serve add chilled Champagne and the Claret for color. Serve with berries in each glass.

"Dracula has a Zombie"
by Brad 'Tiki Shark' Parker For over a decade Stephen and I have been fans of the Hawaiian-themed phantasmagorical world of Brad's low brow pop culture tiki art. Brad illustrated my husband's two island novels, **"Atomic Dreams at the Red Tiki Lounge"** and, yes, a culinary mystery that became a best-seller, **"Captain Cooked"**.

MY COOKBOOK PASSION

CHAPTER FOUR
More Barrows -- Mixed Drinks

Barrows Books Make Better Cooks...
I enjoy coincidence. In **"Wine Lover's Cook Book"** the Forward is written by Richardson Wright, Editor of **House and Garden,** who happened to be one of the host tasters at the Oscar's Golden Wedding Anniversary at the Waldorf a few pages earlier. **"The Man's Cookbook"** was originally published as **"200 Dishes For Men to Cook"**. Author Marion ClydeMcCarroll **("Summer")** was Woman's Editor for King Features Syndicate.

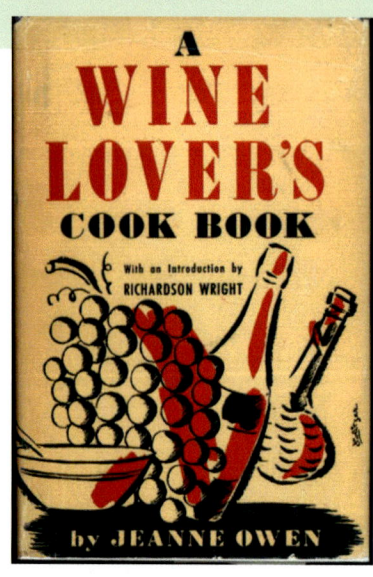

1940

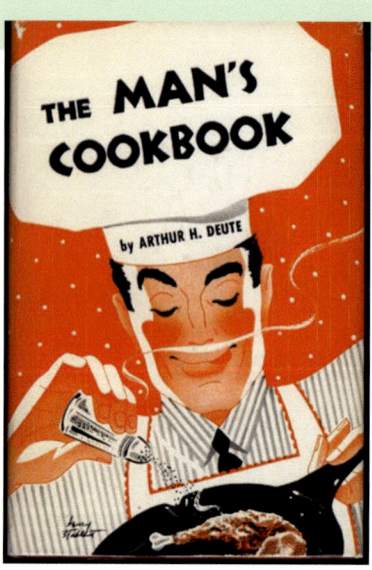

1944

1954

1959

PAMELA KURE GROGAN

CHAPTER FOUR
More Barrows -- Mixed Drinks

Taste Buddies

Just because books of today are coffee table sized with gloss photos of scrumptious looking foods artistically arranged on plates we ourselves could never hope to duplicate, don't give up on the previous generations of cook book writers whose meals remain tasty and easy on our minds and pocket books. Let's wander down memory lane of cookbooks I believe still retain kitchen values.

*Note: repeat authors Florence Brobeck and Jeanne Owen. Brobeck's **Curry** is touted as the first curry cook book ever published. **Sour Cream** stretches its dairy ingredients to include recipes using cottage cheese, buttermilk and sour milk.*

1936

1941

1941

1947

1952

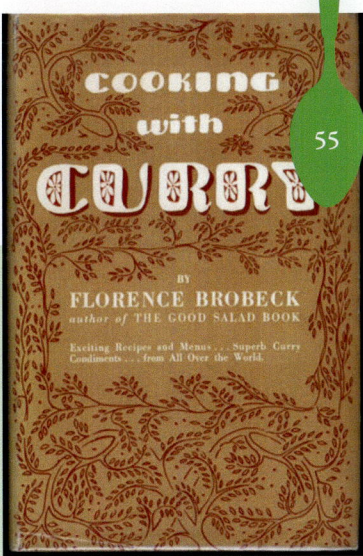
1952

MY COOKBOOK PASSION

CHAPTER FOUR
More Barrows -- Mixed Drinks

Let the Chips Fall…

Here is an example of the transition between the privately published cookbook to promote an inn and the invention of a popular food: *Toll House Chocolate Chip Cookies*. Here is the story with a little myth mixed in:

Ruth Wakefield (1903-1977) and her husband bought an old toll house in Whitman, Massachusetts, built in 1709, that was located on Route 18 halfway between Boston and New Bedford. Historically, people had stopped, paid a toll, changed horses and enjoyed home cooked meals. The Wakefields opened the place as the "Toll House Inn", started as Ruth explained, 'with more courage than capital'. With her background as a dietician and her husband in the food business they served meals and became especially known for their desserts.

As the legend goes, one of her favorite recipes was for Chocolate Crunch cookies. Baker's chocolate was called for in the recipe but that one fateful day she had run out of the ingredient. A semi-sweet chocolate bar was instead used and cut up in to small bits. Ruth discovered that the chopped up chocolate bar did not melt in the cookies but instead went soft to a 'chip' status.

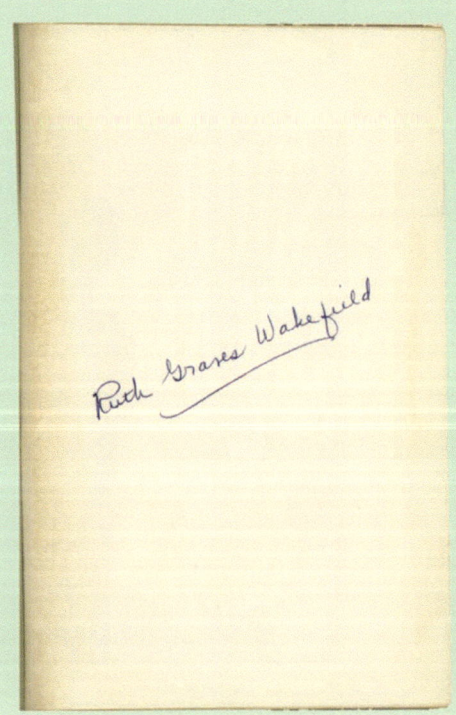

CHAPTER FOUR
More Barrows -- Mixed Drinks

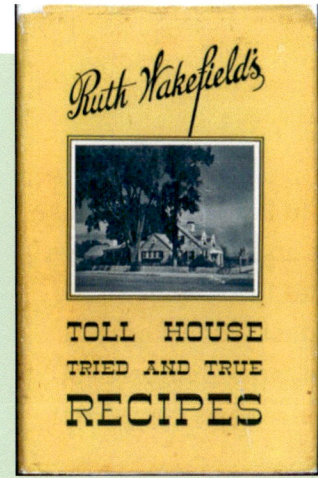
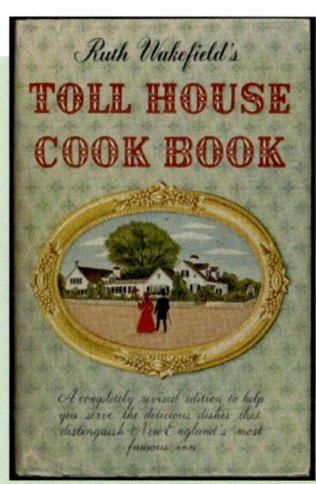
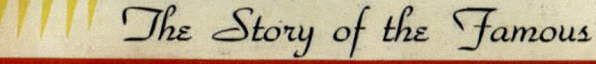

These cookies became popular at the inn, the recipe spread to the public and the Nestlé Chocolate Company started to see a spike in sales of their semi-sweet chocolate bars. Obvious to a good thing they struck a deal: Ruth Wakefield's recipe would be printed on all of their semi-sweet chocolate bars and in return she gained a lifetime supply of chocolate for her baking.

Ruth Wakefield died in 1977 and did not live to see her beloved Toll House Inn burn down on New Year's Eve, 1984. I guess without her we wouldn't have Debbie Fields and Famous Amos.

MY COOKBOOK PASSION

CHAPTER FOUR
More Barrows -- Mixed Drinks

It has always been sad to look back at those restaurants where time and circumstances have removed them from the scene. To me, cookbooks from these past places give us a remembered snapshot, and memories of pleasant times and their recipes revive our spirits with a good meal.

Collector's Corner

Ruth Graves Wakefield's central cookbook went through multiple printings, many times expanding with new recipes. Her first book, **Ruth Wakefield's Tried and True Recipes**, was first printed in December, 1930 (with a 1931 copyright), in a red binding, no dust jacket. Barrows begin publishing revised editions, **Toll House Tried and True Recipes**, with colored photos in 1937 at which time her chocolate chip recipe was noted as "Toll House Chocolate Crunch Cookies." In 1952, after twenty seven printings, the book went into a 'New Edition Completely Revised' version published by Little, Brown & Company. I have this last edition, second printing, 1955, signed by Mrs. Wakefield, and a signed seventh printing, 1938.

PAMELA KURE GROGAN

CHAPTER FOUR
More Barrows -- Mixed Drinks

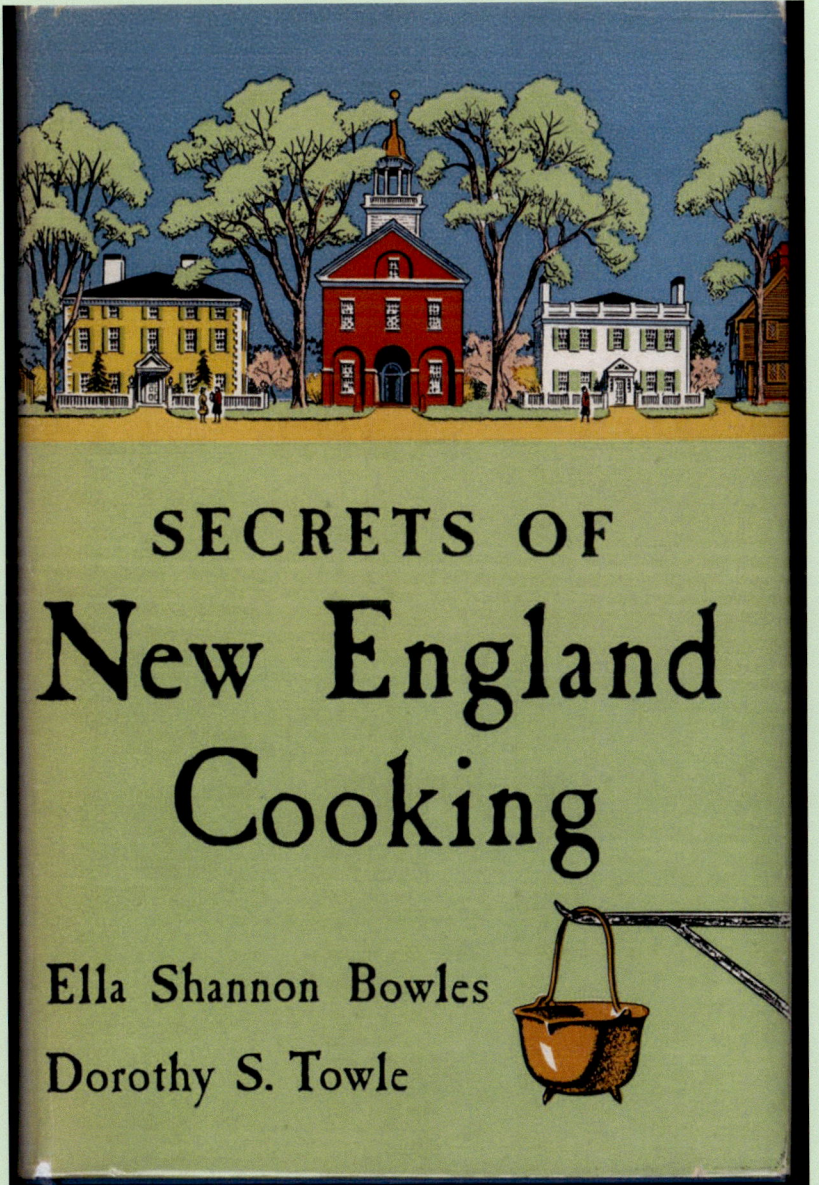
1947

Franconia Baked Strawberry Dumplings

"This recipe is the prized possession of a lifelong resident of the White Mountains. She serves it on very special occasions during the strawberry season, and for the first time has given the recipe away".

Make a rich biscuit dough. Roll out about half an inch thick and cut in three-inch squares. In the center of each square put about two tablespoons of wild or cultivated strawberries cut in pieces.

Cover with one-half tablespoon of sugar and add a tiny pinch of salt. Fold the squares over to form dumplings and brush the tops with a little milk. Bake in a hot oven, 400 degrees F., about fifteen minutes. Serve piping hot with the following sauce.

Strawberry Butter Sauce
1 cup strawberries
1 cup sugar
1/2 cup butter

Mash the strawberries thoroughly. Cream the butter and sugar and mix with the berries. This sauce should be turned over the dumplings while they are hot enough to melt the butter. Serves six. Strawberry butter sauce is also delicious on pot popovers and hot rice. In season, raspberries and blackberries may be substituted for the strawberries.

MY COOKBOOK PASSION

CHAPTER FOUR
More Barrows -- Mixed Drinks

OLD HUNDRED CHICKEN PIE

Clean a large fowl, cover with hot water, add one-quarter pound salt pork and simmer until nearly tender. Add salt and cook until done. Cool. Remove skin, discard bones and cut meat in rather large pieces. In the meantime, simmer the broth until it is strong and reduced one-half. Melt two tablespoons butter, add two tablespoons flour and cook until crumbly. Add one and one-half cups chicken broth, cook until thick and season to taste. If more gravy is needed, increase butter, flour and broth.

Roll light biscuit dough one-half inch thick, cut a round to fit your baking dish by inverting dish on dough. Bake biscuit top on a separate pan. Place chicken covered with gravy in baking dish, heat and when the biscuit is cooked, place on top. Cooked separately, the crust is always crisp and perfect. This old family recipe is that used for my famous Saturday Night "Old Fashioned New England Dinner." It is luscious. [P.K.G.--Notice there are no vegetables, the chicken is the central taste]

Did you know? Old One Hundred Inn was named from people practicing church singing in the building where they sang the 100th Psalm of David, the melody known as the "Old One Hundredth". In its heyday of the late 1930's, the restaurant held 215 seats and served over 80,000 meals a year. World War II rationing of staples like butter and sugar led to the restaurant's demise. All that's left today of the Inn is the old wishing well.

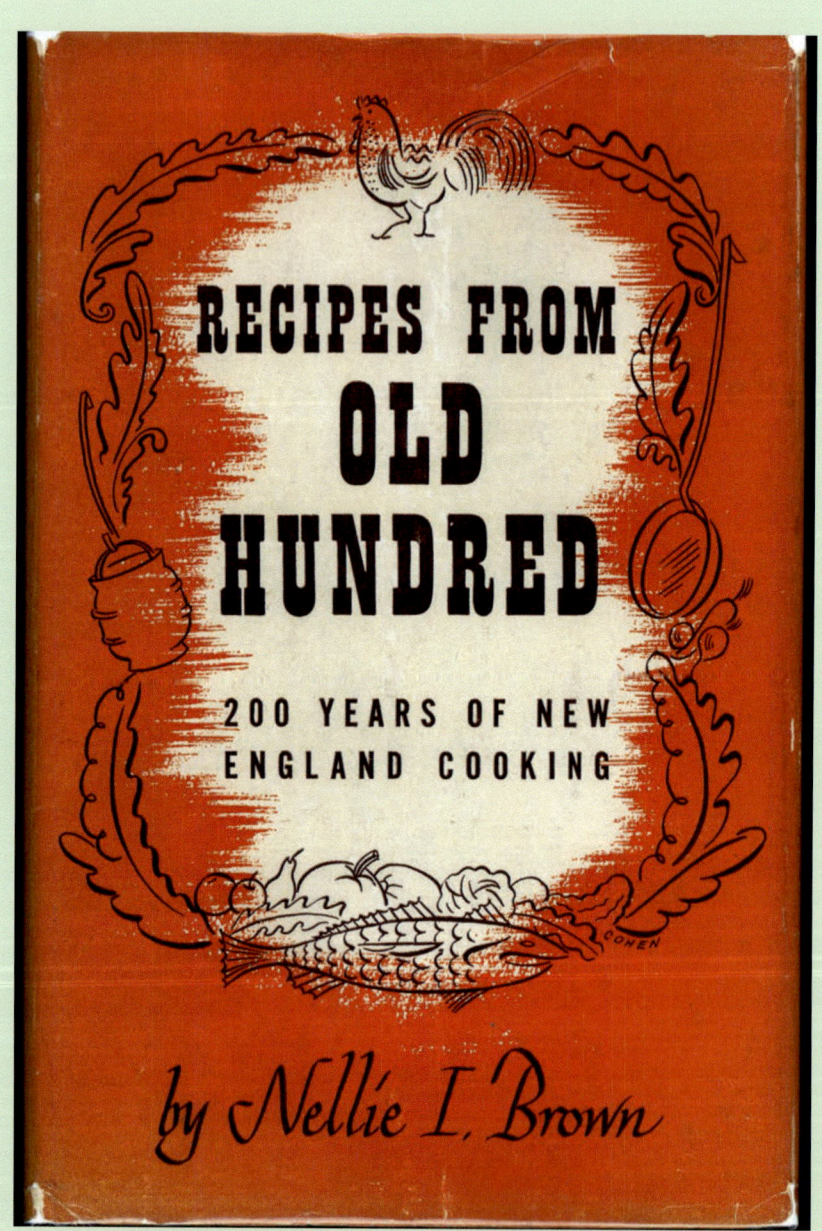

1939

CHAPTER FOUR
More Barrows -- Mixed Drinks

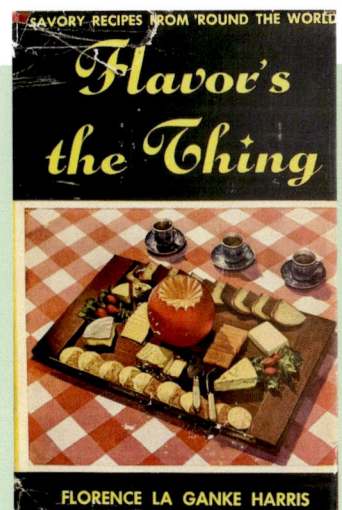 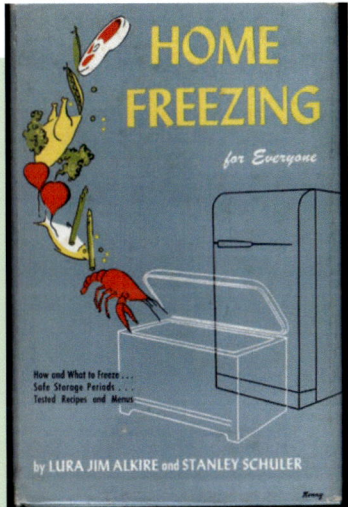 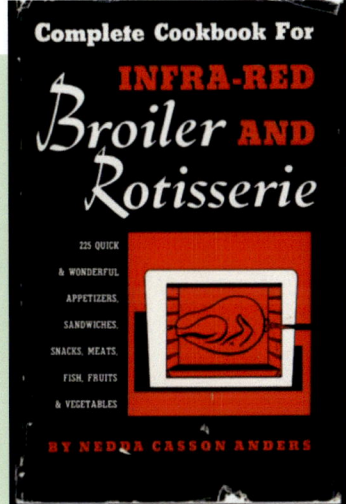 

1939   *1950*   *1953*   *1954*

Sift dry ingredients, cut in lard until the mixture is the consistency of coarse meal, add milk and mix well. Knead thirty seconds. Roll or pat with the palm of the hand until one-quarter inch thick for crisp biscuits and one-half inch thick for dinner biscuits. Cut with a lightly-floured round cutter. Bake in a well-greased baking pan in a hot oven, 425°F., until brown, about twelve minutes. Makes two dozen small biscuits. These biscuits may be prepared an hour in advance, covered with wax paper, stored in the refrigerator and baked at service time.

Baking powder biscuits

2 cups flour – 3 tablespoons lard – 3/4 cup milk – 4 teaspoons tartrate baking powder or 2 teaspoons combination type
1 teaspoon salt

1. Peel onions, and slice.
2. Leave skins on cored apples. Slice into one-quarter inch thick slices.
3. Place butter in frying pan. Arrange layers of apples and of onions.
4. Sprinkle lightly with salt.
If desired, about two tablespoons sugar may be sprinkled on top. Cook over low fire until onions and apples are soft.
5. *Baked ham or sautéed ham slices and this dish pair happily.* -- **Flavor's the Thing**

Apples and onions

Onions – Apples, cored – sugar – 2 tablespoons butter
Salt

COOKBOOK PASSION

CHAPTER FIVE
International

CHAPTER FIVE

GOOD FOOD INTERNATIONAL

1939 — 1950 — 1950 — 1952 — 1957

PAMELA KURE GROGAN

CHAPTER FIVE
International

States of Epicurean Delight

G. Callahan: "This is my version of one of the most famous and popular salads served at the Palace Hotel in San Francisco. It was named in honor of George Arlis when he was appearing in the play, "The Green Goddess".

Green Goddess Dressing

1 clove garlic, grated – 1/2 cup heavy cream (preferably soured)
3 tablespoons finely chopped anchovies, or anchovy paste – 1 cup mayonnaise
1/3 cup finely chopped parsley
3 tablespoons finely chopped chives or green onions – Salt and coarse black pepper tablespoon lemon juice
3 tablespoons tarragon wine vinegar

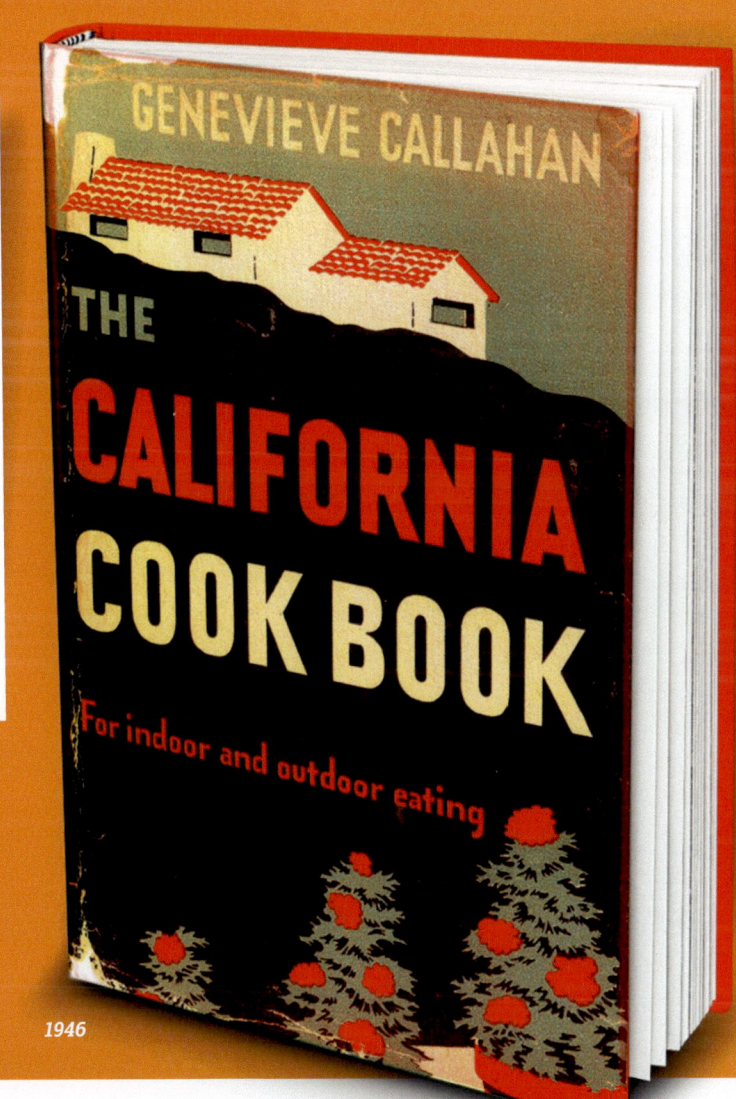

1946

Combine ingredients in order given. Chill, then pour liberally over coarsely torn mixed greens—romaine, chicory, and escarole, or head lettuce and leaf lettuce. Toss until well coated, adding more salt and pepper as needed. Serve in individual plates or bowls, to accompany the main course. You'll mop up your salad plate with French bread when you finish! Makes about a pint.

CHAPTER FIVE
International

Will you come to my *hale* for *kaukau*? First printed in 1940, this book must have been popular as it went through 8 printings to 1960. Authored by a professor who was the Chairman of Department of Home Economics at the University of Hawaii, what's between the page covers is a brief history of the multi-cultures who settled in the islands and their recipes reflect these diverse nationalities: Samoan, Portuguese, Korean, Chinese, Japanese, and old Hawaiian. Here's a recipe I have yet to acquire a taste for. You be the brave one.

1946

PICKLED OPIHI
(LAPAS CONSERVADAS EM VINAGRE)

2 1/2 pounds opihi in shells
6 whole cloves
1 cup vinegar
6 cloves garlic
6 small red peppers

Wash the opihis thoroughly in water. Pour hot water over them to remove the shells. Discard the shells and seaweed. Wash the opihi and drain. Combine all the ingredients and allow mixture to stand for two hours. Simmer it for 5 minutes. Drain the opihis and serve hot or cold. (1 serving, approximately 1/4 cup, 63 grams. 6 servings.)

[On Kaua'i we watched opihi being gathered—a dangerous craft. Between crashing waves local collectors knife scraped the limpet mollusks off algae-slippery rocks. Offered, like oysters, we ate opihi raw. I love the Islands and annually make a culinary trek; these days my menu choices are more 'Asian fusion' & imu-prepared Kalua pig. -pkg]

PAMELA KURE GROGAN

CHAPTER FIVE
International

BANANA POI (POI FAT)

3 1/2 cups mashed very ripe banana – 1 1/2 cups coconut cream (3 to 4 coconuts) – 1 1/2 tablespoons lime juice or 2 tablespoons lemon juice

Press the banana pulp through a coarse sleeve or squeeze it with the hands until a smooth paste is obtained. Add the fruit juice. See directions for Coconut Cream*. Gradually add the coconut cream to the banana, stirring constantly. Chill and serve in glasses or coconut shells. 9 servings.

*A substitute for coconut cream made from fresh coconut may be prepared by soaking 1 1/2 cups packaged coconut in 1 cup coffee cream for 30 minutes, simmering for 10 minutes, cooling, and straining several thicknesses of cheesecloth, squeezing out as much liquid as possible.

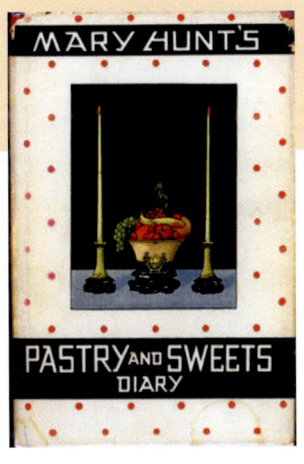
1939

1940

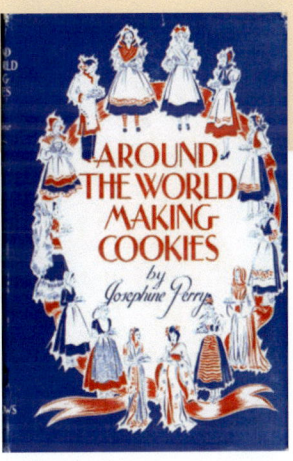
1940

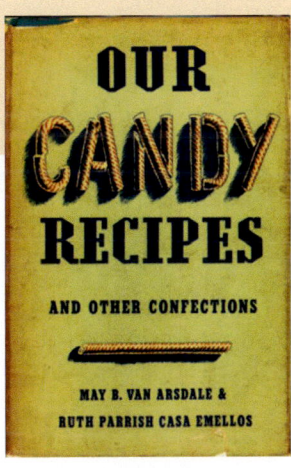
1941

1950

Sometimes the simplistic writing style would catch my attention.

POP CORN CANDIES
General Directions for Popping Corn.— Corn can be popped either in a regular popper or in an iron frying pan. When using the popper, do not put in too much unpopped corn at one time, because the popper will be so full that the last of the batch will not have room to pop. It is better to pop over a covered low flame so that the pop corn will not be scorched. Shake the popper constantly during the process.

Many persons prefer to use an iron frying pan, believing that the popped corn has a better flavor and is less dry. Melt one tablespoon of lard or any vegetable shortening and one of butter in a large frying pan over the fire until the corn is popped. Bacon fat can be substituted if the flavor is desired.

MY COOKBOOK PASSION

CHAPTER FIVE
International

If the corn does not pop well it can be covered with water for about three minutes, drained, and dried on clean tea towels. This additional moisture often causes the corn to pop.

After corn is popped it can be salted, or salted and buttered. Melt the butter and pour it over the corn, stirring the corn as you pour. The amount of butter to be used depends upon personal taste. *[Who said they didn't have 'Cooking for Dummies' way back when.]*

PINK POP CORN BALLS
LARGE RECIPE

Sugar, 2 cups – Light corn syrup, 2 tablespoons – Water, 1 1/4 cups – Pink coloring, few drops – Vanilla, 1 teaspoon – Popped corn, 3 quarts – Salt, 1 teaspoon

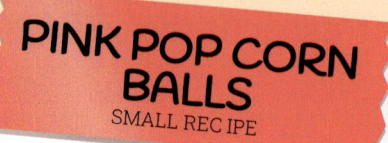

PINK POP CORN BALLS
SMALL RECIPE

Sugar, 1 cup – Light corn syrup, 1 tablespoon – Water, 3/4 cup – Pink coloring, few drop – Vanilla, 1/2 teaspoon – Popped corn, 1 1/2 quarts – Salt, 1/2 teaspoon

Put the sugar, corn syrup, and water into a saucepan and cook, stirring until the sugar is dissolved. Continue cooking, without stirring, until the temperature 290º F. is reached (brittle in cold water). Add the vanilla and the coloring paste which has been dissolved in as little water as possible. Stir only enough to mix the coloring evenly.

Have the popped corn in a large bowl and sprinkle with the salt. Pour the cooked syrup slowly over the salted popped corn, stirring well.

Form into balls with the hands, using little pressure. Cold water test when syrup reaches 290º F.: brittle. Yield (large recipe): number of balls—twenty (two and one-half inches in diameter) -- From **Our Candy Recipes**

CHAPTER FIVE
International

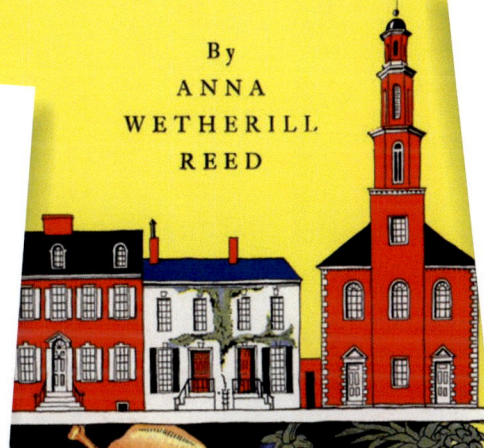

The PHILADELPHIA COOK BOOK *of* TOWN and COUNTRY

By ANNA WETHERILL REED

Famous dishes and celebrated menus from Colonial days to the present

1940

Welsh Rabbit a la Yale Club

12 slices bacon
6 slices broiled tomato
6 slices toast

Place broiled tomato slice on a piece of toast, cover with Welsh Rabbit, and top with 2 slices of broiled bacon.

Welsh Rabbit
THE SHELBURNE

1 ½ pounds American cheese, chopped fine – 3 teaspoons English Mustard – 3 teaspoons Worcestershire sauce – 12 ounces beer – ½ teaspoon paprika

Place cheese in saucepan and add to it the mustard, Worcestershire sauce, beer and paprika. Stir over slow fire until cheese is melted. Serve on toast.

A. W. Reed: We use these days the term 'rarebit' instead of 'rabbit'. The idea of calling it 'Welsh' goes back to England where in the 17th and 18th centuries it was common to use the adjective "Welsh" for things of inferior quality, especially if these had been substituted for something better. So, what we have here is basic 'cheese on toast'. Although you can use chedder, try English cheeses like Lancashire, Double Gloucester, or better yet, Red Leicester. And though we are dealing with old Philadelphia recipes, I believe this previous dish was 'loaned' to the author by Mr. Paul Arnswalde of the then glamorous Shelburne Hotel in Atlantic City. Close enough. [PG side note: The old grande dame hotel, where Diamond Jim Brady used to indulge his vices, went under the wrecking ball in 1984 to make way for casinos. Something to remember: over their doorway, the hotel's Latin motto: "Virtute non Verbis" *(Deeds, not Words)*].

MY COOKBOOK PASSION

CHAPTER FIVE
International

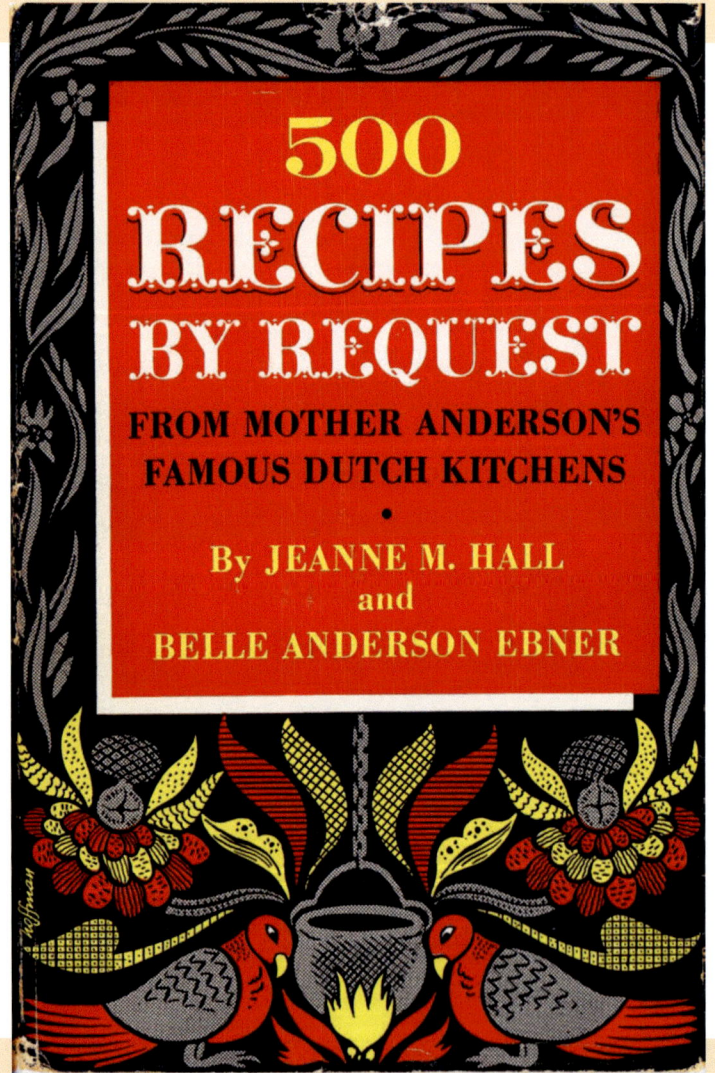

This is a family cookbook (1948) with both authors related to the matriarch originally from Perry County, Pennsylvania, thus the book's subtitle, 'From Mother Anderson's Famous Dutch Kitchens'. The dishes prepared "are still served to the hoards of hungry guests who throng the Anderson Hotel and beg for the recipes."

I'll show you more restaurant cookbooks, but unlike the Old Hundred Inn which disappeared over time, the Anderson Hotel, now the Historic Anderson House (a claim -1856- to being 'the oldest country inn west of the Mississippi') located in Wabasha, Minnesota operates under new ownership yet proudly continues the tradition of Grandma Anderson's Dutch oven recipes. A nice touch: If a guest stays at this inn today they can request one of several friendly cats to keep them company in their rooms.

Where are they now? 500 Recipes By Request (1948) by Jeanne Hall and Belle Anderson Ebner over time evolved to **500 More Recipes By Request** by (1960) and finally into **The Anderson House Cook book** by Jeanne M. Hall and son John Hall (1986), and a softcover, **Bread & Breakfasts --Notes & Recipes from a Country Inn** (1985).

CHAPTER FIVE
International

CHERRY BREAD
(GRANDMA'S RECIPE)

1 cup sugar – 1 bottle (8-ounce) maraschino cherries, 2 eggs beaten drained and halved
1 cup milk – 2 tablespoons melted butter – 3 cups sifted flour
4 teaspoons baking powder
1 teaspoon salt

FRESH STRAWBERRY MOUSSE

1 cup crushed strawberries
1 egg white – 2/3 cup sugar 2 cups heavy cream, whipped –
1/3 cup light corn syrup
Pinch of salt – 2 tablespoons orange juice

Add the sugar to the eggs and beat well. Add the milk alternately with two cups of the flour. Sift the baking powder and salt with the remaining cup of flour and add. Stir the cherries and the butter. Beat well and turn into a well-greased bread pan. Bake in a moderate oven, 350° F., for one hour. Makes one loaf.

Combine the strawberries and the sugar, reserving one tablespoon of the sugar for the egg white. Add the syrup and the orange juice and allow to stand until the sugar is dissolved. Beat the egg white with the remaining sugar until stiff. Combine the two mixtures, add the salt, and fold in the whipped cream. Place in the freezing tray of an automatic refrigerator and freeze for two to four hours, until firm. Serves eight. - From **500 Recipes By Request**

Collector's Corner: You may run across in a cookbook where the publisher's price on the inside cookbook flap has been cut-off. That's usually to reflect a store's change in pricing. A purist collector of fine literature will seek first editions, no price-clipping, and book covers in better than fair condition. With cookbooks if you can find a pristine copy, sure, but not so much. Here, outstanding recipes are the goal. Cookbooks in this chapter are from publisher Barrows Co. and dates shown here are first year of publication.

MY COOKBOOK PASSION

CHAPTER SIX

MEN AT WORK
(IN THE KITCHEN)

PAMELA KURE GROGAN

CHAPTER SIX
Men at Work

Our Wild Wild West
Room in our first Las Vegas home filled with autographed photos of cowboy movie stars and signed Zane Grey novels. Shelved here are the western motif cookbooks. Sam Arnold's *The Fort Restaurant Cookbook* is one of my picks, but not the Rocky Mountain Oyster recipe within. First Edition of the *Colorado Cache Cookbook* by the Denver Junior League ranks top choice in fundraiser spiral softcovers.

MY COOKBOOK PASSION

CHAPTER SIX
Men at Work

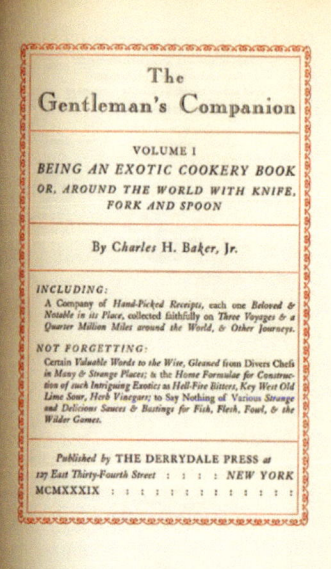

Charles H. Baker, Jr.
It would be very easy to gender bash when starting a chapter on men in the kitchen or before the grille, delivering such jabs as 'You have to look in a cookbook to boil water' or 'when you BBQ I have to hold the water hose in one hand while my other hand holds the phone on speed dial to 911'. Face it, men have moved from prehistoric hunters into epicureans with finesse at garnishment and a palate for fine wines. My husband is more in the **Gentleman's Companion** style. What can you say to a dinner date at his house when he prepared home-made vichyssoise in a cold half cut honey dew melon, followed by wok stir fried apricot brandied shrimp with snow peas, and dessert of fresh raspberries over vanilla bean ice cream with a dash of Grand Marnier. My, how that man can seduce by cuisine!

Still one has to watch him closely. His idea of creating edible art from refrigerator leftovers can be reckless. Any meat dish he prepares I demand to know what critter was used as I have been surprised--after the fact--to ostrich steak with a blueberry sauce (delicious, I must say) and warm rattlesnake salad (let's not go there!). And if he deserves any plaque hanging in the kitchen it would read: 'I'm creative, you can't expect me to be neat, too.' So, here's to the men and their recipes.

I consider Charles H. Baker, Jr. one of the great men of high epicurean living. During his career he was the Food and Drink Editor of *Town and Country Magazine* and the drink editor of *Gourmet* Magazine and later contributed articles to *Esquire*, among others. In the late 1930's for a two year period he traveled the world seeking out the best restaurants and watering holes with the culmination of such tough duty a two set volume:

The Gentleman's Companion, Volume I, and "An Exotic Cookery Book", and Volume II, "Being an Exotic Drinking Book or, Around the World with Jigger, Beaker and Flask". I'll deal with his drinking book when we sip into bar books. Suffice it to say, this is one of the greatest armchair drinking books of all times and when modern bartenders started looking for exotic new concoctions, they returned to Baker's **"Gentleman's Companion,"** as the acolyte might sit at the feet of the wise seer.

Here is a little of his flavoring:

SAUCE No. II, Sea Island Georgia Style

Sailing south in the Fall of 1935 in Marmion we flirted with the edge of a November hurricane, crossed the bar at Fernandian with waves breaking in 23 feet, and coasted up back of a friend's dock on Cumberland Island, in the Andy

PAMELA KURE GROGAN

CHAPTER SIX
Men at Work

Carnegie estate, and found notable bourbon, a half acre mint bed, and many fine fresh shrimp in the tide creeks just waiting for our 5 foot cast net. Served chilled, this local sauce went instantly into the log...Sour cream, 4 tbsp; 1/2 cup mayonnaise, 2 tbsp chili sauce, lime or lemon juice, 3 or 4 tsp; rub in a little sweet marjoram between palms. Put in The Mixer or use egg beater. The sour cream adds the "touch;" marjoram points up the delicate whole...Excellent for cold boiled fish.

Baker enjoyed an era before war smothered the world. His language seems stilted, the writing Olde English styled but that creates his persona and the light heartedness innocence of the traveling observer. One wonders what his wife was doing at the time of his tasting, imbibing frivolity. Here's a black-and-white cover front piece photo of him lying in his hammock, fanned cool presumably by his wife while served his cocktail by his young daughter, both in island garb. *The false fantasy of all men.* Listen to his book's dedication: "Contrary to current routine this volume is not dedicated to Publisher, Wife, Friend, Mistress or Patron, but to our own handsome digestive tract without which it never could have seen the light of day."

Let's try another excerpt from **The Gentleman's Companion**

THE AUTHOR DISCOVERED THAT GATHERING MATERIAL FOR AN EXOTIC BOOK ON COOKERY WAS PLEASANT AS WELL AS TECHNICALLY INFORMATIVE

MY COOKBOOK PASSION

CHAPTER SIX
Men at Work

Just to the eastward of our own St. Thomas lies the British island of Tortola, with Road Town—which, by the ways has no road!—its main town, and capital of the British Virgins. The outdoor and indoor sports of Tortola seem to be fishing, treasure hunting, begetting children—both black, white and khaki—and fishing. Their cuisine is slim.

Finding the dish there was an accident and we report it in that location simply because a rambling yachting friend who pokes the bowsprit of his ketch in many strange spots had recently explored the rocky shores of Sir Francis Drake's Channel from Norman Island to Virgin Gordo—the "Fat One" mentioned by Christopher Columbus—and sent the formula back to us a scant week before it came in by mail from two spots in the South Seas!

CHICKEN TORTOLA, which Is as Good a Name as any for Chicken Baked in the Shells of Ripe Coconuts, Tropical Style

Again basic indications point toward a fowl of tender years, although this is not essential. Cut into fairly small pieces and discard bones and skin. Fry out 4 rashers of diced bacon and brown chicken lightly; salting light, to taste. Take out chicken and reserve… Now dice a big onion fine, do the same to a seeded green pepper, and along with a speck of garlic toss these items in the same hot grease until fairly tender—further adding 1 tsp brown sugar, 2 dashes Tabasco, and salt to taste. Put this with the chicken.

TO OPEN the RIPE COCONUT SHELLS, a Tricky Proceeding yet Simple if Instruction Is Honest

We've fixed this dish ourselves on several occasions when gourmets were impending as guests and can assure you that no man born of woman can take a saw and saw a cap off a batch of coconuts without hours of wasted time, blistered palms, slashed fingers, and discovery of additional vocabulary which, strictly, should be used only in prayer…. No, and even a vise won't hold them tightly without crackling, or popping them half way across the lot.

First puncture 2 "eyes" and drain milk into a bowl. Just hold coconut with end having the 3 "eyes" touching hard rock, concrete, or metal at a point 1/4 of the way back. Strike smartly with a hammer on the top side, more or less vertically above the lower bearing point, and the nut will crack all the way around in a rough but clean circle.

Fill 2/3 full of the chicken-vegetable blend, introduce 1 bayleaf and 1tbsp white wine into each nut. Season, finally, to taste. Tie lids back on with a bight of string, and stand in a baking pan having 1" of water on the bottom. Put in a medium oven for 45 minutes, and serve one to each person….Other vegetables also will do, such as okra, cut in slices, green corn off the cob, palm hearts, cucumber, egg plant, mushrooms, or what not. If sherry is used do not add until 10 minutes before service—removing the shell caps and allowing 1 tbsp to each coconut. This one of the most attractive and delicious chicken dishes we know, for during roasting the coconut kernel donates a rich bouquet to the cooking chicken.

PAMELA KURE GROGAN

CHAPTER SIX
Men at Work

"Dining With My Friends" by Crosby Gaige
Another worldly gentleman, we've run across before is Crosby Gaige his cookbooks published by Barrows. In **Dining with My Friends, Adventures with Epicures,** [1949, Crown Publishers] by Crosby Gaige he turned to friends and acquaintances he had known through the years and asked them to contribute a meal's menu and their associated recipes with interesting anecdotal tidbits on how the dish came to be. Instead of listing a few of the book recipes, I've decided to tease you with the menus and focus on the contributors who themselves have published cookbooks, many of the authors to likewise be found in my book. Mr. Gaige's intros may be light pandering to the cooking stars of the day but with his own extensive cookbook collection you will read he sought out the best for inclusion, 123 epicurean friends and their menus and meals (recipes included). 'It is not a book for the pedestrian cook but the true lover of good food'.

"**Merle Armitage** has lived for many years in close association with the Arts. He is an impresario, a designer of fine books, and a writer of distinction. I first made pleasant acquaintance with him through his book on good living and good eating, **Fit For a King**, which deserves an honored place in any collection of volumes devoted to the arts of the table. From his studio where he acts as Art Director for Look Magazine he scents a scenario for a winter meal for six people."

Dinner for A Winter Evening
SHERRY
Tomato Soup – Tossed Salad with Roquefort Dressing Bitki, Served with Kasha Toast and a burgundy type wine – String Beans Solov
Lemon Ice with Crème de Menthe
Coffee

CHAPTER SIX
Men at Work

Papa Cooks in the Garden

An Outdoor Luncheon or Dinner for Eight
Oversize Rum Collins for the Onlookers.
Marinated Hip Steaks, Genoese Inspiration
Garden Provender in Ice with an Herbed sour
Cream Dunking Bowl Garlicked French and
Italian Bread Griddle Shortcakes with Heavy
Cream Coffee

"The friendly and well-upholstered gentleman [**James Beard**] who is responsible for this offering needs little or no introduction to American gastronomes. His magnum opus **Hors-d'Oeuvre and Canapés**, published by Barrows, is required reading for the successful hostess, and his guide to charcoal cuisine, **Cook It Outdoors**, is the acknowledged authority for those who like to dine al fresco."

Gaige listed the menu from his 'friends' then provided the recipes. Here, I tease and give a few menu examples.

Breakfast

Sliced Oranges with Rosemary
California Omelette – Bacon Curls
Toasted English Muffins – Feioja
Marmalade – Cream Cheese – Coffee

"No account of contemporary hospitality in southern California would be either authentic or authoritative without a visit to the home of **Mrs. Neil McCarthy**. She is not only a famous hostess, a creative and inventive cook, but she writes of food with intelligence and enthusiasm. Her recent book, *The Cook Is in the Parlor,* may well be taken as a guide for those who wish to practice at their tables the art of effortless entertaining."

CHAPTER SIX
Men at Work

Menu

Hot Hungarian Goose Liver on Toast

RY MARTINIS or CHAMPAGNE
Boiled Chicken – with Chive and Butter Sauce

DRY WHITE WINE
*Asparagus or String Bean Salad Vinaigrette
Hazelnut Torte*

CHATEAU YQUEM
French Roast Coffee

GREEN CHART REUSE LIQUEUR
Tangerines

"…I once wrote: '**June Platt** is one of the best informed and more graceful writers upon the eternal subject of food and drink. I have followed her contributions to *House and Garden* with admiration and respect. If it were within my power to award her an American *cordon bleu*, I would certainly enclose it herewith'."

MY COOKBOOK PASSION

CHAPTER SIX
Men at Work

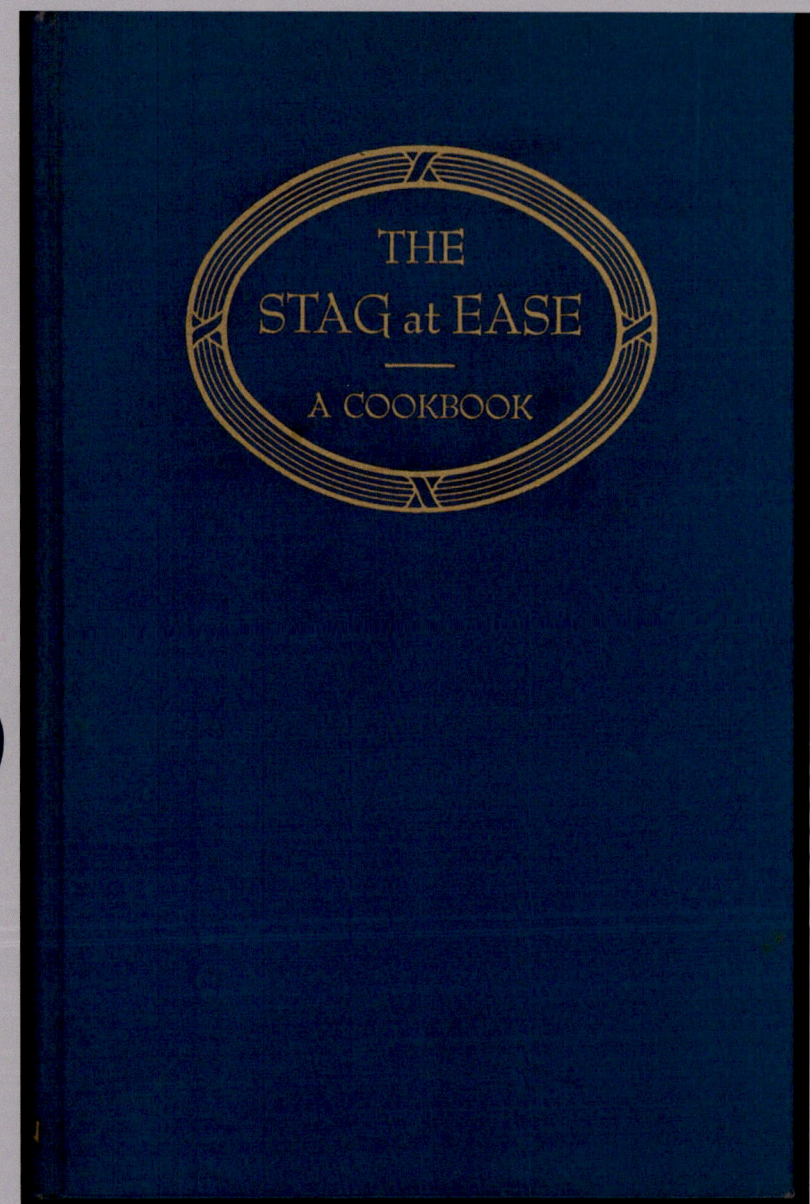

The Famous, and not so famous

"Being the Culinary Preferences of a Number of Distinguished Male Citizens of the World", including President Franklin Delano Roosevelt, Carl Sandburg, H. L. Mencken, Walter Winchell, Jack Dempsey, Charles Dana Gibson, Robinson Jeffers, A. A. Milne [Winnie the Pooh fame], Ed Sullivan [radio to future TV], William S. Hart [silent film cowboy star]. To me this cookbook comes off flat, the attempt at wit discouraging. It's like the author sent out mass mailing requesting recipes and then adlibbed to fill in for any minor response received.

The Stag at Ease
Compiled by Marian Squire (1938)

CHAPTER SIX
Men at Work

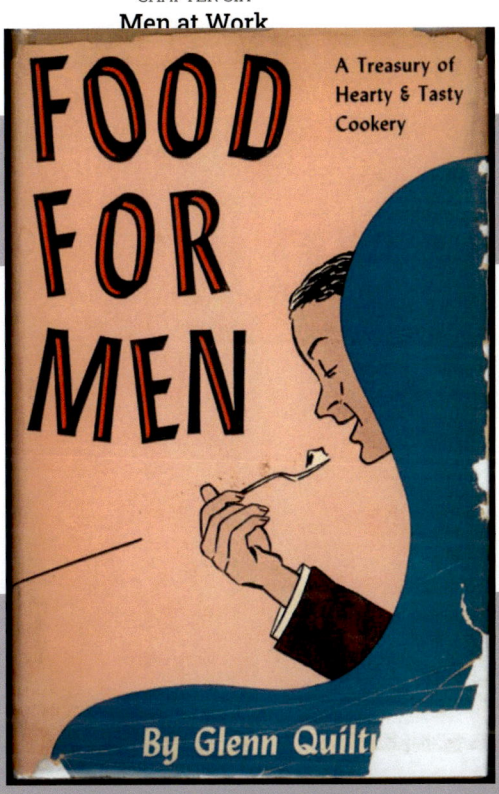

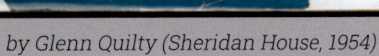
by Glenn Quilty (Sheridan House, 1954)

In 1940, Sunset Magazine invited the men among its hundreds of thousands of Western Readers to send in their best recipes. *Sunset* explained "the heritage of these chefs comes from the early Western men who, by necessity, cooked on the open trail…" Culinary experts from the magazine selected the "best of the best" who went into a featured column and received a chef's hat. If they were selected a second time, they received a special apron. I agree with *Sunset's* selection process: "These Chefs of the West are men who are deadly serious about their cooking. They may joke about their methods and their mistakes, but they are serious about their final accomplishments." The 474 men selected came from all walks of life in the West. Later editions were published as *Sunset's* **Cooking Bold and Fearless**.

A humorous book, 1949 with Lew Lehr's wit ("Monkies is the cwaziest people!"), the self-proclaimed head of The Society of Amateur Chefs. He's better known as the sourpuss narrator-producer behind 300 Fox Movietone News shorts beginning in 1932. Recipe contributors include: Fred Allen, Mel Allen, Kenny Delmar [Who? Senator Claghorn champion of the Old South], Arthur Godfrey, Rube Goldberg, J. Edgar Hoover, and Lowell Thomas, among the VIP fifty. There's a grouping of cartoonists that I may draw attention to in a chapter on cookbook illustrations. Most of the writing is dialogue versus straight ingredient talk. Interesting cover art, that's about it.

MY COOKBOOK PASSION

CHAPTER SIX
Men at Work

Let Crosby Gaige master the introduction: "If any American ever justly deserved the title of High Priest in the Lamasery of Good Living it was the late Charles Browne of Princeton, New Jersey. He was a doctor of medicine, however, and not of divinity. For more years than one could count on an abacus he presided at feast and festival not only as arbiter elegantiarum but as an able and active master of the marmite and the skillet. He was at one time mayor of Princeton and overseer of the poor of that city. In 1919, the neighbors sent him to Congress to act as a counter-irritant to the late Andrew Volstead of Granite Falls, Minnesota. Dr. Browne's efforts were followed by the repeal of the Volstead Act in 1933 [Prohibition]. "Two outstanding contributions Dr. Browne made to the culture of his time are **The Gun Club Cookbook, The Gun Club Drink Book,** both published by Charles Scribner's Sons. They are highly regarded by persons like myself who like a dash of the literate with the lettuce in the salad bowl."

Dr. Browne's recipes are not of ingredients but of setting atmosphere as one might discourse in front of a roaring fire at the hunting lodge, brandy snifter in hand. Here are two examples:

POTATOES ANNA
Potatoes "Anna" are raw sliced potatoes baked in the oven (Pyrex dish, why not?) with butter and seasoning. In a hot oven (450°) they will take about 1 hour. Grated cheese is a grateful addition and this would probably give them another name and if milk is added they are called "Delmonico."

PAMELA KURE GROGAN

CHAPTER SIX
Men at Work

LOBSTER "PAUL"

As a change from Newburg, lobster cooked in a chafing dish after the manner of Paul of the Shelbourne Grill (Atlantic City) [see page 57] is quite to be recommended and it might be added that the "kitchen" in this hotel is not surpassed by any other in these United States. The receipt is simple and effective. Blend equal parts of butter and chili sauce in a chafing dish. When hot add Worcestershire sauce, 2 teaspoonfuls to a cupful of the mixture, then the cut up boiled lobster. Heat thoroughly and just before removing add some very finely chopped parsley, say 2 teaspoonfuls to a cupful of the same. Mix and serve. A dash of lemon juice is optional. Paul himself steams the lobsters, un-shells them at the table and uses neither Worcestershire sauce nor lemon juice.

Men at their Best

Founded in 1933 by Arnold Gingrich as a men's racy magazine *Esquire* evolved into a refined periodical with an emphasis on men's fashions and literary contributions by prose giants as F. Scott Fitzgerald and Ernest Hemingway. Both **Esquire's Handbook for Hosts** (1949) and **Esquire Cook-Book** (1955) retained the light banter of the debonair man-about-town and usually on-the- make. Cartoons and artwork were always important and add the humor reinforcing the image of the swinging bachelor of the early fifties, featured illustrators were L.J. Allen in **Esquire Hosts** and Charmatz in **Esquire Cook- Book**.

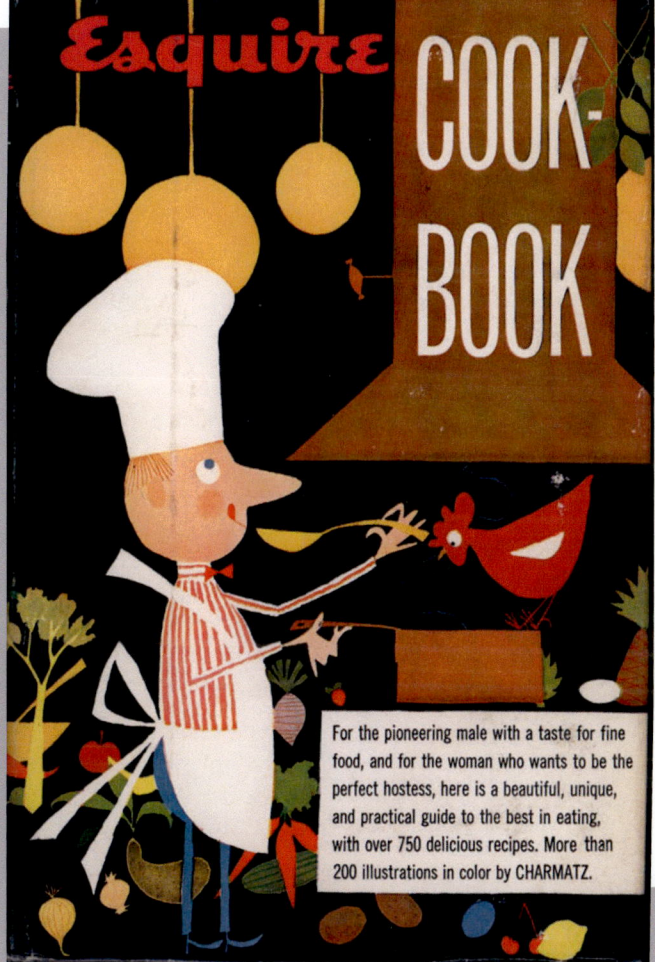

Esquire's Handbook for Hosts sets forth meals, drinks, and even games to play at a party (bridge, canasta, puzzle games were of that era) even 365 reasons to throw a party. I especially liked October 17, Anniversary of Walgreen Super-Value Days or how about April 5, birthday of actor Spencer Tracy. Any event sets the party in motion. One specific chapter is a must in reading, even today: Professor Adler's "How to Talk Sense in Company".

MY COOKBOOK PASSION

CHAPTER SIX
Men at Work

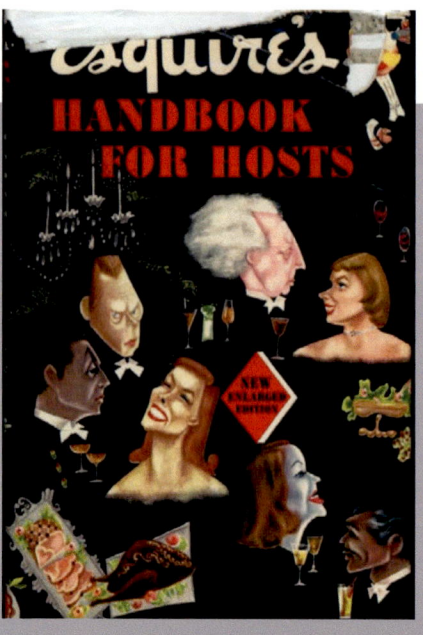

For some obscure reason, many outdoor cooks cherish the notion that a barbecue sauce should be as hot as the fires of Hades. They often use it with entirely unnecessary liberality, thus they destroy the basic natural flavor of the meats, poultry and fish.

BARBECUE SAUCE #1

In cooking pan place 1/2 cup tarragon vinegar, 1/2 cup catsup, 1 tablespoon Worcestershire sauce, 1 large onion, finely minced, 2 crushed garlic cloves (large), juice of 1 lemon, half of the peel, 4 drops of Tabasco, 2 heaping tablespoons brown sugar, 1 teaspoon salt, 1/2 teaspoon chili powder, a pinch of sage. Bring to a slow boil, reduce heat, let simmer for 15 minutes. Keep warm until using. If sauce needs thinning add just a little red wine. This sauce may be made ahead of time and refrigerated. But heat it up before applying to spare ribs.

Who says cookbooks can't rise to literary achievement? Founder Gingrich came up with the magazine's name when he received a letter addressed to "Arnold Gingrich, Esq." *Esquire* set the stage for the proliferation of men's magazines, where it is said, **Playboy Magazine** is *Esquire* with nude photographs. Writer Dorothy Parker wrote book reviews for *Esquire* and was credited for discovering young writer Harlan Ellison, a future sci-fi master. In *Esquire Cook-Book* there are witty essays by writers Paul Gallico ('The Poisedon Adventure' and 'The Snow Goose') and James M. Cain ('The Postman Always Rings Twice' and 'Double Indemnity').

PAMELA KURE GROGAN

CHAPTER SIX
Men at Work

RISOTTO
...from Imperial House, Chicago

Sauté 1 finely diced onion in 1/4 pound butter until brown, then add 2 cups raw rice, 5 cups chicken broth, and boil briskly for 2 minutes. Add 1 bay leaf, 1 pinch saffron, salt and pepper to taste. Cover pan and place in a medium oven for 20 minutes, or until all broth is absorbed. Stir in 1/8 pound butter and sprinkle with grated Parmesan cheese.

CHERRIES JUBILEE
...do them at the table in your chafing dish; dramatic!

Pour the juice from a pint can of pitted Bing cherries into the blazer of your chafing dish and bring to a quick boil; then add a sprinkle of sugar and stir. Add cherries and let them heat thoroughly while you dim the room lights and bring on individual dishes of French vanilla ice cream. When cherries are hot, warm and add 2–3 ounces of kirsch; set afire. As soon as the flames die (or even before, if you like) ladle the cherries and juice over the ice cream and serve.

from Esquire Cook-Book

Henry Holt & Co., 1947

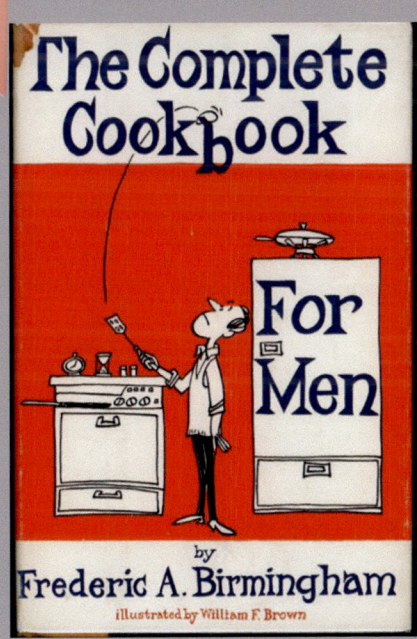

Houghton Mifflin, 1946

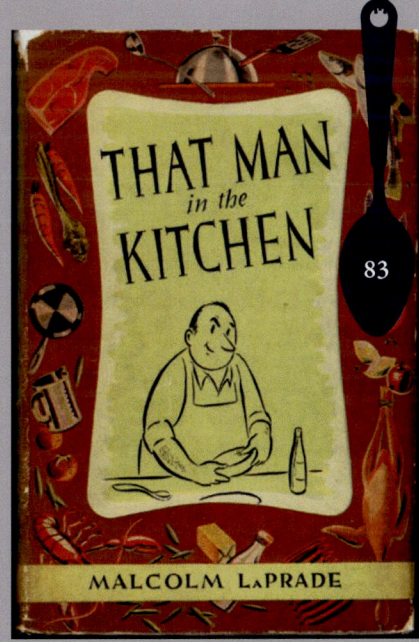

Harper & Brothers, 1961

MY COOKBOOK PASSION

CHAPTER SEVEN
Inns & Farms

CHAPTER SEVEN

INNS & FARMS

PAMELA KURE GROGAN

CHAPTER SEVEN
Inns & Farms

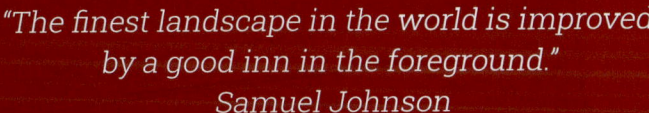

"The finest landscape in the world is improved by a good inn in the foreground."
Samuel Johnson

Before restaurants there were the coach inns on the dirt tracks between village and castle, way stations that sprung from farms, places for changing horse teams, resting weary passengers, offering a night's lodging and a warm supper.

The White Turkey Inn, outside of Danbury, Connecticut, had been built for a bridal couple in 1760 and gained the reputation as being 'haunted by Happiness.' The house at the turn of the century became an English-style tea house, later an inn owned by Harry and Dorothy Davega. When the Second World War, as we have seen with other rural eateries, imposed gas and food rationing, the Davegas shifted the New England theme into New York City and opened a White Turkey Town House, and after 1948 several other White Turkey locations sprang up in the city.

Of days gone by, a letter writer in www.Visiting New England.com commented about restaurants no longer with us: *The White Turkey Inn was a wonderful New England restaurant in the heart of New York City that I still remember from my boyhood days in the late 1940's and early 1950's. It was my first experience with an assortment of relishes and a dollop of cottage cheese, and interesting breads and rolls, instead of the usual white bread and butter fare most restaurants offered as starters when you first sat down. I remember there being an impeccably clean atmosphere, and excellent service, with what I now know to be an unimaginative menu but which, at the time, felt as though I was dining among kings. Was it the restaurant itself, or a nostalgic longing for youth, that brings a smile to my face when I recall my family's visits to this restaurant, which I believe was part of a chain, that I thought would be there forever.*

The author of this cookbook, **Let's Talk Turkey**, by F. Meredith Dietz, had previously penned **The Gay Nineties Cook Book** and **Ol' Virginia Hambook** when she ran across the original White Turkey Inn with its charming cottages and talked the Davegas into letting her turn history into 'adventures and recipes'. It is the historical narrative and tone of the holiday feasts written by Mrs. Dietz which gives Let's Talk Turkey sentimental warmth and worth the read.

CHAPTER SEVEN
Inns & Farms

CHICKEN PIE, LADY BALTIMORE

(Serves 4 to 6)

4-pound or smaller dressed chicken

2 cups raw rice

1 tablespoon butter 1 ½ cup milk

2 eggs

1 medium onion

Cook chicken in only enough water to cover until tender. Remove chicken and cook rice in this broth until it is tender. Stir into the rice mixture, butter, milk, chopped onion, salt and pepper. Stir the eggs in a bowl and slowly, drop by drop at first, add a little of the thin part of the rice mixture. Then turn eggs and mixture into rice and stir well to keep eggs from curdling. Don't cook this again over flame. Cut chicken into large pieces and place in a casserole, cover with a layer of rice, then another layer of chicken with a layer of rice on top. Pour remainder of broth over all and bake one hour in a moderate oven.

Did you know?

'The Lady Baltimore' as referred to here is actually more famous as applied to a rich frosting wedding-type cake with several lost-in-history stories of how it came to be. The most probable as stated in **Let's Talk Turkey** was from the generous recipe contribution by the ladies of the Lady Baltimore Tea Room in Charleston, South Carolina, who in turn, say the cake and tea room nom de plume originally sprung from a flirtateous 1906 novel, 'Lady Baltimore', by author Owen Wister (of **The Virginian** fame). The book held no recipe and the tea room ladies devised their own trademark cake. *"Miss Nina cautions that 'a good Lady Baltimore cake requires time, particularly in the icing which should be carefully beaten and quite thick."*

Wrote novelist Wister: *"I should like a slice, if you please, of Lady Baltimore," I said with extreme formality...I returned to the table and she brought me the cake, and I had my first felicitous meeting with Lady Baltimore. Oh, my goodness! Did you ever taste it? It's all soft, and it's in layers, and it has nuts--but I can't write any more about it; my mouth waters too much."*

Collector's Corner: In my library I have this first edition cookbook signed by Mrs. Dietz. Her books are plentiful in the marketplace.

PAMELA KURE GROGAN

CHAPTER SEVEN
Inns & Farms

Actor Charles Boyer inscribes to Jean Dalrymple. 'To Jean, my fondest wishes. Charles.' In author's collection.

Well, well. Here I go trying to organize my books. When I think I pegged the **'Pinafore Farm Cookbook'** I realize it could go equally into the 'celebrity' category. This is what excites me. Going beyond the recipes to realize the author led an extraordinary life we knew nothing about, discovering nuances of world experiences which influenced the cook's repertoire.

Jean Van Kirk Dalrymple (1902-1998) is one such lady, a Broadway star, producer, theater owner/operator and publicist for the stage. She helped to found the New York City Center in 1943 creating a theatre powerhouse by attracting actors like Charles Boyer, Jose Ferrar and Orson Wells and held the prestigious position of Director of the New York City Center Light Opera. Gossip wise she was one of the most beautiful women of her day and supposedly had an affair with Time-Life founder, Henry Luce. She produced over 100 New York productions. I am guessing that Pinafore Farm was named after Gilbert & Sullivan's musical, *H.M.S. Pinafore*. In fact she named everything Pinafore, her television production company and Pinafore Products was the brand name of her preserves and pickles. And that comes full circle to her being a *rural epicurean*. I found a tidbit article about her in 1960 cooking pancakes with Gypsy Rose Lee at Michael Tree's Country Emporium in West Redding, Connecticut. More facts show her as treasurer and a stockholder in Tree's Emporium and in her cookbook she touts the Emporium's Chili and the Dilly Rolls.

MY COOKBOOK PASSION

CHAPTER SEVEN
Inns & Farms

Dalrymple wrote: *People came from miles around to the Country Cousin which is what Mike has named the Emporium's dining room. They come for the dilly burgers and also to buy the delicious dilly rolls which give the dish its name. They consist simply of a split dilly roll, heated or toasted, with a juicy hamburger placed on it, topped with a dollop of sour cream flavored with prepared horseradish.*

Serving dillyburgers at my house I go a step further, putting a good serving of heated chili over the hamburger and roll, and topping all that with the sour cream and horseradish.

Dilly Rolls

2 packages active dry yeast – 2 teaspoons and 2 tablespoons sugar – 1 3/4 cups lukewarm water – 2 tablespoons soft butter – 2 tablespoons salt – 4 1/2 cups flour – 2 tablespoons dill weed – 2 tablespoons dry onion flakes – 1/2 pint cottage cheese

Soften the yeast in lukewarm water with 2 teaspoons sugar. After about 15 minutes, or when the yeast and sugar are dissolved, add the butter, salt and additional sugar and mix until well blended. Sift 2 1/2 cups of flour into the yeast mixture, mixing thoroughly. Add the cottage cheese and continue mixing until very well blended.

Put one cup of flour on a board and turn the soft dough on to it. Knead the dough, mixing in some of flour, until it is smooth. Form it into a ball, place it in an oiled bowl, turning once, cover with a clean cloth and let rise in a warm place for about 3 hours.

Grease 2 cookie sheets. Punch down the dough, cut off small chunks, roll them between floured hands into balls and place on sheets. Set in a warm place to rise for about 1 1/2 hours. Cook when risen in 375º oven for about 30 minutes, or until nicely browned.

Collector's Corner: Autographed photo of actor Charles Boyer inscribed to Jean Dalrymple are called 'association pieces' and help to enhance value. I own another example: West Coast cookbook author, Helen Brown, sends a copy of her book, **Holiday Cook Book,** to famed food writer, M.F.K. Fisher, inscribing a personal *thank you* for Fisher writing the book's Forward.

CHAPTER SEVEN
Inns & Farms

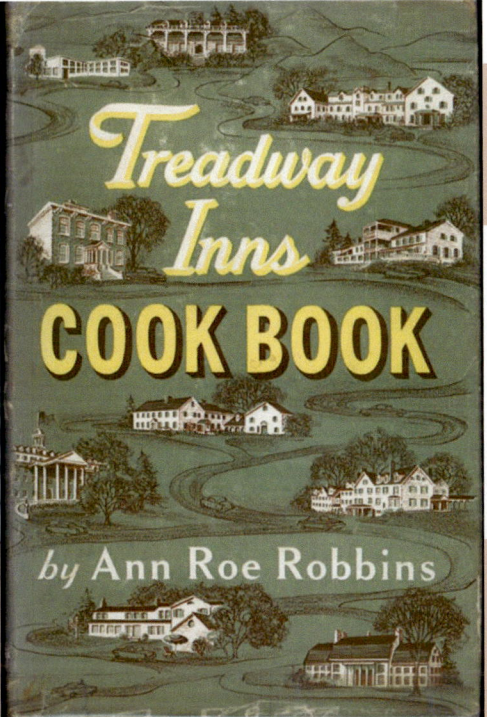

1912 with only two rules: bedrooms should always be built around a good dining room and all executives should have kitchen training. "Good hotelmen," proffered Treadway, "start in the kitchen."

CLAM FRITTERS
Dozen littleneck clams, shucked
1 tsp salt — 7/8 cup sifted flour
1 egg — 1/2 tsp baking powder
1 tsp grated onion — 1 tbsp salad oil

You can see the march, or rather roadie of progress, when you visit the **Treadway Inns Cookbook** (1958) by Ann Roe Robbins . Treadway Inns in 1965 were the crème de la crème of colonial inns, 28 of them, yet at the same time facing the economic pressure competing against the freeway motor lodges of Howard Johnson and Holiday Inns. Treadway Inns stood out among their peers by acquiring older, historic preservation type structures, with names like Publick House and Toy Town Tavern.

To my interest the founder, L.G. Treadway, would want a cookbook bearing his name to reflect his own culinary knowledge. He worked his way through Dartmouth (Class of '08) in the college kitchen. He bought his first inn in

Drain the clams, push out the black bellies if you wish, and chop the clams coarsely. Sift together into a mixing bowl 7/8 cup of flour, 1/2 teaspoon of baking powder, 1/4 teaspoon of nutmeg, and 1 teaspoon of salt. Beat 1 egg well. Beat in 1/2 cup of milk, 1 teaspoon of grated onion, and 1 tablespoon of salad oil. Blend in the clams. Pour into the dry ingredients and stir quickly until smooth. Drop by spoonfuls into hot deep fat at 350° and cook until golden brown, turning once, about 3 minutes. Drain on absorbent paper. Serves 4.

MY COOKBOOK PASSION

CHAPTER SEVEN
Inns & Farms

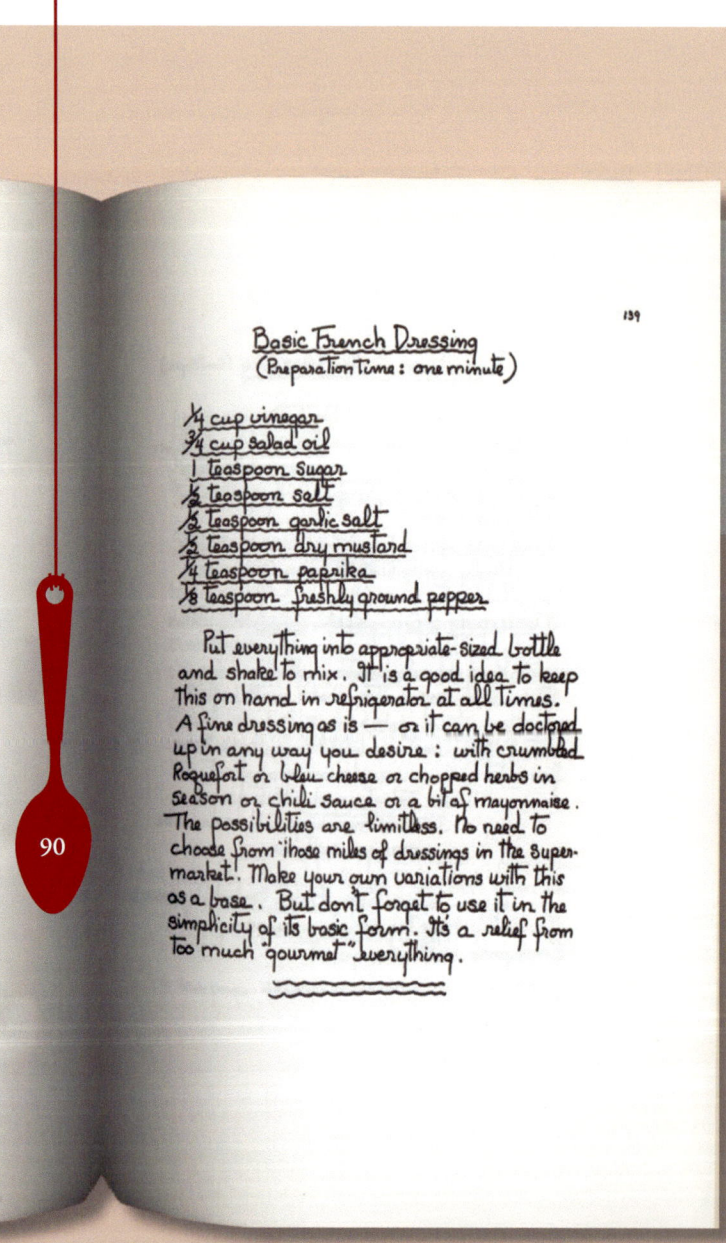

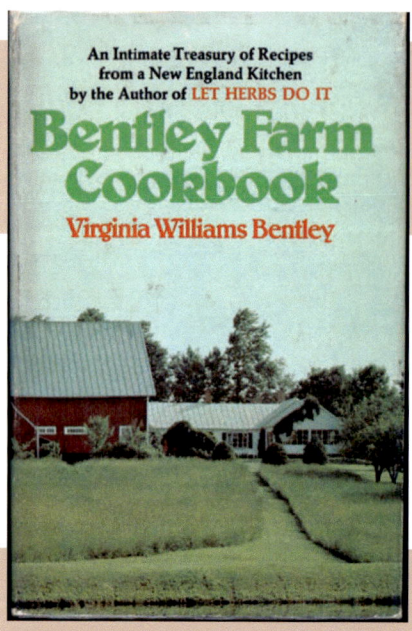

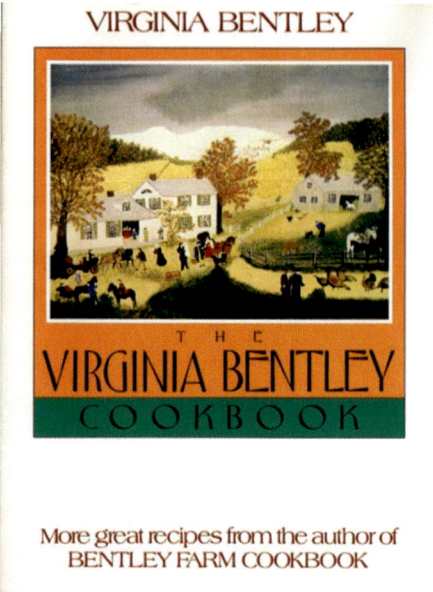

These books strain the eyes since all writing is in script as you see by this one recipe. Virginia Williams Bentley likewise wrote **Let Herbs Do It** which went through several printings. In **Bentley Farm Cookbook** (1974) she wrote: "Cooking, to me, is one of the fine arts, and the limitless creativity it involves has sustained me in sickness and health, joy and sorrow. It's also a magic carpet to making others happy, so the cry of certain over-zealous Women's Liberationists to 'get out of the kitchen' puzzles me. In a far more subtle and lasting way, the power and action are with the hand that stirs the kettle, rather than one that pounds a typewriter (though many women successfully do both). And if it isn't one of women's chief roles to feed people, then Mother Nature certainly gave us the wrong signal."

PAMELA KURE GROGAN

CHAPTER SEVEN
Inns & Farms

CRUNCH DROPS
FROM OLD MCDONALD'S INNS

1 cups sifted flour – 1 cup granulated sugar – 1 teaspoon baking soda – 2 cups quick cooking oats – 1/2 teaspoon salt – 2 cups Rice Krispies (2 small boxes) – 1 cup shortening – 1 cup pecans, chopped fine – 1 cup brown sugar (packed)

MARSHMALLOW DATE PUDDING
FROM GREEN PARROT

2 doz. Graham crackers – 1 lb dates, chopped fine – 24 marshmallows (cut in small pieces) – 1 cup nuts, chopped fine – 3 tbsp. cream

Preheat oven to 350°. Cream shortening and add both kinds of sugar until mixture is smooth and creamy. Add flour, soda and salt. Add eggs one at a time with flour – then cereal and nuts. Batter will be stiff. Drop by teaspoonfuls on greased baking sheet.

Bake 12 to 15 minutes. Cookies spread during baking. Yield: About 5 dozen.

With hands, mix ingredients into loaf, using the cream for moistening. Place loaf in pan and set in refrigerator overnight. Serve with both hot vanilla sauce and whipped cream.

MY COOKBOOK PASSION

CHAPTER SEVEN
Inns & Farms

These two books exampled here are what you usually find in the farm and inn category, the cook wanting to capture family recipes to pass on to their loved ones, special gifts to remember the good times and hold the memories. Both books are self-published.

The Green Parrot Cook Book 'is a compilation of recipes collected during more than thirty years in the restaurant business by Mrs. J.B. Dowd who operated the Green Parrot Inn, Kansas City, from 1929 to 1955.' She went on to open other Green Parrot Inns in the St. Louis, Missouri area and Houston, Texas.

"Yes, there is an Old McDonald's Farm." The farm was located along the Ouachita River five miles south of the city limits of Monroe, Louisiana. It served as a refugee camp during floods in the late 1800's because of its elevation on the banks of the river, the land known as Refugio Plantation. In 1918 the property was purchased by the McDonald Family.

Old McDonald's Farm Recipes (softcover, 1971) by Miss Rosa Belle McDonald is part family collection, part recipes from friends and neighbors. Today we would call most of these foods 'comfort foods'. Found within are many hidden nuggets of rural Americana. Miss Rosa sprinkles throughout a Southern style cornucopia the likes of 'Hogshead Cheese', 'Okra and Tomatoes', 'Garlic Grits', 'Beef Jambalaya', 'Guinea Stew with Drop Dumplings', to name the more interesting.

And on that farm he had some cooks, E-I-E-I-O!

With a pinch, pinch here, and a spoon-full there,

Here a cup, there a pinch, every-where a cook, cook- Old McDonald had a farm, E-I-E-I-O!

CHAPTER SEVEN
Inns & Farms

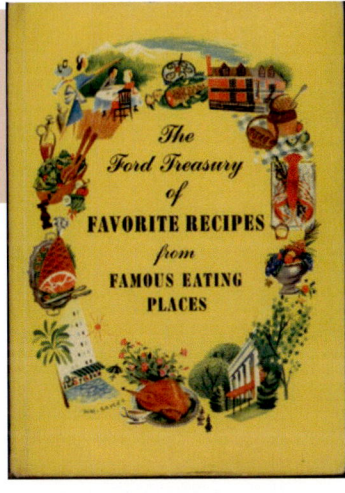 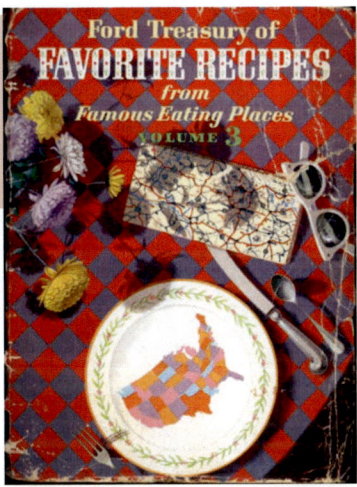 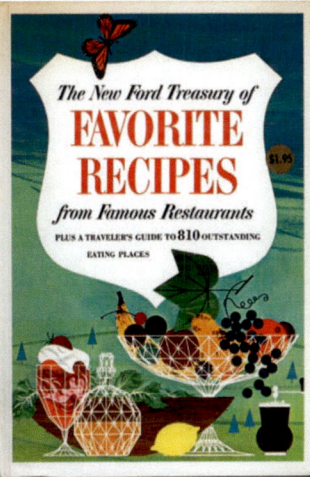 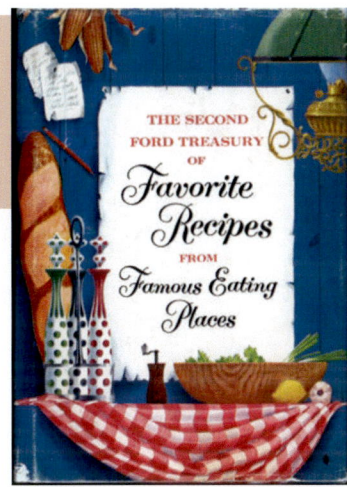

Road Trip

Since I can't catalogue all cookbooks devoted to inns and farm house cookery it would be best to turn to the Marketing Department of Ford Motor Company who created a series entitled, **Ford Treasury of Favorite Recipes From Famous Eating Places** compiled out of *Ford-Lincoln Times* magazines by William and Nancy Kennedy dedicated to 'the Ford and Lincoln-Mercury Dealers of the United States'. We can pooh-pooh a corporate cookbook but this series gives us a long since departed snapshot of the restaurants and inns of the 1950's when American motorists were topping off their gas tanks at 35 cents a gallon! I vividly recall my parents loading us six kids in the station wagon, somehow surviving map stops of tourist landmarks and amusement parks. For that endurance my parents deserve the Congressional Medal of Honor.

I have four of the **Ford Treasury** books, editions being: 1950 (Simon & Schuster), 1954 (Simon & Schuster), 1959 (Volume 3, spiral, Golden Press), and 1963 (Golden Press). Art work is timeless. Each book divides into geographical sections across the country, a road map to locate good dining spots. For sentimental reasons I included a page featuring the Brown Palace Restaurant in Denver, Colorado. The city my husband grew up in and where his late father, Doyle Grogan crossed the street from his office to enjoy his customary lunch at the Brown Palace. That's what fuels the passion, reading through these pages, and you can relate. My husband, Stephen, thumbing through pages said: "Oh, here is the Hotel Taneycomo in Southern Missouri. My Dad was camp counselor and then I attended as a kid and then my daughter Holiday went to the nearby Kanakuk Kamp in Branson. My Dad and I ate at this place!"

MY COOKBOOK PASSION

Restaurant closed 2020

In my own page turning I found Mattei's Tavern, founded 1886, located in Los Olivos, California. On a tasting weekend to the Santa Ynez wine country we ate there (Brothers Restaurant in the Mattei's Tavern). Seeing the artist sketch (50 years old!) memory floods back, sitting on the veranda of the old stage coach stop, large oak trees sheltering, sipping wine bottled just down the vineyard road. If you acquire these **Ford Treasury** books, let me know what places and recipes reignites your road trip memories. Any of these?

Red Snapper at The Lighthouse (Miami Beach), *Chocolate Rum Pie* -- Sunset Farm (Whittier, North Carolina), *Fruit Cookies* – Wentworth-by-the- Sea (Portsmouth, New Hampshire), *Columbia River Salmon* – Columbia Gorge Hotel (Hood River, Oregon).

PAMELA KURE GROGAN

CHAPTER SEVEN
Inns & Farms

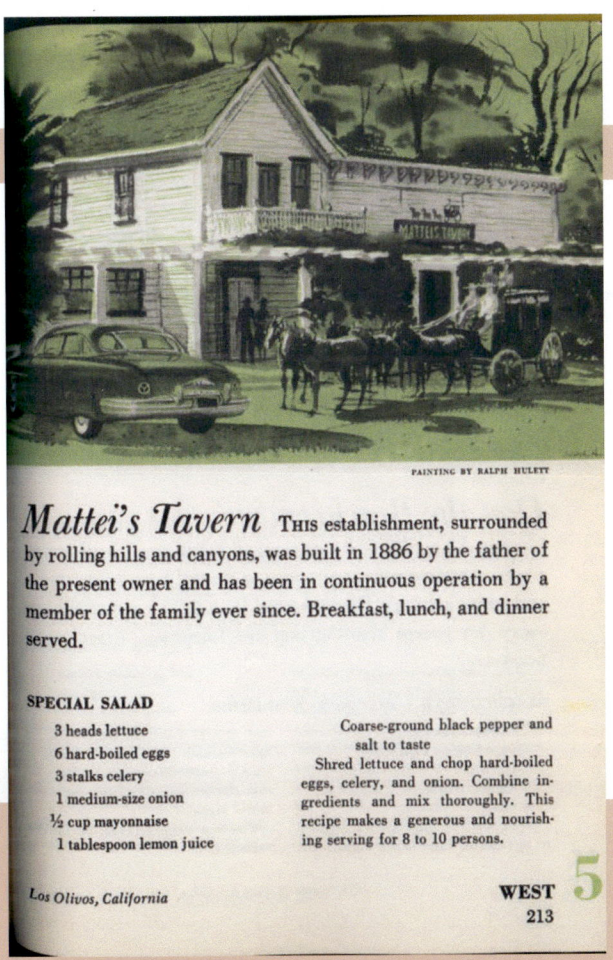

Wait! In the **1963 Ford Treasury (810 eating places)**, South Central, Texas, page 99, here's Chocolate Fudge Pecan from the Green Parrot Restaurant. Why, this restaurant is owned by Mrs. Vira Fredericks, sister to Mrs. J.B. Dowd of the Kansas City Green Parrot [page 92]. This is what makes the search fun!

The Ford Times Cookbook, Volume 6, Signed by Nancy Kennedy, 1977

MY COOKBOOK PASSION

CHAPTER SEVEN
Inns & Farms

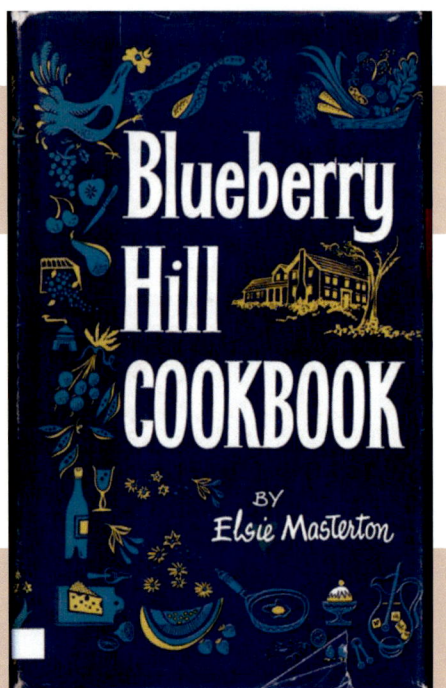
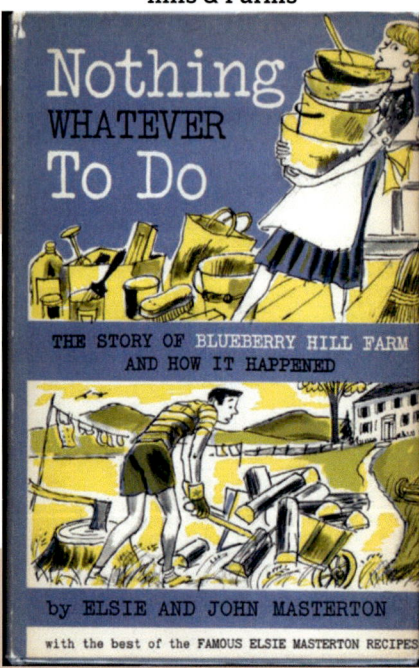
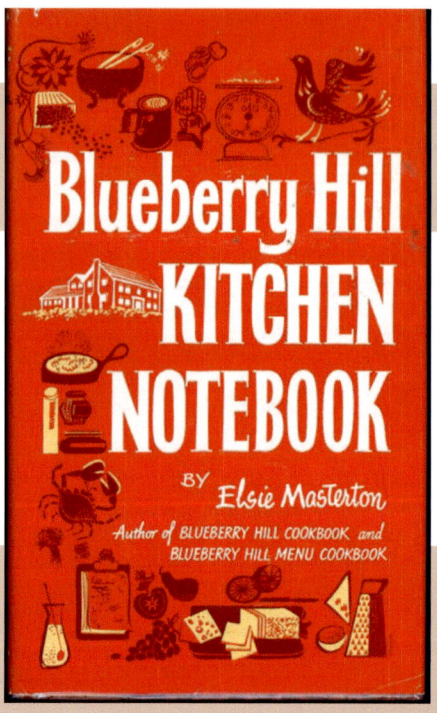

Blueberry Hill

Elsie Masterton did not cook when she and her husband John made that mid-career change and moved from fast-paced New York to the wild environs of Vermont. They bought land and thought a small ski area might work. It snowed at the wrong time of the year, sadly, several years in a row. Facing the loss of all their savings friends suggested they drop the ski angle, try instead running an inn. That's when Elsie found out she had to cook for strangers, the resort, gaining recognition as Blueberry Hill Farm, outside of Goshen, Vermont.

It seems a preponderance of fact, but not a scientific poll, that brave people who own inns versus city restaurants have a tendency as writers to become quaint story tellers with a doctorate in home-spun, practical philosophies.

Elsie's first book, a 'how-to-survive' in rural start-up business is entitled **Nothing Whatever To Do** (1956), the 'story of Blueberry Hill Farm and how it happened'. The book title comes from their advertising to the hustle bustling city dwellers: "come visit where you can do absolutely nothing". By Chapter Twenty One she got around to include the most famous of Elsie Masterson recipes which "have been consistently successful". *Cinnamon Consomme, Blueberry Hill; French Fried Shrimp, Tempura; Sweet and Pungent Duck with Pineapple; Roast Pheasant with Wild Rice and Artichokes;* and of course, several dishes based on locally picked blueberries. No surprise that Elsie found herself in the mail-order blueberry jam business every season and swamped with rising customer demand as the Farm's reputation grew.

CHAPTER SEVEN
Inns & Farms

What cemented the fame of Elsie and John Masterton as they became assimilated into the local northern New England culture and their voices acquired a native brogue was publishing Elsie's **Blueberry Hill Cookbook** (1959) which went into multiple printings and is still available today. Mine is a signed 7th 1964 printing and cherished. She then followed with: **Off My Toes** (1961), **Blueberry Hill Menu Cookbook** (1963), and **Blueberry Hill Kitchen Notebook** (1964). Elsie even did a guest appearance on television's "To Tell The Truth".

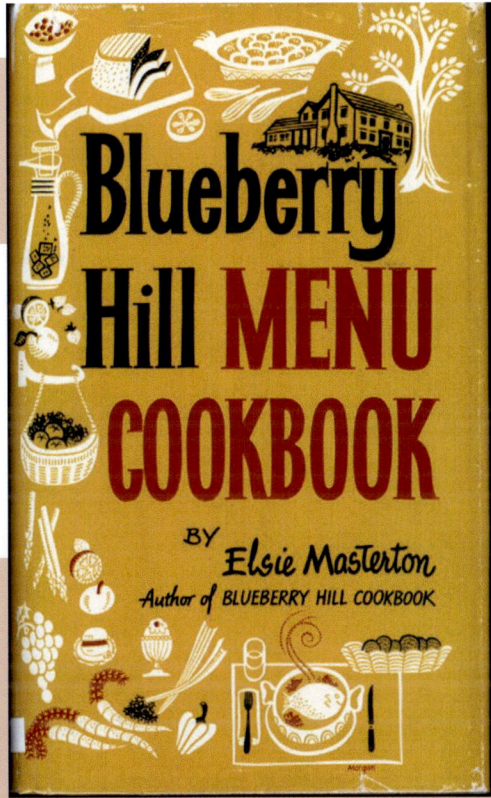

MAMA'S RICE PUDDING

"This is my mother's recipe for creamy rice pudding. Do not try any of the quick-cooking types of rice with this. It's an old-fashion kind of pudding, creamy and full of memories."

3 1/2 cups milk – 1/2 cup sugar – 1/2 teaspoon salt – 1/2 teaspoon vanilla – 1/4 cup long grained rice – 1/4 cup raisins – 2 eggs

Rinse a saucepan with cold water, drain, but do not dry it. Pour into this saucepan 2 cups milk; add salt and bring to boiling. Add rice, stirring constantly. Cover and let simmer over low heat until the rice is tender and the milk absorbed. This will take about 45 minutes, but be sure you keep your eye on it. When the rice is soft and the milk completely absorbed, remove it from stove and let it cool to lukewarm.

Beat together eggs and sugar. Add this to the rice with remaining 1 1/2 cups cold milk, vanilla, and raisins. Wet a 1-quart casserole with cold water. Drain it, but do not dry it. Set it in a pan of cold water. Spoon the pudding into the casserole. Bake in a hot (400°F.) oven until pudding has a light brown crust on top. Test it after it has been in the oven 20 minutes. Don't let it get too dry; it is important that it have a creamy consistency. 4 Servings.

CHAPTER SEVEN
Inns & Farms

ELSIE'S BISCUITS

"I'm going to give you the recipe for my biscuits. I'm a little proud of this recipe because, like all my recipes, it started out with somebody else's combined with somebody else's and, under the eyes of some pretty good Vermont cooks who frowned on my fooling around, I just went ahead and fooled around. Blueberry Hill biscuits are more than a conversation piece.

They are, now, part of every dinner we serve to guests and we hear about if we forget them. Here we go."

Sift
3 cups flour – 2 tablespoons baking powder – 2 teaspoon salt. Cut in **1/4** lb. margarine (and this I mean. They are not the same with any other shortening).

Add 1/2 cup milk – 1/2 cup butter milk – 1/3 cup sour cream – 1/8 teaspoon vanilla – 1/8 teaspoon sugar. Stir until just mixed.

Bake 12 minutes in 450°-500° oven. This depends on the kind of oven you have. My biscuits don't burn in a 500° oven, but maybe yours will, so try it warily. If you should cut your biscuits small as I do, with a whiskey glass, they need to bake only 7 minutes.

Eat these right away!

PAMELA KURE GROGAN

CHAPTER SEVEN
Inns & Farms

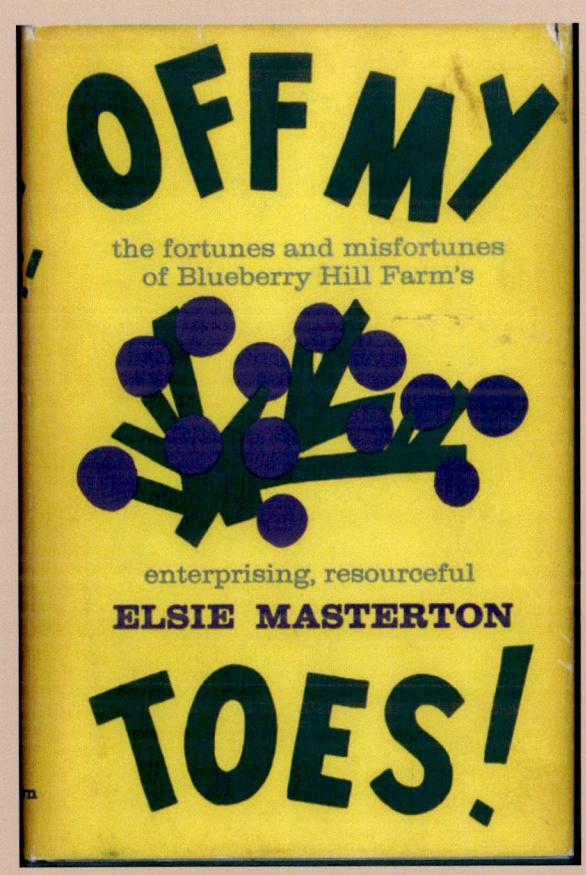

Where are they now?
As much as I believe: whatever might befall you in a personal life crisis, make the best and keep moving. Still, life to some is just not fair. **In Off My Toes**, Elsie recounts her battle with breast cancer resulting in radical surgery. I got teary eyed at the part where she is dictating a cookbook from bed while recovering as her husband types out the manuscript pages in the next room. Having knee replacement surgery while writing this book I reflect on the mutual strength of a strong husband-wife team fighting unfair obstacles.

Three years later she and her husband, John, will die within months of each other leaving three wonderful children from their marriage in the world alone. The kids, as teenage orphans, battled on to survive and flourished.

One of mother's helpers, Laurey Masterton ("who makes fabulous brownies", said Elsie), carried on the family tradition in Asheville, North Carolina active in the catering business. In 2006, she penned a soft cover autobiographical sketch, *Elsie's Biscuits, 'Simple Stories of Me, My Mother, and Food'*. In her writing Laurey says of Elsie's Biscuits, "We make a bazillion of these things each year. Sometimes we add grated Vermont Cheddar Cheese and Fresh Dill, which makes a delicious foundation for a savory hors d'oeurve like a Maple-Glazed Ham Biscuit." Laurey, as a child, with her sisters, entertained guests with songs at Blueberry Hill. In 2014, she passed away from cancer. And like her mother she lived the positive, even with a trademark slogan, 'Don't Postpone Joy'

Today at the same location is Blueberry Hill Inn, a Nordic Ski retreat in winter, a summer outdoorsy get-away, and in 1990 they produced a softcover cookbook! I hope the Inn continues to appreciate the true culinary history of the Mastertons and regale in the home spun story-telling, honor those tasting traditions and pass around a few plates of Elsie's biscuits.

MY COOKBOOK PASSION

CHAPTER SEVEN
Inns & Farms

Coventry Forge Inn

With cooking schools abounding it is my firm belief that part of the curriculum, especially those wishing to open a restaurant, that required reading is **Fine Food, Wine, and Pickled Pine: The Story of Coventry Forge Inn** (1962) by Ann Kilborn Cole (pseudonym of free lance writer, Mrs. Claire Wallis Callahan—also writing in other books as Nancy Hartwell). Once again this is casual story telling ending with recipes but well worth the read, learning the 'inns' and outs of starting a restaurant post-Depression and in the boondocks, 33 miles outside of Philadelphia.

There are two heroes to this story, the matriarch, Mrs. C., and her son Wallis Callahan. After his stint in World War II in the Merchant Marine, the story goes: *"Well, I said, passing a second helping of Sour Cream Apple pie across the table let's take stock, everything being equal...what would you most like to do? What are you most interested in?"*

"Food," he said promptly and forked a piece of pie as if it were his first bite.

Purchased as a derelict property in 1937 to be used for her own writing retreat she turned the place over to her son and his wild idea of fine dining in the back woods, and the Inn opened in May, 1954 with thirty two guests tasting Shrimp Remoulade and Chicken Coventry Forge. The place had gained its name because it might have been owned by the

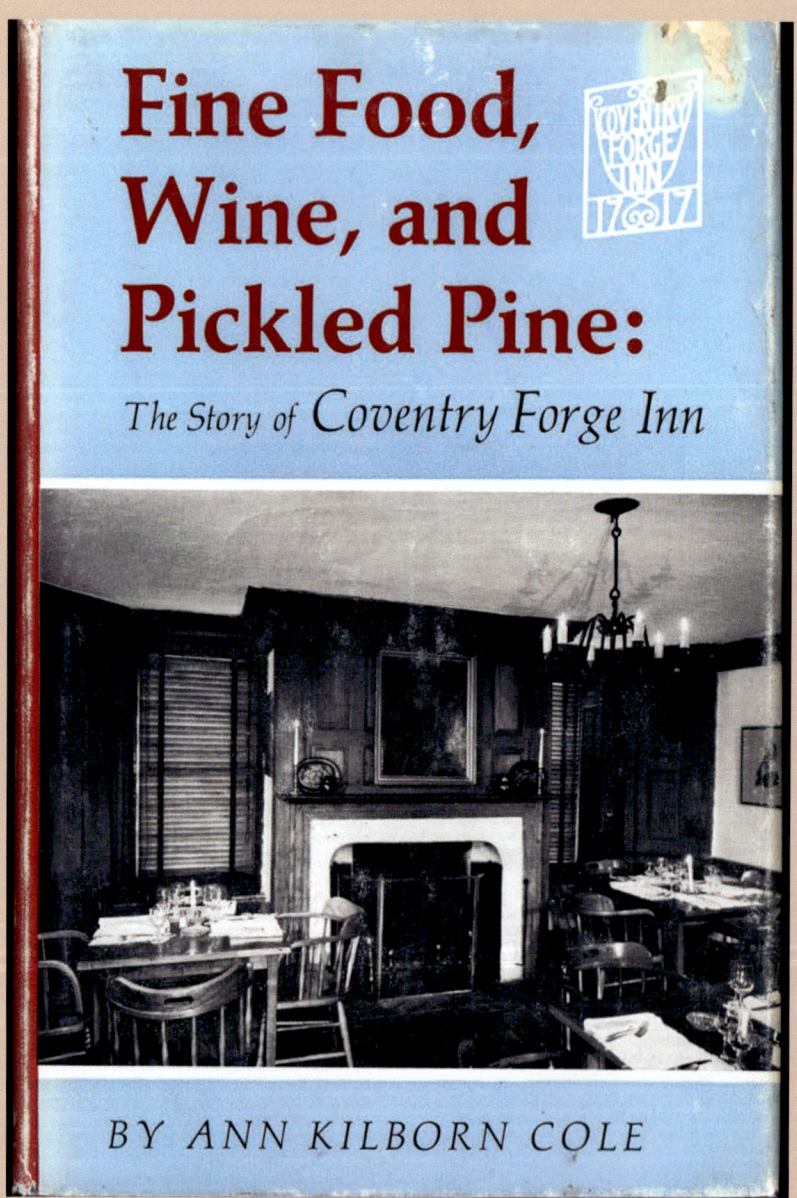

CHAPTER SEVEN
Inns & Farms

ironmaster who in 1717 operated the first forge and furnace for steel in the county.

Because steel made weapons, George Washington and his troops camped nearby at Valley Forge. Between 1758 to 1818 the building had the name of Rising Sun Inn, a wagoner's tavern, where the oxen drivers camped on blankets in front of a large fireplace.

What made the place successful and a willing place to travel out from Philadelphia was the cooking of Wallis Callahan who introduced, nay, 'pioneered', French haute cuisine to the Philadelphia area. Where the Inn started with basic staple dinners to attract guests over time Wallis as a world traveler, a former Merchant Marine cook with vagabond curiosity in sniffing out the best European kitchens evolved his food as French, more Continental. It is best said by the Chapter: *Our Recipes—Haute and Not So Haute*.

Veal Carbonade

This is a Flemish dish made traditionally with beef but by substituting veal Wallis has turned out a very delicate and pleasing addition to his cuisine.

Use 3 pounds of shoulder of veal cut into thin, short slices. Brown this quickly in a combination of butter and olive oil. Brown lightly 1 1/4 pounds of minced onion in butter. Lay in alternate layers in saucepan with a *bouquet garni.* **Now clean out the pan in which the veal was browned (draining off any fat) with 1 pint of beer. Add 1 pint of brown stock (or substitute a bouillon cube or canned bouillon) and thicken with 4 ounces of brown roux (made with 1 1/4 ounces of butter and 1 ¾ ounces of flour). Add 1 ounce of powdered sugar. Set to boil, stirring to keep from sticking and strain over veal and onions. Cover and cook in a 350° oven for about 1 1/2 hours. Eight to ten servings.**

Coquille St. Jacques Parisienne

A good old stand-by for any French menu. Every chef has his own version of it.

Scallops have to be washed very carefully to remove all sand. Cover 1 pound with white wine, add 1 small sliced onion and 1 sliced shallot with a bouquet garni (a sprig of thyme, 1 of parsley, a stalk of celery and a bay leaf all tied together), salt and pepper to taste. Simmer 10 minutes. Make a roux of 1 tablespoon of butter and 1 tablespoon of flour, and enough milk for a thick sauce, cook for a few minutes over low heat. Cook 5 ounces of mushrooms cut into small pieces in water made acid with a tablespoon of lemon juice for 5 minutes. Add these with the scallops also cut into small pieces to the sauce, mix and season highly. Add 2 ounces grated Gruyére cheese. Put into shells, cover not too thickly with bread crumbs and brown in a hot oven. Serves six.

CHAPTER SEVEN
Inns & Farms

Culinary Chain Reaction
Passing the Flambé Torch!

According a Philadelphia visitor travel site: *Most locals agree that the city's first "Restaurant Renaissance" began in the 1970s. The original "Restaurant Renaissance" man was the late Wallis Callahan, whose superb and elegant Coventry Forge Inn opened in 1954 outside the city. When the restaurateur hired esteemed Peter von Starck as sous chef, Callahan set off a culinary chain reaction.*

While studying in France, von Starck met rising star and future partner Georges Perrier. The pair opened Philadelphia's acclaimed **La Panetiere** in a small townhouse on Spruce Street in 1967 [with Perrier as Head Chef]. They were ushering in the country's first new wave of fine dining. In 1970, von Starck moved **La Panetiere** to a larger space on Locust Street. Perrier, however, remained and opened **Le Bec-Fin**. In 1983, **Le Bec-Fin** also outgrew its original townhouse and relocated to its current address on Walnut Street, where it currently anchors a neighborhood known as Restaurant Row. A Mobile five-star restaurant, Le Bec-Fin, one of the country's finest dining destinations, closed in 2013..

Did You Know? Ann Kilborn Cole, as an author, made her reputation not for cookbooks or free-lance work but as an expert in antique collecting, writing three books on the subject, and myriads of magazine articles

the ancient custom of "tipping"

The word TIP was derived from a small sign that appeared over coin boxes in British Inns centuries ago. The sign, "To Insure Promptness," was advice to travelers that a coin in the box meant immediate attention. Not everyone agrees with this custom, however, it is a practice that is here to stay and it is customary to reward good service with a tip. The following may be used as a guide to gratuities for waiters or waitresses in the dining rooms . . .

35¢ per person for breakfast
30¢ per person for buffet lunch
35¢ per person for a la carte lunch
75¢ per person for dinner

Must have been the good ol' days...

Omelete Dining Conversation

One beautiful spring day of the early 17th Century Prince Giovanni of Italy was hunting in the woods of Asis. After an extensive chase of the deer, he and his entourage became lost and were soon hungry. They sent their bush beaters ahead to find food. They came across a lonely cottage occupied by Mr. and Mrs. Mellette. They requested food and Mr. Mellette prepared eggs. He broke the eggs in his pan, and when he heard his guest was to be the popular Prince, he got so nervous his hand would not stop shaking. Oh! Mellette, oh! Mellette, what is happening to you, cried his wife. However, the eggs came out so well, the Prince was delighted and decided to call the scrambled eggs Omelets after "Oh! Mellette."

'Tip Card'. Two vintage items were a restaurant pyramid table top card for the customer's notice

PAMELA KURE GROGAN

CHAPTER SEVEN
Inns & Farms

Mercedes the Cat

"Mercedes the Chef bakes Mouse Cookies"

'On a trip to Port Townsend, Washington after a store mangers' conference for Sur La Table in Seattle, I ran across an extraordinary children's artist, Richard Jesse Watson. I bought a cartoon-styled sketch and several copies of his marvelous illustrated **'The Night Before Christmas'** to give to family members. Staying in touch, I later asked him to create a painting in memory of my beloved cat, Mercedes, and he did so as a 'chef' with book titles in background: *Fish for the Feline, Cat Cookery, Meow Muffins, Fast Meals to Purr About, Cat Nip Casseroles*, among others. Richard also painted the cover art for my husband's first mystery, **'Vegas Die.'**

Illustration by Richard Jesse Watson

MY COOKBOOK PASSION

CHAPTER EIGHT

PUBLISHING HOUSES: FARM JOURNAL

PAMELA KURE GROGAN

CHAPTER EIGHT
Publishers Houses: Farm Journal

"For people who really love it, food is the lens through which we view the world. For us, the way people cook and eat, how they set their tables, the utensils that they use all tell a story. If you choose to pay attention, cooking is an important cultural artifact, an expression of time, place and personality."
Ruth Reichl-- Chef, Food Writer (Gourmet Magazine Editor-in-Chief 1999-2009)

America in its infancy grew first into childhood as an agrarian nation. Journalism for farmers, beginning with Benjamin Franklin's *Poor Richard's Almanac* entered adulthood with the founding by Wilmer Atkinson of *Farm Journal*, an agricultural newspaper intended for farmers within a day's ride of Philadelphia and dedicated to "practical, not fancy farming." The first issue, priced at 25 cents, was published in March 1877 with an initial press run of 25,000 copies. In a rare pledge of integrity for early publications, Atkinson in his premiere issue made the pledge not to accept any 'quack medical advertisements'.

What led to the Farm Journal considering cookbooks was its acquisition in 1939 of *The Farmer's Wife*, a national women's magazine, which was then included as a magazine within *Farm Journal*. The women's section was eventually replaced by *Farm Family Living* which catered to all members of the family. Women were becoming a major role in the farm and as far back as the 1900's Publisher-Founder Atkinson stood out as one of the few male suffragettes supporting women's right to vote, as well as seeking to repeal the Widow's Tax which kept many women holding on to the family farm after a husband's death.

To take the editorial spatula for the cookbook division the right person had to come along, and she did. Nell Nichols published in 1952, her own **Home Cooking Across the U.S.A**., no doubt an asset on her resume (likewise didn't hurt she grew up in the middle of Kansas). Hired as Food Editor for the *Farm Journal* she held this position for many years, and would edit in this time over 25 *Farm Journal* cooking and kitchen books.

How this book came to be is interesting as it required twelve years in the making supported by a questionnaire sent to 500 farm women making up the FJ's Family Test Group. What did they want? The consensus: "Farm life has changed in the past decade or two; so have ingredients on the grocers' shelves. So have pots and pans and equipment! The cellar pantry has been replaced by a refrigerator and, in half the farm homes of the U.S., a freezer..." Inside this book published in 1959 (Doubleday & Co.), *Farm Journal's* **Country Cookbook** creates recipes around 'what country women think of food'. All recipes were tested in their Countryside Kitchens consisting of four complete kitchens.

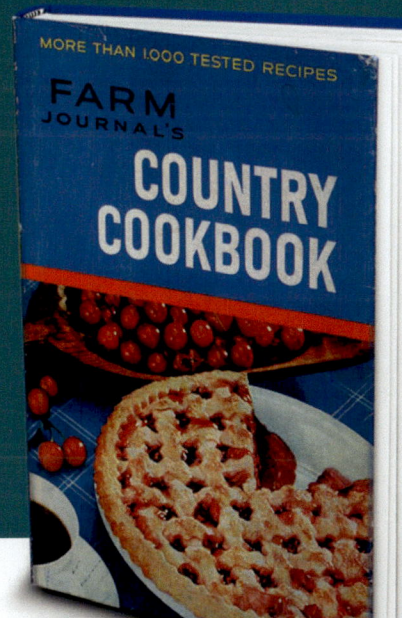

MY COOKBOOK PASSION

CHAPTER EIGHT
Publishers Houses: F...

They have a chapter called: *Money Makers*. Nell B. Nichols says: "Some of you tell us you earn money by selling homemade foods…these recipes are from farm women who have best sellers." To foster entrepreneurial spirit we need a few modern cookbooks with chapters like this.

Did you know? *Farm Journal* reached its peak in 1953 with 3.7 million subscriptions. Times were changing, for the farm family and for mass communication via magazines (*Life, Look, Saturday Evening Post* are other bygone examples). Believe it or not, *Farm Journal* survives today as a diversified corporation, lean and mean, providing farm information via online, newsletters and via livestock/agriculture specific industry publications.

Old-Fashioned Recipes

Few farm women have the ingredients or time these busy days to fix the tedious dishes Grandmother used to make. But sometimes nostalgia nudges all of us to turn back the clock long enough to make a few old-time favorites to treat our families and friends…

When you've a lot of windfall apples, cook up some old-time apple butter—its appeal is difficult to resist, especially if you remember hot biscuits topped with this spicy, cider-flavored spread. – N.B. Nichols

OVEN APPLE BUTTER

Everyone used to take a turn stirring the purple-russet goodness

2 qts. Water – 2 tblsp. salt – 6 lbs. apples, cored, peeled and sliced – 2 qts. sweet cider – 3 1/2 to 4 c. sugar – 1 tsp. cinnamon – 1/2 tsp. cloves – 1/2 tsp. allspice

- Combine water and salt. Add apples. Drain well but do not rinse slices.

- Grind through fines blade of food grinder. Measure pulp and juice (should be 2 qts.).

- Combine with cider. Place in large enamel pan. Center pan in moderate oven (350°). Let mixture simmer until cooked down about half and is thick and mushy (about 3 to 3 1/2 hours). Stir thoroughly every half hour.

- Put mixture through sieve or food mill; should yield 2 1/4 to 2 1/2 quarts.

- Combine sugar and spices; add to sauce and return to oven. Continue simmering about 1 1/2 hours or until thick, stirring every half hour. To test, pour small amount onto cold plate. If no liquid oozes around edge, apple butter is cooked.

- Pour into hot, sterilized jars and seal at once. Makes 2 quarts.

CHAPTER EIGHT
Publishers Houses: Farm Journal

Collector's Corner

I like this series of books by *Farm Journal* for the simple reason they are wholesome, well constructed recipes, economical in that ingredients are interchangeable to make varied dishes. Plus, it's real 'old fashion country style'. Books are out there and affordable. **Country Cookbook** was reprinted as a paperback in 1981.

It is almost impossible to find Nell Beaubien Nichol's **Home Cooking Across the U.S.A**. (1952, Iowa State College Press). Appreciated in value is *Farm Journal's* **Complete Pie Cookbook** (1965, Doubleday & Co.). Now, that does go for a pretty penny. Start your own Search/Wish list. Somewhere, sitting unnoticed and under-priced in a dusty book store, is your long- lost treasure. Many used bookstores don't have a value system to price old cookbooks.

Bargains exist. For searching and price comparisons I use www.abe.com (American Book Exchange). Sometimes Ebay provides books the general buyer is unaware of true values. Outside general searching go to their *Advance Search* of what has sold to see what buyers actually paid. Recently, I started putting unwanted books for sale onto various Facebook group marketplaces.

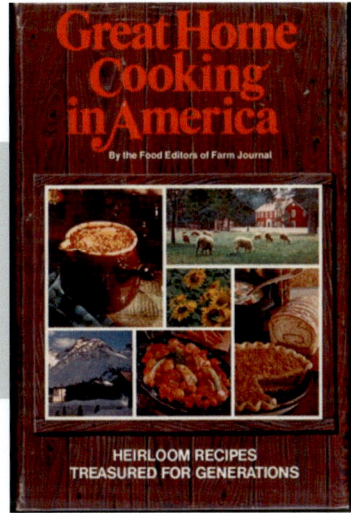

MY COOKBOOK PASSION

CHAPTER EIGHT
Publishers Houses: Farm Journal

BANANA-SWEET POTATO BAKE

Excellent take-along dish—pretty, too

3 c. mashed cooked sweet potatoes (6 medium) 2 ripe bananas, mashed – 1 tsp. salt – 1/4 to 1/2 c. light cream – 1 c. miniature marshmallows

- Combine hot sweet potatoes (mashed until smooth) and bananas. Add salt and sufficient cream to make a soft, fluffy mixture.

- Place in buttered 1-qt. casserole. Dot top with marshmallows. Heat in slow overn (325°) long enough to brown marshmallows, about 45 minutes. Serve piping hot. Makes 6 servings.

- Note: You can make 2 casseroles of this vegetable treat for 10 to 12 servings.

PAMELA KURE GROGAN

CHAPTER EIGHT
Publishers Houses: Farm Journal

PINEAPPLE BEETS
Pleasing way to perk up beets when you serve them often. Good flavor blend

(13½ oz.) can pineapple chunks — 1/2 c. water — 1/3 c. cider vinegar — 4 tblsp. brown sugar 1 tblsp. Cornstarch — 1/2 tsp. salt — 1/8 tsp. ground ginger — 2 (1 lb.) cans sliced beets, drained (4 cups)

FRENCH ONIONS AND RICE
Absolutely delicious with poultry

1/4 c. long grain rice — 2 qts. boiling water — 1 tsp. salt — 1/4 c. butter or margarine 4 c. thinly sliced large white or yellow onions (about 3) — 1/2 tsp. salt — 1/8 tsp. paprika — 2 tblsp. grated Parmesan cheese

- Drain syrup from pineapple and mix with water and vinegar. Mix brown sugar, cornstarch, salt and ginger; add vinegar mixture. Cook until thickened, stirring constantly. Add beets, then heat to boiling. Just before serving mix pineapple into hot mixture. Makes 8 servings.

"Refrain from mentioning that vegetables are good-for-you foods. This approach, tried for years, seems to have failed in many homes. Concentrate instead on making vegetable dishes so tempting and tasty that everyone will enjoy them."

- Drop rice into rapidly boiling water with 1 tsp. salt added; boil uncovered 5 minutes; drain at once.

- Melt butter in 2 qt. casserole in oven; stir in onions. Add 1/2 tsp. Salt and stir in onions. Add 1/2 tsp. salt and stir onions in butter until nicely yellowed and coated. Then add rice and stir to distribute evenly. Cover and bake in slow oven (325°) 1 hour. Sprinkle with paprika and cheese. Makes 8 servings.

Note: Large onions are easier to slice if first cut in halves lengthwise and then placed on a flat surface and sliced. (Cut a thick slice from top and bottom, enough to remove top and root growth; save this for seasoning another dish.)

MY COOKBOOK PASSION

POTATO-MACADAMIA NUT PUFFS

Consider these distinctive potato puffs when you want to splurge a bit

6 medium potatoes – 1/2 c. milk – 1 egg – 1/4 c. soft butter or margarine – 1/2 c. finely chopped macadamia nuts or walnuts – 2 tsp salt
2 tsp. baking powder
1/4 tsp. white pepper

- Cook peeled potatoes in boiling water until done; drain. Put through a ricer or mash well. Turn into large bowl of electric mixer; add remaining ingredients and whip at medium speed until fluffy.

- Drop large spoonfuls onto well-greased baking sheet. Bake in moderate oven (375º) to 10 to 156 minutes. Makes 8 servings.

SOUTHWESTERN CORN SCALLOP

2 eggs, slightly beaten – 1 (1 lb.) can cream-style corn – 2/3 c. milk – 1/2 c. coarsely crushed soda crackers – 1 tsp. sugar – 1 tsp. salt – 1/8 tsp. pepper – 1 c. grated sharp Cheddar cheese – 1 tblsp. chopped canned green chili peppers

Combine all ingredients. Place in greased 1-qt. casserole. Bake in moderate oven (350º) until set, 60 to 70 minutes. Makes 6 servings.

DATE NUT BARS *These cake-like cookies and coffee make great evening refreshments*

1 c. sifted confectioners sugar – 1/2 tsp. baking powder – 1 tblsp. oil – 3/4 chopped nuts – 2 eggs, beaten – 1 c. chopped dates – 1/4 c. sifted cake flour – 1 tsp. vanilla – 1/4 tsp. salt – Confectioners sugar (for tops)

Add 1 c. confectioners sugar and oil to eggs; blend well. Add sifted dry ingredients. Stir in nuts, dates and vanilla.

Pour into grease 9" square pan. Bake in slow oven (325º) 25 minutes. Cool slightly in pan on rack. Cut in 3x1" bars; sprinkle with confectioners sugar. Makes 27.

CHAPTER EIGHT
Publishers Houses: Farm Journal

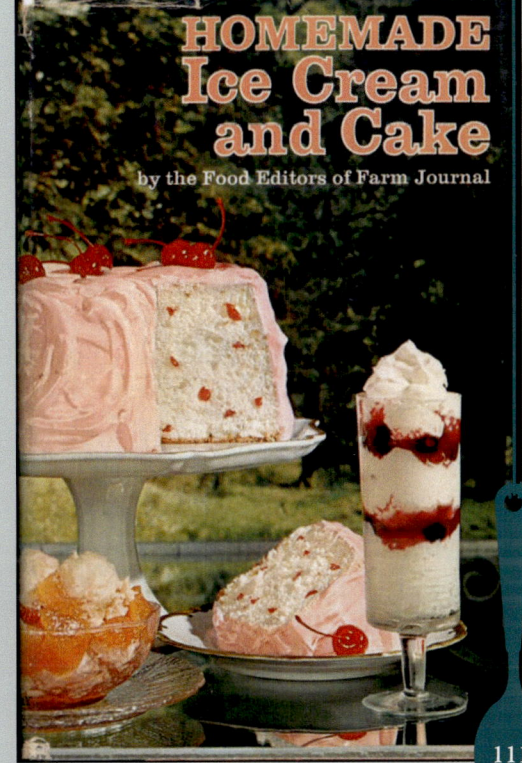

CREAMY LIME SHERBET

Garnish each serving with two bright red strawberry halves

1 (3 oz.) pkg. lime flavor gelatin – 1 (6 oz.) can frozen limeade concentrate – 1c. boiling water – 8 drops green food color – 1 1/4 c. sugar – 4 c. milk – 1/8 tsp. salt – 2 c. light cream

- Dissolve gelatin in boiling water. Add sugar and salt. Add limeade, stirring until thawed. Stir in food color, milk and light cream.

- Pour into 1-gal. freezer can. Freeze by basic directions.* Makes 1 gallon.

*[They ask you to refer to a section on "Freezing and Ripening Ice Cream". This means using the old fashion ice cream crank mixer, with ice and rock salt to create the freezing brine. My husband remembers as a kid being told that cranking the handle until it couldn't turn was a passage rite into manhood. His family recipe was pineapple sherbet. Nowadays, the store has several modern varieties of ice cream makers and better to use today's version unless you are really into a nostalgia demonstration for the kids. Ripening ice cream refers to letting it stand and expand. –pkg]

MY COOKBOOK PASSION

PIONEER POTATO CANDY

Potato candy is an "I remember" sweet—there was bustling excitement in grandmothers' kitchens when this treat was made for the Christmas holidays. Grandchildren of those days haven't forgotten how wonderful it tasted.

A FARM JOURNAL reader recently wrote from Iowa: "Last year the kids came home from Grandma's with the recipe for potato candy and a sample of it. I hardly could believe you could make such wonderful candy with potatoes. I tried the recipe and had success with it."

Our recipe for Pioneer Candy, contributed by a Wisconsin homemaker, gives the measurement of cooked, unseasoned, mashed potato. Potatoes have a high water content, which depends on the climate (dry or wet season), the time of year (new potatoes contain more water than old ones), and the variety. The amount of water in the potato affects the quantity of confectioners sugar you need to add.

The trick is to add enough sugar to produce a candy mixture with the consistency of a stiff dough so that you can knead it. The result is a type of fondant that you can dip in melted chocolate and roll in chopped nuts or coconut. Or you can omit the dipping and decorate the candy pieces with nuts. This, like all other potato candies, is at its best when eaten fresh.

This is a big recipe; you may wish to make half of it the first time

1 c. warm unseasoned mashed potato – 1 lb. chocolate confection or chocolate for dipping – 1/2 tsp. salt – 2/3 c. ground salted peanuts, or 1 c. shredded coconut – 2 tsp. vanilla – 2 lbs. confectioners sugar

- Combine potato, salt and vanilla in a 4-qt mixing bowl. Sift confectioners sugar over potato, stirring and adding about 1 c. at a time. Mixture will liquefy when first sugar is added, then gradually begin to thicken. When it becomes the consistency of stiff dough, knead it even though all the sugar has not been added (likewise, add more sugar if needed).

- After kneading, cover with a damp cloth; chill until a small spoonful can be rolled into a ball.

- Shape in small (1/2") balls. Dip balls in melted chocolate, then roll in peanuts or coconut. Makes about 8 dozen 1/2" balls or 2 pounds.

CHAPTER EIGHT
Publishers Houses: Farm Journal

WONDERFUL OKLAHOMA BROWN CANDY

You'll never put more delicious candy in your mouth. The recipe for it originated in the Sooner State, where the candy is a favorite.

You may want a helper standing by, at least the first time you make this candy. The trick is to get the sugar caramelized and ready to pour at the same time the sugar-milk mixture reaches the boil. Also, it's helpful to have someone share the beating.

6 c. sugar – 1 tsp. vanilla – 2 c. milk or dairy half-and-half – 2 lbs pecans, broken (about 8 1/2 c.) – 1/4 tsp. baking soda – 1/2 c. butter or margarine (1 stick)

- Combine 4 c. sugar and milk in 4-qt. heavy saucepan. Stir and set aside.

- Put remaining 2 c. sugar in 10" heavy skillet over medium heat. Stir constantly until sugar starts to melt. Then place sugar-milk mixture over low heat, stirring occasionally until sugar dissolves.

- Continue melting sugar in skillet, stirring, until all is melted and is the color of light brown sugar. (Melting sugar scorches easily so watch carefully). This may take almost 30 minutes.

- Pour melted sugar in a fine stream into the boiling sugar-milk mixture stirring constantly. The secret to success is to pour in a very fine stream.

- Cook combined mixture to the firm ball stage (246°). Remove from heat at once. Stir in baking soda. The mixture foams vigorously when soda is added. Add butter and let stand 30 minutes.

- Add vanilla and beat with wooden spoon until mixture loses its gloss and begins to thicken. Add pecans, and stir to mix.

- Pour into lightly buttered 13X9X2" pan. Cool slightly and cut in pieces of the desired size. Makes 4 1/2 to 5 pounds.

MY COOKBOOK PASSION

CHAPTER EIGHT
Publishers Houses: Farm Journal

Five decades ago, the epitome of the special occasion dinner meal seems very *comfort food* oriented today.

REGAL BEEF DINNER
Stuffed Baked Potatoes/ Favorite Green Beans/ Fiesta Relish Tray/ Strawberry Cheese Pie.

This is a splendid menu for your husband's birthday dinner, an impressive selection for many other occasions. You get off to a good start with the meal because a standing rib roast commands great respect.

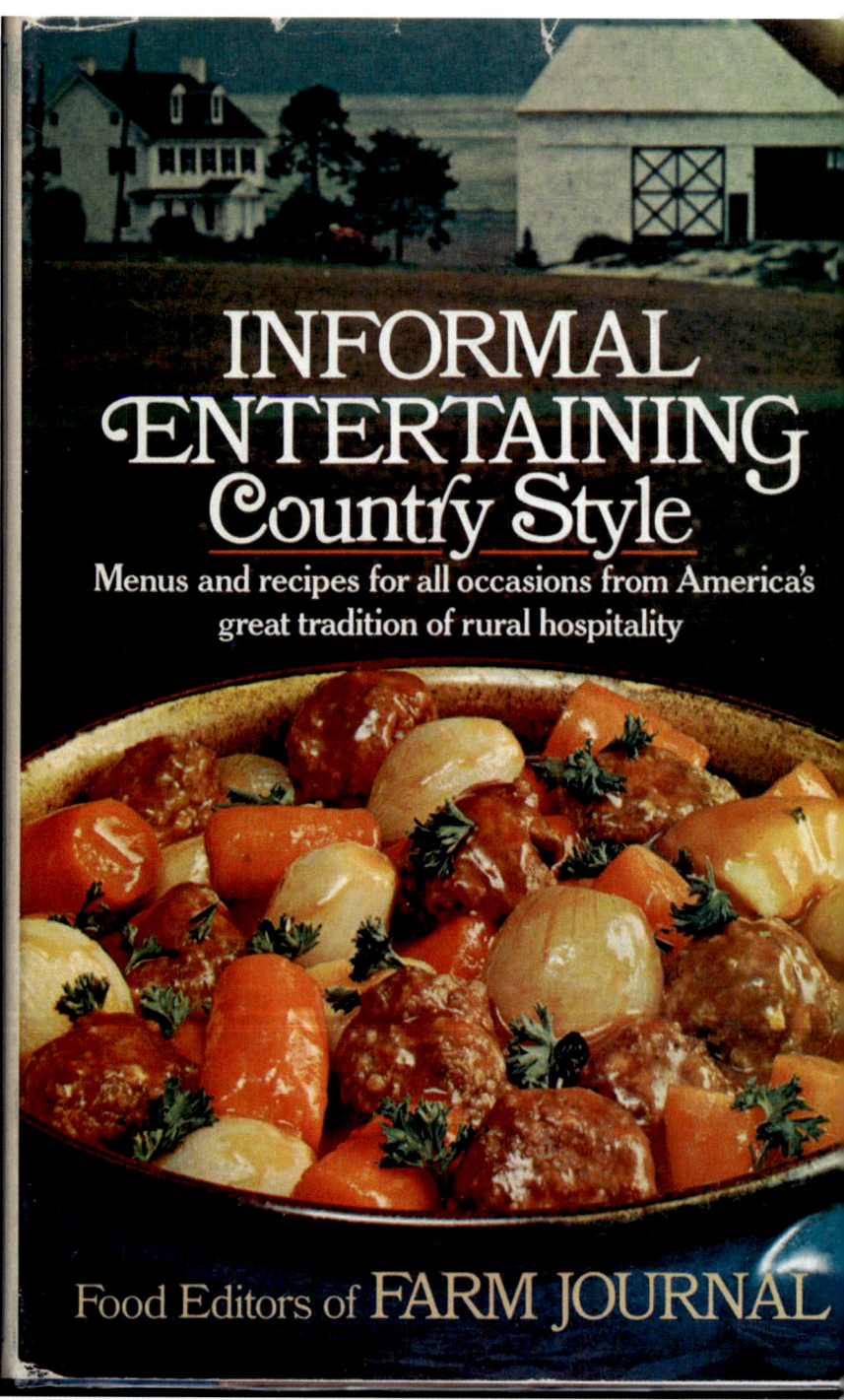

PAMELA KURE GROGAN

SPECIAL STUFFED BAKED POTATOES

Cumin, a seasoning used since biblical times and an ingredient in chili powder, gives potatoes a subtle new flavor

8 medium baking potatoes – 1 1/2 c. milk – 2 (1 1/2 oz.) envelopes sour cream – 1/4 c. butter or regular margarine sauce mix – 6 tblsp. grated process American cheese – 1 tsp. ground cumin – 4 slices bacon – 1 tsp. salt – Dash of pepper

- Bake potatoes in hot oven (425°), 50 to 60 minutes until tender.

- Meanwhile, combine sauce mix, cumin, salt, pepper and milk. Let stand 10 minutes to blend flavors.

- Cut a slice from top of potatoes and discard. Scoop out potatoes, saving shells. Place in large electric mixer bowl and beat, adding the sauce mixture and butter. Beat until light and fluffy, adding more milk if necessary. The amount needed varies with the potatoes.

- Fill potato shells with fluffy potatoes, sprinkle with grated cheese and heat in slow oven (325°) 40 to 45 minutes, or until thoroughly heated. Cook bacon until crisp; drain and crumble. Sprinkle over tops of potatoes. Makes 8 servings.

FAVORITE GREEN BEANS

Seasonings from Italian-American kitchens make this special

1 (10 ox.) pkgs. frozen green beans – 3/4 tsp. garlic salt –1 tblsp. salad oil – 1/4 c. croutons – 1 tblsp. wine vinegar – 2 to 3 tblsp. grated Parmesan cheese – 1 tsp. chopped shallots or green onion

- Cook beans by package directions; drain if necessary.

- Combine oil, vinegar, shallots and garlic salt. Pour over beans. Add croutons; heat and stir until well heated. Pour into serving dish and sprinkle with cheese. Makes 6 to 8 servings

COCONUT SNACK CAKE

So good! This cake was given a Purple Ribbon in Nebraska

2 c. sifted flour – 1 tsp baking soda – 1 tsp ground cinnamon, 6 tsp salt – 2/3 c. shortening – 1 c. brown sugar, firmly packed, 2 eggs – 1 tsp vanilla – 1 c. buttermilk – 1 c. flaked coconut, 1 c. sugar – 1 tsp ground cinnamon – 1/2 tsp ground nutmeg – 1/4 c. light cream

- Sift together flour, baking soda, cinnamon and salt.

- Cream together shortening and brown sugar until light and fluffy. Beat in eggs, one at a time beating well after each addition. Beat in vanilla.

- Add dry ingredients alternately with buttermilk, beating well after each addition. Spread in greased 13X9X2" cake pan.

- Combine coconut, sugar, cinnamon, nutmeg and light cream. Sprinkle over top of batter.

- Bake in 350° oven 35 minutes or until cake tests done. Cool in pan on rack. Makes 16 servings.

Edited in 1975 by Elise W. Manning, *Farm Journal* Food Editor who took over from Nell Nichols.

CHAPTER EIGHT
rs Houses: Farm Journal

CHAPTER EIGHT
Publishers Houses: Farm Journal

Here we have Gwen Berryman known as 'Mrs. Archer' of the British Broadcasting Company's radio show about her family's own country recipes. Book stamped *'From the Cookery Collection of Marshall Blum'*. I'd like to know more about this collector. Is he also an author? 'Collection of Cookery & Gastronomy' **Doris Archer's Farm Cookery Book** (1958) Museum Press Limited, London

Before beginning her editor's career at Farm Journal, here is her outpouring of twenty years on the editorial staff of *Women's Home Companion*. **Nell Nichols Reports --Good Home Cooking Across the U.S.A.** (1953) The Iowa State College Press, Ames

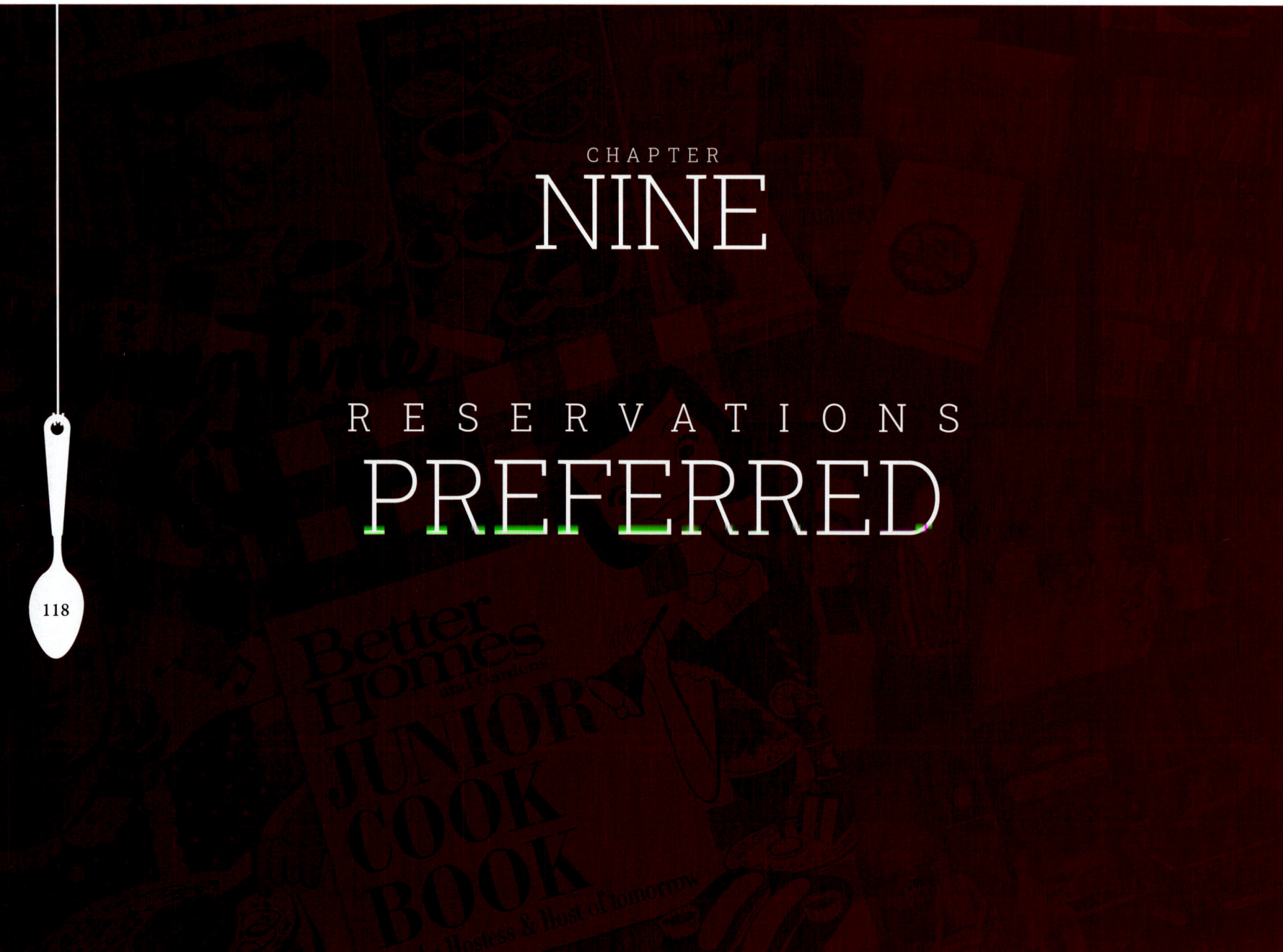

CHAPTER NINE
RESERVATIONS PREFERRED

PAMELA KURE GROGAN

CHAPTER NINE
Reservations Preferred

"Come unto me, all ye that labor in the stomach, and I will restore you"

--M. Boulanger, 1765. Motto over door of first European restaurant

I don't know about you but I can sit and relax and recall special meals, those restaurants where they were created and presented, where ambiance in candle-lit rooms or outside terraces with distant views vividly rekindles my thoughts. At times these recollections sense smells of a kitchen and inhaled into my subconscious savoring tingles wander my tongue.

We all love restaurants. They are places to explore, to enjoy new adventures. Yet we always leave as critics, voicing pro or con. Our mental list stars the best for return visits while we never cross again the threshold where we pushed mediocre food around on the plate, where the service staff worried more about their own daily problems than concentrate on creating for guests a menu world of suspended disbelief.

I want to recall past (some still present) restaurants and the cookbooks which highlighted their success.

- As to our dining out, the word 'restaurant' springs from the French, restaurer, meaning 'to restore' and first applied in 1765 to an eating establishment in Paris run by a soup-seller named Boulanger. By 1782, history tells us a place called *Grand Taverne de Londres* was seating guests at individual tables, offering menus, and stating fixed operating hours.

Let's start off with a cookbook created not by a chef but by the ultimate maitre d'hotel, anywhere, anytime, past or present: **Oscar Tschirky** (1866- 1950). The best way to present him is with scatter shot of trivia.

- He was known as "Oscar of the Waldorf", or "Mr. Oscar" and served as the ultimate host of the old Waldorf-Astoria, 1893-1928, until the building was torn down to make way for the Empire State Building. Three years later he continued his duties at the new Waldorf Astoria when it opened in 1931. He retired in 1943.

- When he came to America from Switzerland he gained a job at Delmonico's supposedly because he saw Diamond Jim Brady escorting in actress Lillian Russell, and Oscar wanted to meet her. Oscar eventually moved up to be the Head Waiter at Delmonico's before moving over to the Waldorf.

- *Maitre d'hotel* means Master of the Hall. In lesser restaurants the position would be called a 'host'.

CHAPTER NINE
Reservations Preferred

- In restaurant lore the following dishes have been attributed to his creative skills: *Waldorf Salad, Thousand Island Dressing, Eggs Benedict, and Veal Oscar*. Closer to the truth, these recipes probably showed up in the kitchen at the Waldorf and he made the most in promoting them (others lay better territorial claims of how the dishes came to be).

- Composer Cole Porter's 1934 song, "You're the Top", contains the lyric, 'You're the top, you're a Waldorf salad...' Porter lived for a while in the Waldorf Towers.

- Tschirky's home in New Paltz, New York eventually became a retirement home for chefs, called the Culinarians' Home.

- Today, you can find his statuary likeness in the hotel and the Waldorf's coffee shop is named 'Oscar's'. Yes, you can get there stylized Eggs Benedict.

- Over the years he accumulated one of the largest collection of menus and today these and his personal papers are housed at Cornell University. [Don't forget we also visited him on page 31 ,the fancy anniversary dinner feted for he and his wife]

As to **The Cook Book by "Oscar" of the Waldorf** (1896,) it is an encyclopedia tome of 900 pages of the culinary tastes of the 1890's, gourmet as well as exotic to our current standards. *Sheep's Tongues in Papers, Fricasseed Pigeons* or various stewed- baked-pickled preparations of *Carp* don't resonate well with me. For historical meandering my first edition 1896 copy is an enjoyable read of the Gay Nineties palate and as far as I am concerned, if food be music, it is the Overture to all future fine dining cookbooks.

Oscar's Waldorf Salad. (p.433)
Peel two raw apples and cut them into small pieces, say about half an inch square, also cut some celery the same way, and mix it with the apple. Be very careful not to let any seeds of the apples be mixed with it. The salad must be dressed with a good mayonnaise.

Is that it? Over the years, as we know, other styles and ingredients have made their way into the base foundation of the Waldorf Salad and we find modern kitchen artists dropping in oddities from Cajun chili powder to grapefruit to pine nuts to dried cherries. My personal choices are the middle safe ground of raisins, chopped pecans or walnuts, perhaps small pear slices. With apples, I leave on the skins. You could put ontop of a bed of lettuce—but not then the 'original'.

Maintenon Sauce
Chop fine a slice of lean ham and put it into a saucepan with a sprig of parsley, two mushrooms and two shallots, all finely chopped, one-half tablespoonful of butter, two lumps of sugar and the juice of a lemon, and toss them over the fire for a few minutes. Mix well one tablespoonful of flour with a small quantity of water then stir in with it gradually one-half pint of stock and mix it in with the other ingredients in the saucepan; season to taste and continue stirring the sauce over the fire for twenty minutes. Move the saucepan to the side of the fire and thicken the sauce with the beaten yolks of four eggs. When thick the sauce is ready for serving.

CHAPTER NINE
Reservations Preferred

For their Golden Anniversary the hotel produced **The Waldorf-Astoria Cook book** *(1969) by Ted James and Rosalind Cole, updated history mixed with current recipes. Oscar stories are included.*

Still Going Strong? You be the judge...

You take a gamble on acquiring a restaurant cookbook. Was it hurried to publication? Are the recipes too commercial in production and not kitchen tested? In my mind you need something special attached to a good restaurant cookbook—history, chef's credentials, easy-to-create masterpieces (with exquisite and proven tasting). To my mind, most essential to a restaurant cookbook—*a touch of literary ambiance*-- to seep out from the writing and recipes.

Here I have chosen three cookbooks of restaurants which exist today, even after a national epidemic and still steeped in tradition, maintain their food fame, where you can gain a surrounding ambiance: theatre district (Sardi's), the classic resort (Greenbrier) and a tried and true downtown seafood bistro (Bookbinders).

Known affectionately as "Bookies" the restaurant was founded in 1865 down by the Delaware River in

CHAPTER NINE
Reservations Preferred

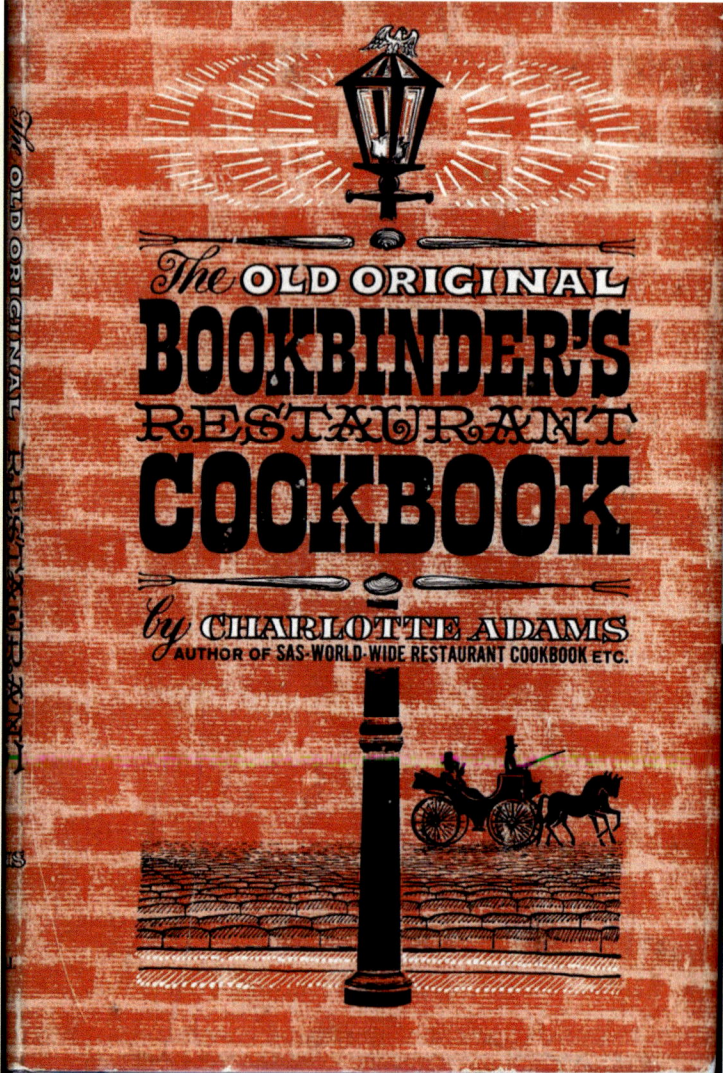

Philadelphia. Each noon time, Samuel Bookbinder's wife, Sarah, would ring a bell to announce the main meal of the day. John Taxin acquired the restaurant from the Bookbinder family during the during the Depression. In 2009 the restaurant closed though a namesake still operates in Richmond, Virginia. And Taxin family's branded Bookbinders food division today sells retail cocktail and tartar sauces. In the past location, a restaurant 'The Olde Bar' specializes in seafood. The restaurants claim to fame is seafood. The **Old Original Bookbinder's Restaurant Cookbook** (1961) by Charlotte Adams is not elaborate and recipes give minimal instructions suggesting she has faith in you as the cook.

CHAPTER NINE
Reservations Preferred

LOBSTER BISQUE

1 tablespoon finely minced celery – 1 tablespoon finely minced onion – 3 tablespoons butter – 1/4 cup flour – 4 cups lobster stock – 1/4 cup cream – Salt and white pepper – Dash of freshly ground nutmeg – 1 cup diced lobster meat

Author: "Creating the lobster stock for the bisque is a time-consuming art but well worth it." For a short period of time I was the Food Editor for an on-line 'buy live lobsters from Maine' site.

Sauté celery and onion in butter until soft, but not brown. Sprinkle with the flour and mix well. Add lobster stock and cream and stir until thickened. Season to taste with salt, white pepper, and nutmeg. Add lobster meat and heat through. Serves 4.

CHAPTER NINE
Reservations Preferred

Founded in 1778 around a sulphur spring where visitors came to 'take the waters' the Greenbrier Hotel, the 'Old White', located in White Sulphur Springs, West Virginia, has evolved through a very colorful history of war and important guests, too lengthy to detail here. Suffice it to say, today, among the refined opulence of the many amenities is the ability to participate in the hotel's Culinary Arts Center where the guests, at any cooking level, can take a variety of courses from experts. Sign me up! Call the masseuse while you're at it! Before you get to the gourmet recipes laid out in the **Greenbrier Cookbook** you have to accept that it is **Hermann Rusch's Greenbrier Cookbook** (1975) and 6 pages of his curriculum vitae at the book's beginning puts you in your place. You come to accept he does have the pedigree of the Swiss expatriate and is the epitome of the grand resort master chef when he writes as the Executive Food Director of the Greenbrier backed up by co-author, Martina Neely. After all Chef Rusch (1907-1997), among many deserved titles, achieved status as Honorary President of the Societe Culinaire Philanthropique and Honorary Chairman of the Salon of Culinary Art of New York and one of the founders of the international Resort Food Executive Committee. Today in the American Culinary Federation chefs around the country vie for the Hermann G. Rusch Humanitarian Award which honors chefs who have demonstrated the highest level of commitment to the culinary profession. Okay, whatever he is going to show us is going to be well worth it. Here are two of my favorites.

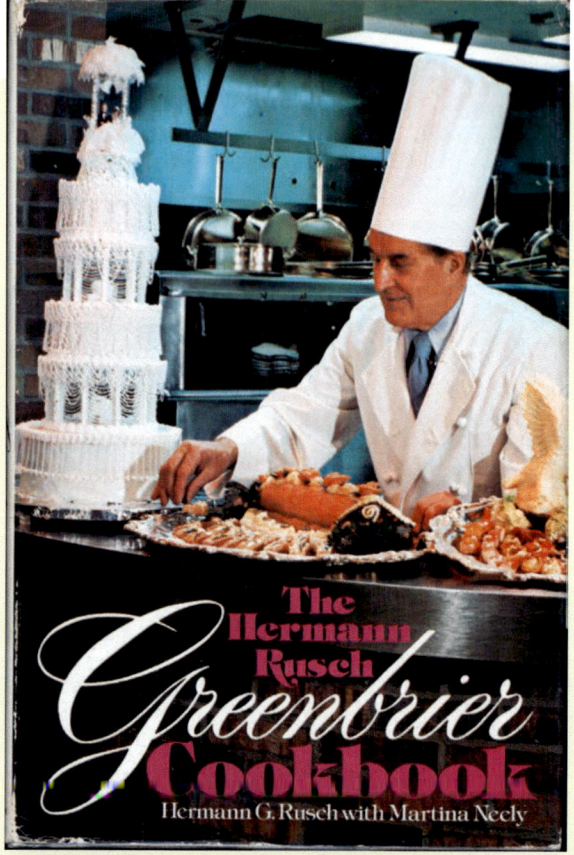

PAMELA KURE GROGAN

CHAPTER NINE
Reservations Preferred

One of the most spectacular and delicious main courses served at The Greenbrier.

FILET DE BOEUF WELLINGTON
(Beef Wellington)

1 beef tenderloin, about 5 pounds – 1/2 teaspoon salt – 1/2 teaspoon pepper 2 tablespoons butter – 1/2 cup peeled, chopped onion – 1 pound fresh mushrooms, chopped – 1/2 pound ground pork 1 cup chicken livers, sliced – 1/2 pound goose liver pâté – 2 eggs – 1/3 cup brandy pastry for 9-inch, 2-crust pie – 3 sheets pork fat (or 6 strips bacon)

Preheat oven to 450º F. Sprinkle beef lightly with salt and pepper, and place on rack in shallow roasting pan. Roast about 20 minutes per pound for rare. Remove from oven and let cool to room temperature. Melt butter in a skillet and sauté onions until golden brown. Add mushrooms and sauté until browned. Add ground pork and chicken livers and let cook for 3 minutes. Remove from heat and cool mixture to room temperature. Place onion mixture in an electric blender. Add goose liver pâté, one of the eggs and brandy. Blend until s mooth. Set this mixture aside for the filling. Prepare pastry dough. Roll dough on a lightly floured board into a rectangle about 1/8-inch thick and large enough to completely enclose tenderloin.

Place cooled tenderloin on pastry about 2 inches from one long side. Spread pâté mixture on meat and cover with pork fat or bacon strips. Fold pastry over meat, and seal seam and ends carefully. Place roll in a shallow roasting pan. Lightly beat remaining egg, and brush pasty with it. Preheat oven to 350º F. Bake tenderloin 50 minutes until pastry is golden brown. Serves eight.

CHAPTER NINE
Reservations Preferred

CRABES MOUX A LA MEUNIERE
(Soft Shell Crabs Meuniere)

12 soft shell crabs, cleaned
1/2 cup light cream
1/2 cup all-purpose flour
1/2 cup vegetable oil
3 table spoons butter lemon juice
1/2 cup chopped fresh parsley

If the Chef will give me his recipe for his Bisquit Tortoni, I'll give him mine for apple jelly!

Wash crabs well. Dip each one in cream, and roll in flour to coat both sides lightly. Heat oil in large skillet, and sauté crabs until brown on both sides (about 5 minutes on each side). Put on heated platter. Drain oil from skillet. Add butter and heat until it is melted. Pour butter over crabs; squeeze lemon juAice over them, and sprinkle with parsley. Serves four.

PAMELA KURE GROGAN

CHAPTER NINE
Reservations Preferred

Another Opening, Another Show at Sardi's

Like Father, like son, Vince Sardi and his son, Vince, Jr. stand before artist Alex Gard's caricature of actor-epicurean-art collector Vincent Price (photo from the Prices' restaurant tour de force, **A Treasury of Great Recipes** (page 225). [see menu right]

Special promotional gathering at Sardi's, April, 1958. Singer Abbe Lane is crowned as Rheinhof May Wine Queen of 1958. Coronation Luncheon menu signed by Abbe Lane, and her husband, Cuban band leader Xavier Cugat. Main entrée: English Sole, 'fit for a queen'. Recipe printed on back of menu. [Author's Collection]

Pop culture trivia: known as a femme fatale, Abbe Lane once said, "Jayne Mansfield might make boys into men, but I take them from there." Xavier Cugat's band opened the Waldorf Astoria and stayed on as the resident musical group. Their marriage lasted from 1952 to 1964. Two years later Cugat would marry salsa performer/flamenco guitarist Charo, the first nuptials held at the opening of Ceasar's Palace in Las Vegas.

Vincent Sardi, Sr. and his wife Jenny opened a restaurant in 1921 but faced eviction in 1926, their building slated for demolition. Theatre impresarios, the Shubert brothers, offered Sardi a lease in a new building they were erecting at 234 W. 44th in the New York theatre district, across the street from what we know these days as Shubert Alley. The restaurant, opening in 1927, has become an institution for pre and post theatre goers, and late, late

night for unwinding performers. Vincent Sardi, Jr. died in 2007 at 91, and the restaurant recently was severely impacted by the 2020 epidemic which shut down the Broadway shows and kept away theatre-goers who came for their pre-opening dinner reservations. Hope they bounce back.

MY COOKBOOK PASSION

CHAPTER NINE
Reservations Preferred

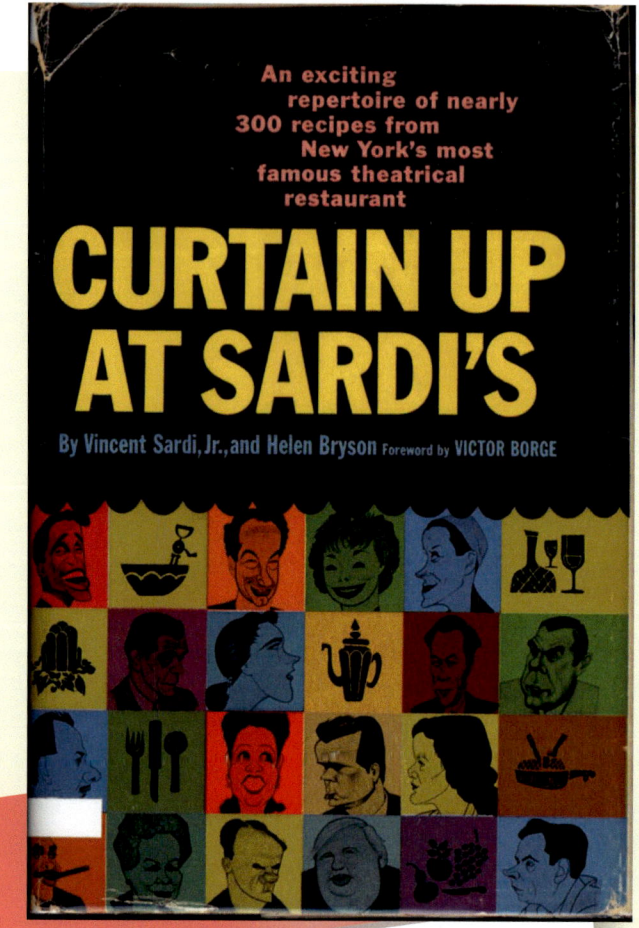

Curtain Up at Sardi's (1957) by Vincent Sardi, Jr. and Helen Bryson with forward by comedian- pianist Victor Borge is touted as divulging "for the first time the secrets of the Sardi menu and makes it possible for you to enjoy at home. Co-author Helen Bryson spent months in the kitchen and in consultation with Vincent Sardi Jr., evolving methods and measurements tailored to family-size menus." 300 recipes are presented.

Though the Sardi family came on the scene with Italian culinary background the cuisine of today's restaurant and 'Curtains Up' recipes tends to be a continental menu with a slant towards 'English-American food'. So I shall indulge:

BRAISED YANKEE POT ROAST OF BEEF

A well-known dish served with a rich sauce, the result of careful and long marination. Peas, carrots, potato balls, turnips and whole onions are the accompaniment. Especially good when cooked a day in advance.

3 pounds top round or sirloin beef – 1 cup red wine – 2 tablespoons vinegar – 3 peppercorns, crushed – 1 bay leaf – 1 clove garlic, crushed – 1/4 teaspoon sage 1 tablespoon salt – 1/4 cup shortening – 2 cups tomatoes (canned) 1 cup tomato purée – 1 cup beef consommé (or 1 bouillon cube in 1 cup boiling water) – Salt and pepper to taste – 1 tablespoon chopped parsley

CHAPTER NINE
Reservations Preferred

Yankee Pot Roast Preparation: Blend together in a large mixing bowl the wine, vinegar, peppercorns, bay leaf, garlic and sage. Place the meat in this and turn occasionally. Allow to marinate overnight. If this is not possible, allow not less than 4 hours for marination. Remove meat from wine marinade and brown in 1/4 cup of melted fat. Reserve marinade. Brown meat on all sides about 15 minutes. Season with salt. Place the meat and the marinade in a large saucepan. Add the tomatoes and tomato purée, stir well and bring to a boil. Cover and simmer gently for 1 hour. Add 1 cup consommé and continue simmering for 2 hours. When the meat is cooked, remove from pot and put to one side to keep warm. Boil sauce 20 minutes to reduce. Strain the sauce through a strainer. Taste and season with salt if necessary. Pour some of the sauce over the meat, sprinkle with chopped parsley.

At Sardi's: The meat is served sliced, surrounded by potato balls, whole small boiled onions, carrots, peas and turnips. The sauce is poured over the meat and the whole dish sprinkled with parsley.

Did You Know?
For the tourist in and about Manhattan the drawn caricatures up on the walls at Sardi's is a famous hallmark worth the stop. As the story goes, Sardi Senior found business was a little slow when he first made the move into his new restaurant and decided he needed a gimmick. He recalled the celebrity sketches on the walls of a Paris jazz restaurant and hired Alex Gard, a Russian artist, to do the sketches. On the walls today there are over 1,200 caricatures of the famous and near famous. When actor James Cagney's caricature was stolen on his death, it became the standard that three celebrity likenesses were made: the original into a vault, a copy to the star, and one copy for the wall. Various artists over the years have had the privilege but Alex Gard had the most unusual deal. He would do the drawings for one free meal a day. When Vincent Junior took over operations in 1947 he tried to change the arrangement but artist Gard wouldn't budge and the free meal deal continued until Gard's death a year later.

Trivia
The Tony Award was conceived at a table at Sardis and for many years the Tony Award nominations were announced at the restaurant.

Both Sardi Senior and Junior each received special Tony Awards for their community service to the theatre industry. Who was the first official caricature drawn for Sardis? Never in a million years would you guess—Ted Healy, vaudeville performer and actor, remembered these days for being the originator and first employer of a comedy team called The Three Stooges.

CHAPTER TEN
Jovial Ghosts of Dining

CHAPTER
TEN

JOVIAL GHOSTS
OF DINING

PAMELA KURE GROGAN

CHAPTER TEN
Jovial Ghosts of Dining

I want to run through a series of famous restaurants and sad to say are no longer with us. Why did they disappear? As we noted World War II rationing shuttered many of the inns and mom-and-pop diners. I feel the demise of the city restaurants, those of great notoriety closed because of two factors: the passing of the primary owner whose dynamics and personal touch brought personality to the table by his or her food service, and more so, the pressure of economics when land and lease costs became prohibitive.

I have multiple examples of the Golden Age of Restaurants, and offer here a few gems, selected because of the recipes, and as said before, because their cultural ambiance made these establishments hits in the social world.

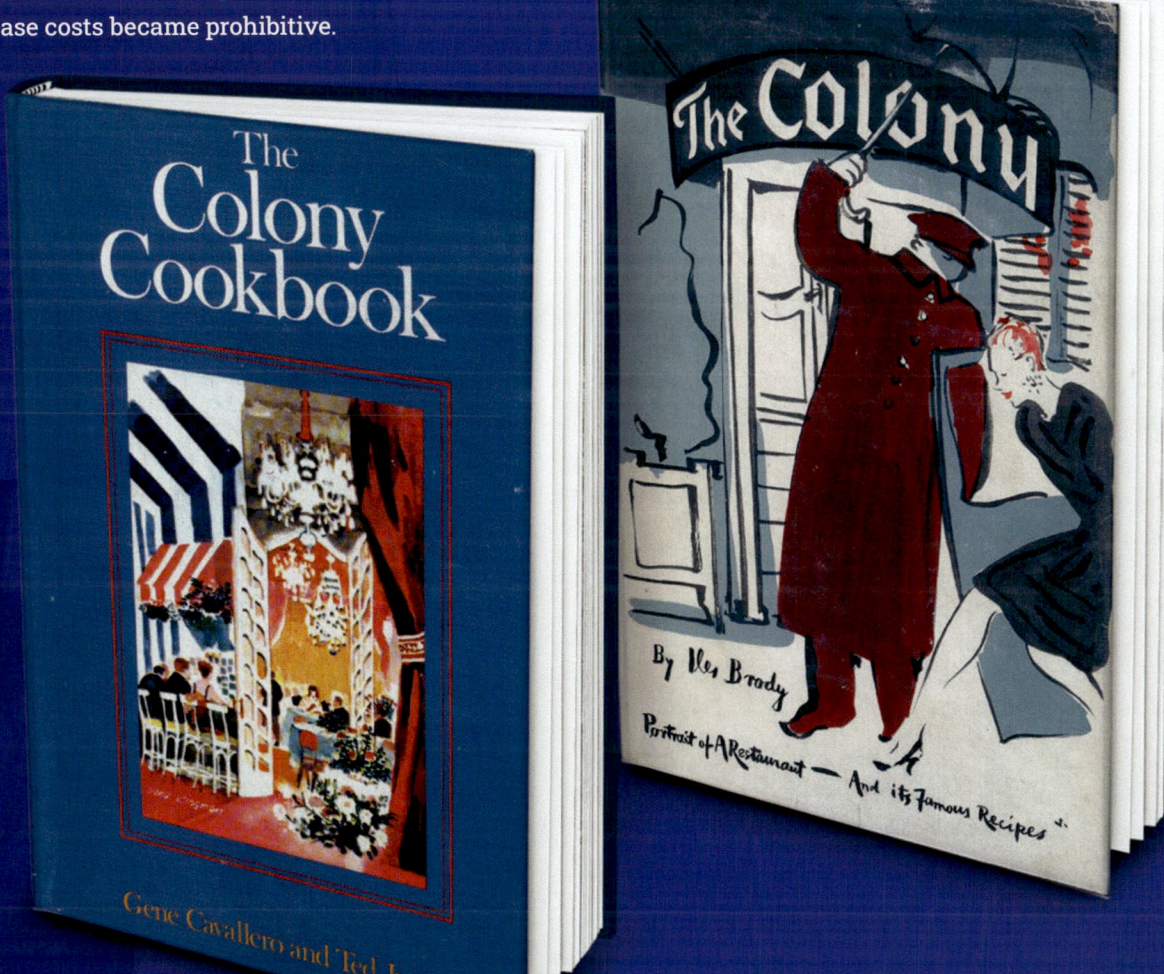

CHAPTER TEN
Jovial Ghosts of Dining

The Colony

In the 1920's a small bistro called **The Colony** served two-bit gamblers and flappers of the Roaring Twenties, and became the perfect place for a businessman to bring his mistress, but that reputation couldn't make a profit and the owner wanted to turn it into a cheap nightclub. Three members of the head wait staff felt this would be its doom and went directly to the landlord and had him act as a straw buyer for the Colony. The new owners struggled to find a clientele. Two factors worked in their favor, the superb food and the service which bordered on dramatic showmanship. And as it came down in lore, one night it happened. Mrs. William K. Vanderbilt was having dinner with a lady friend. The next night, William K. Vanderbilt himself decided to see if his wife's praise had been accurate. He became a regular and the society and celebrity crowd soon followed. The primary owner of The Colony after ownership changes fell to Gene Cavallero whose son later took over the helm as owner host. There are two Colony books, one irreverent and fun (1945) by writer Iles Brody, 'a portrait of a restaurant—and its famous recipes" and the other (1972) by Gene Cavallero Jr. and Ted James (of the anniversary Waldorf cookbook). Brody, when he writes his Colony book is the Food Editor for *Esquire* Magazine and one of *Gourmet* Magazine's early food critics. He will write books such as **On the Tip of My Tongue** and the historical, **Gone with the Windsors**. Brody in Chapter Five of **The Colony**, sub titled, 'The Dining Room, where a Vanderbilt is ready to give battle to a princess for a tiny table', writes: *"Elsa Maxwell, when she comes to the Dining Room, table-hops all over the place, for her popularity matches that of Mr. Bernard Baruch's [Table No. 37 is Mr. Baruch's]. It is rumored that Miss Maxwell, who has to take great care of her figure, always dines at home on a plainly broiled piece of steak before accepting an invitation to dinner and thus she is able to forego the fattening and foppish food usually served at dinner parties. Lady Mendl, the famous Elsie de Wolfe, eats very sparingly but of the finest things; she knows her food thoroughly. She never touches soup, claiming she does not wish to make a lake out of her tummy."*

As to what goes on in the renowned kitchen, Brody gives the secret: "Cuisine is strictly *au beurre*. But just simply *au beurre* is not enough; they use double butter, in case you didn't know. For example, let us say, that the chefs are busy with an order of *cote de veau chez soi*. It is a simple veal cutlet. And just like yourself, the chefs at the Colony brown the veal cutlet in butter. But while you are serving this veal cutlet as soon as it is done, and pour over it the few drops of liquid butter (burned in the process of cooking, as a rule) the chefs at the Colony throw the browned butter out. While the veal cutlet was being cooked, they have prepared another butter sauce in another pan together with spices, seasoning, and herbs, and at the strategic moment the new sauce is poured over the meat. The result is a better flavor, beautiful color (called *rosé* in culinary parlance), and causes less heartburn."

The Colony Cookbook by Gene Cavallero, Jr. and Ted James repeats Brody's history with a few family stories thrown in, the recipes better presented after 30 years of change in the public's palate.

PAMELA KURE GROGAN

CHAPTER TEN
Jovial Ghosts of Dining

BEIGNETS SOUFFLÉS

1/2 c. butter – 1 c. water – 1 pinch of salt
1 tbsps. sugar – 1 c. sifted flour – 4 eggs

Bring water, butter, salt, and sugar to boiling point in a saucepan over heat. Remove from heat, add flour, and stir. Return to heat, and when mixture boils again and rises somewhat in the pan, remove from heat and add eggs, one at a time, beating continuously. Drop bits of dough, each the size of a small walnut, one at a time into moderately hot deep fat. Gradually increase the heat so that the little dough-walnuts expand as they cook. When they are a deep brown, remove to paper towels. Sprinkle with confectioners' sugar.

Serve with:
SAUCE SABAYON

6 egg yolks – 1 cup sugar – 2 cups Marsala or sherry wine – 1 1/2 ounces rum

Beat egg yolks until light and foamy. Gradually add sugar and beat until mixture has a light, creamy consistency. Add half the wine, beat, then add the rest. Continue beating this in the top of a double boiler over gently simmering water until mixture doubles in volume. Remove from heat and add rum.
Serves 4 to 6.

Collector's Corner
Iles Brody with his 1945 **The Colony** released a boxed limited edition of 750 copies, signed, the book in tissue paper. In older cookbooks you rarely see special editions, limited in numbers, with author signature.

CHAPTER TEN
Jovial Ghosts of Dining

Eat in the Hat

Put it this way, the Brown Derby restaurants not only paralleled the Golden Age of Hollywood, they personified many restaurant chains, fast growth, labor and location problems, eventually succumbing to customer preferences and suburban sprawl. Started at the end of the 1920's by Harry Somborn (ex-husband of Gloria Swanson), Wilson Mizner (a screenwriter) and Sid Graumann (of Chinese theater fame), the restaurants were the place-to-be chain in the 1930's and 1940's, the first on Wilshire Boulevard. Later locations included Hollywood and Beverly Hills. Resembling a bowler hat and built, 28 feet by 17 feet the Wilshire location boasted the only hat architecture and a neon sign, 'Eat in the Hat'.

Associated trivia: At the Hollywood Brown Derby, the restaurant featured celebrity caricatures on the wall, and the stars attended in droves. In 1939, Clark Gable proposed to Carole Lombard in booth #5. In the famous 'I Love Lucy' episode (#114-*L.A. at Last*) Lucy Ricardo, as a tourist (at a studio created Brown Derby), causes a waiter to dump food on actor William Holden. The remaining location, the Los Feliz Derby when slated for demolition was saved by citizens as a historic landmark. The Derby at Los Feliz originally opened with a car café, taking advantage of the popularity of drive-in restaurants. In its faded days, Los Feliz became a hang-out for 'swingers', that is, swing dancers. And yes, that's a replica Brown Derby restaurant at Florida's Disney World.

There are two Derby books, one cover shown here is the first edition, the other in deluxe Mission leather where I'm showing the inside cover pages with photos of their various restaurants.

The first dessert the Brown Derby ever served was a cake made by a former bond salesman named Harry Baker. It was a fluffy, golden cake, neither angel food or sponge, but infinitely lighter and more delicious than either. For almost twenty years Baker baked these cakes for the Derby, refusing to divulge the secret of its recipe. In 1947 he

CHAPTER TEN
Jovial Ghosts of Dining

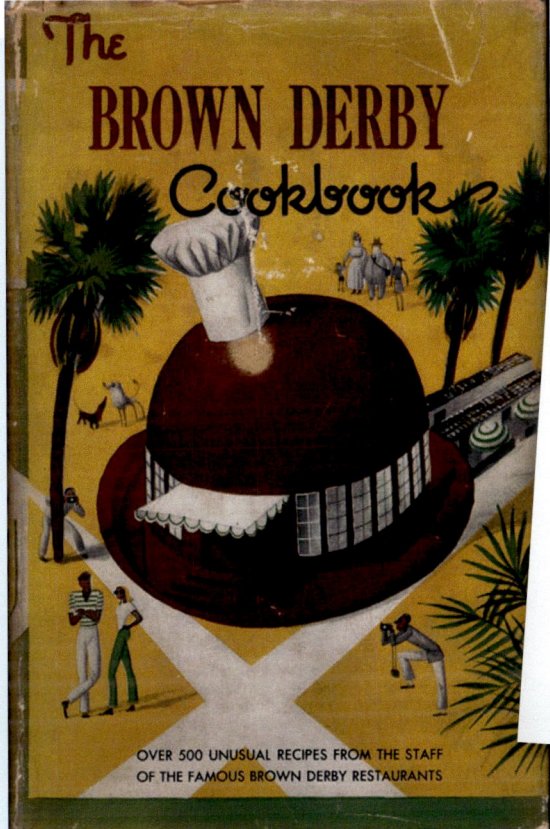

COBB SALAD
Serves 4-6

1/2 head of lettuce - 6 strips crisp bacon - 1/2 bunch watercress - 1 avocado - 1 small bunch chicory 3 hard-cooked eggs - 1/2 head romaine - 2 tbs. chopped chives - 2 medium-sized tomatoes, peeled - 1/2 cup fine grated imported Roquefort cheese - 2 breasts of boiled roasting chicken - 1 cup Brown Derby Old-Fashioned French Dressing

took it to General Mills in Minneapolis, and they paid him handsomely for the recipe. Launched as "the first new cake idea in a hundred years," this is the famous Chiffon Cake, which differs only slightly from the Brown Derby favorite. –
Story of the Brown Derbies

At the Brown Derby Robert 'Bob' Cobb served as the first General Manager and known as the creator of the 'Cobb Salad'.

Cut finely lettuce, watercress, chicory, and romaine and arrange in salad bowl. Cut tomatoes in half, remove seeds, dice finely, and arrange in a strip across the salad. Dice breasts of chicken and arrange over top of chopped greens. Chop bacon finely and sprinkle over the salad. Cut avocado in small pieces and arrange around the edge of the salad. Decorate the salad by sprinkling over the top the chopped eggs, chopped chives, and grated cheese. Just before serving mix the salad thoroughly with French Dressing.

MY COOKBOOK PASSION

CHAPTER TEN
Jovial Ghosts of Dining

BAKED HAM STEAK HAWAIIAN
4 8-oz. center cut ham steaks – 4 tbs. soy sauce – 4 slices pineapple, canned – 1 cup water or fresh – 2 tbs. chutney – 1 tbs. orange peel julienne – 1/2 cup port wine – 2 tbs. toasted shaved almonds – 1/2 cup tomato purée – 2 tbs. honey

Brown the ham steaks under gas broiler or over charcoal. Place them in heavy skillet. Add pineapple, orange peel, almonds, honey, soy sauce, water, chutney, wine, puree. Cover the skillet and simmer until the ham steaks are done—approximately an additional 80 minutes. Should the liquid reduce too fast, add a little water or pineapple juice. Serves 4. --The Brown Derby

The Lobster
"Our location just off Times Square makes us a favorite meeting place of Broadway's brightest stars and most brilliant playwrights, producers and directors; as well as critics, both amateur and professional, who enjoy dissecting deep-sea dinosaurs along with Shelley Winters, Elia Kazan and Tennessee Williams."

"Put me in a corner where no one can see me, and don't tell anyone I'm here," invariably requests Paul Muni.

Most celebrities, we find, like best to be treated the way any other guest is. Don't get excited, boys," Edward G. Robinson will greet some flustered waiters.

"I've played the part of a waiter many times, you know."

"The best lobster thermidor in the world," is the verdict of the Theatre Guild's Lawrence Langer, who invariably orders this rich and sumptuous- looking specialty of ours:

PAMELA KURE GROGAN

CHAPTER TEN
Jovial Ghosts of Dining

LOBSTER THERMIDOR

6 boiled lobsters of about 1 lb. each – 6 mushrooms, finely chopped – 1 medium-size green pepper, finely chopped – 1 pimiento, finely chopped – 6 tablespoons butter – 3 cups cream sauce – 1 teaspoon paprika – 4 oz grated Parmesan cheese – 2 slices bacon, cut into slivers – 12 cooked shrimp – Sherry to tasked (we prefer 1 1/2 cups) – Cracker crumbs for sprinkling

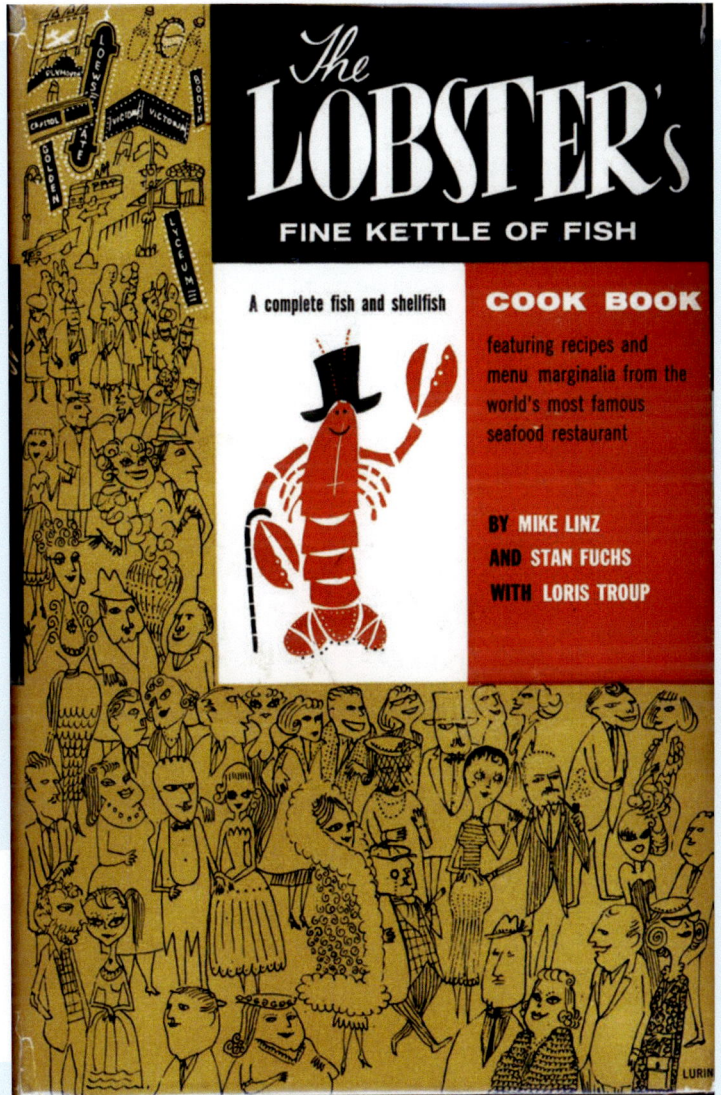

Once Stan was helping Fannie Hurst choose a live lobster from our tank and pointed out which ones were male and which female. "That," parried the famous novelist, "is a matter which could be of interest only to another lobster!"

Split the lobsters, and remove and chop the meat, but keep shells intact for stuffing. Sauté the mushrooms, green pepper, and pimiento lightly in butter. Stir in the cream sauce, paprika and sherry, and simmer gently until the wine has reduced somewhat. Fold in the diced lobster meat, and heat thoroughly. Fill the lobster shells. Top with fine crumbs (only a few) and generously sprinkle with grated Parmesan cheese. Garnish lightly with paprika. Sprinkle lightly with a bit more melted butter. Arrange a few slivers of bacon over tops, and then the cooked shrimp sliced in half. Bake 10 to 12 minutes, or until lightly browned, in a preheated 400º F oven.

CHAPTER TEN
Jovial Ghosts of Dining

A Frenchman, deriding English cuisine not long ago, pointed out that what was wrong with his friends across the Channel was that they had "seventy religions but only one sauce." One of the many great sauces which distinguish *la haute cuisine française* is that named for the 16th century nobleman, Philipe de Mornay. Actually, it's nothing more than ordinary cream sauce with cheese added. You can use it over broiled or fried fish fillets, or as the French do, pour it over uncooked fillets and bake fish and sauce together in the oven.

MORNAY SAUCE

2 tablespoons butter – 2 tablespoons flour – 1 cup milk – 1/4 teaspoon salt – Cayenne – 2 tablespoons butter (additional) – 2 tablespoons grated Parmesan cheese – 2 tablespoons of another kind of cheese – (Swiss is good in this)

Melt 2 tablespoons butter, and stir flour into it. Add milk slowly, stirring constantly until the sauce is thickened, about 3 to 5 minutes. Add salt and cayenne, and then the cheese. Remove from heat and stir in other 2 tablespoons butter.

"Will you walk a little faster?" said a whiting to a snail.
"There's a porpoise close behind us,
and he's treading on my tail.
See how eagerly the lobsters and the turtles all advance!
They are waiting on the shingle
will you come and join the dance?
The Lobster Quadrille
Lewis Carroll, **Alice in Wonderland**

Restaurant cookbooks many times borrow beyond their own limited menus. They will add in a few exotics, most notably seafood or the cuisine from New Orleans Creole or Caribbean. Breaking up the monotony of how one might prepare shrimp these days I can recommend *The Lobster's* choice:

CURRIED SHRIMP WITH BANANAS

1/2 lb. cooked shrimp, split in half (reserve some for garnish) – 2 tbsp butter – 2 tbsp flour – 1 teaspoon curry powder – 1/2 tsp salt – Dash of cayenne – 1 c. chicken stock (or 1 bouillon cube dissolved in 1 c. boiling water – 2 bananas, peeled, cut in half Lengthwise and then each piece in half

CHAPTER TEN
Jovial Ghosts of Dining

Stir flour into melted butter in saucepan over medium heat. Add curry powder. Add chicken stock slowly, stirring constantly until sauce is smooth and thick. Add other seasonings. Add bananas, and cover. Let cook gently stirring frequently, for 5 minutes, or until bananas are tender. Add shrimp, and heat through. Serves 3 to 4.

The Lobster, 145 W. 45th Street, New York City, founded in 1919, by the fathers of authors, Mike Linz and Stan Fuchs, seemed to be going strong when this book, **The Lobster's Fine Kettle of Fish Cook Book,** was published in 1958. A 1964 Hart's Guide said the place seated 450 and the restaurant flew in lobsters daily from Maine. Dinner ran about $4.50 - lunch about $2.25. The restaurant gone, the building many years back was a Hamburger Harry's, location now houses an Irish Pub, and under remodel. Fast food it seems won out over a good crustacean bouillabaisse.

Worldly.

The assignment might be 'worldly' but I don't think I have the stamina as happened when Scandinavian Airlines System (SAS) underwrote author Charlotte Adams and her writing adventure (**The SAS World-Wide Restaurant Cookbook,** 1960) to thirty-six countries to prepare this cookbook. Basically, a restaurant tour guide she states, "My first purpose in visiting any country was to search for 'typical' restaurants, serving primarily native foods. In some countries, there are no such places; in others, very few. The second aim, therefore, was to find the best international restaurants and to endeavor to sample and get the recipes for their own *spécialitiés de maison.*"

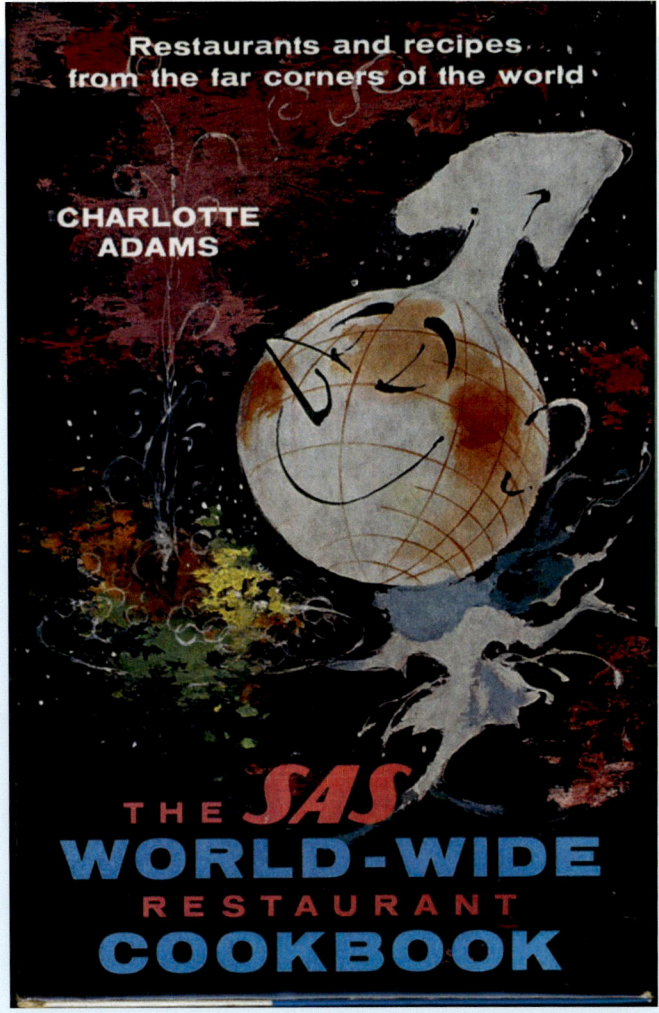

What I like about her reviews is she doesn't mince words, as she observed about one restaurant: "Their boiled beef is considered by many to be the best in the city, but I have eaten better in other restaurants...Service is quite poor—slow and confused, even when they make a great fuss over you if they happen to know well the Viennese with whom you are dining. Prices high."

CHAPTER TEN
Jovial Ghosts of Dining

SALZBURGER NOCKERL

[I was fortunate enough to have this treat when I was on a high school trip to Germany and Austria in 1974. —pkg]

3 egg whites – 1/4 cup sugar – 3/4 cup confectionary sugar
1 teaspoon vanilla sugar – 3 egg yolks, lightly beaten – 1 tablespoon flour – 1/2 cup milk rum

CALF LIVER ON SKEWER

1/3 pound calf liver salt and pepper bacon fresh sage leaves

Cut the calf liver into good-sized cubes and season with salt and pepper. Wrap each with a piece of bacon and stick them on a skewer with sage leaves between each two cubes. Broil them until bacon is crisp and liver is done to your liking. Serves 1. Serve with green beans and Roesti Potatoes.

Beat the egg whites until frothy and continue beating, gradually adding the confectioners sugar. Fold in the yolks and then the flour. In an ovenproof dish bring to the boil the milk, sugar and vanilla sugar. Pour the egg white mixture over this. Sprinkle with confectioners sugar and place in the 350-degree oven. Bake until golden brown (15-18 minutes). --from the Kerzenstürberl restaurant, Austria

Vanilla Sugar. Fill a glass jar with a good screw top with sugar and place in it a vanilla bean.

Close tightly. This may be done with granulated, powdered or confectioners sugar. The vanilla bean will begin to flavor the sugar within a few hours and it gets more redolent as time goes by.

From *Haus Zum Rüden* restaurant, Switzerland – located in an ancient house dating back to 1295 when it was the Zurich mint. "Wine in racks makes an attractive decoration, as always. Waitresses look trim in black dresses with white aprons. The proprietor and his wife are unobtrusively solicitous for their guests' comfort. Service excellent. Prices medium."

In a theme I will be getting to later in this book, Charlotte Adams, was quoted in one of her book introductions: *"Cooking is one of the most satisfying and creative experiences anyone can have. In my opinion, every boy and every girl who's born into this world should learn to cook."*

CHAPTER TEN
Jovial Ghosts of Dining

Behind-the-Ingredients

You never know when you pick up a cook book what the true behind-the-scenes secrets are that brought the book together. I could have just pulled a recipe from this book and wrote a dull sentence—'a food writer got an assignment and went out and wrote a book about restaurants around the world'. End of story? Not quite. A month or so later I'm reading this fast-paced autobiography by food writer Mimi Sheraton, **Eating My Words: An Appetite For Life** (Harper Collins, 2004) and she writes:

"Always thinking up travel boondoggles and inspired by earlier publication of the Pan-American Airways **Complete Round the World Cookbook** by Myra Waldo, I got the idea for the World-Wide Restaurant Cookbook, which just might make it possible for me to eat in every restaurant in the world. SAS agreed to provide me with first-class tickets, and no sooner was the first leg of my journey planned than I discovered that I was pregnant, fate being generously cruel enough to grant me two mutually exclusive wishes. Although SAS said they would wait for me to do the book after the baby was born, I declined, feeling I wanted no such obligation hanging over me at that important time. I gave the project to Charlotte Adams, a friend and much respected food writer, and her dedication in the book reads, 'To Marc Christopher Falcone, whose arrival on this earth gave me a chance to go around it'."

Now, with a giggle of the inside scoop, I appreciate my Charlotte Adams SAS book from an entirely new perspective. Take a look at your cookbooks. What's behind the gloss? Maybe dig a little deeper into the mystery of your older books. How did such and such book come about? Did someone do what to whom? How many copies printed? A literary and financial success? Wondering curiosity always wanders to further adventures.

Collector's Corner

Charlotte Adams (1899- 1980s) gained distinction as a multi-talented food expert in radio, television and publishing. As contributing food editor for *Sports Illustrated* magazine, as well as a Food or Household Editor with *Charm, Collier's, Look* and in 1983 Food Editor for the *Associated Press*. She participated as the food commentator on NBC's *Weekday* show, and had her own Charlotte Adams Program on radio station WOR. **The Four Seasons Cook book**, with James Beard, is one of her best and I'm amazed at her other literary culinary output: **You'll Eat It Up, Home Entertaining, The Eat-Well Diet Book, The Ann McGregor Frozen Foods Cookbook, The ABC's of Cooking** (handbook, no recipes)**, Questions Answered About Cooking,** and **100 Most Honorable Chinese Recipes.** We just visited with her as author of **The Old Original Bookbinders Restaurant Cookbook**.

Remember, we want to feel a restaurant's *ambiance*. Food writer in a pre-blog years ago said this about memories of Lüchow's: "Huge tall ceilings of carved dark wood, on different levels; bannisters separating the areas, oil paintings. A certain scent, absolutely delicious, permeated.

CHAPTER TEN
Jovial Ghosts of Dining

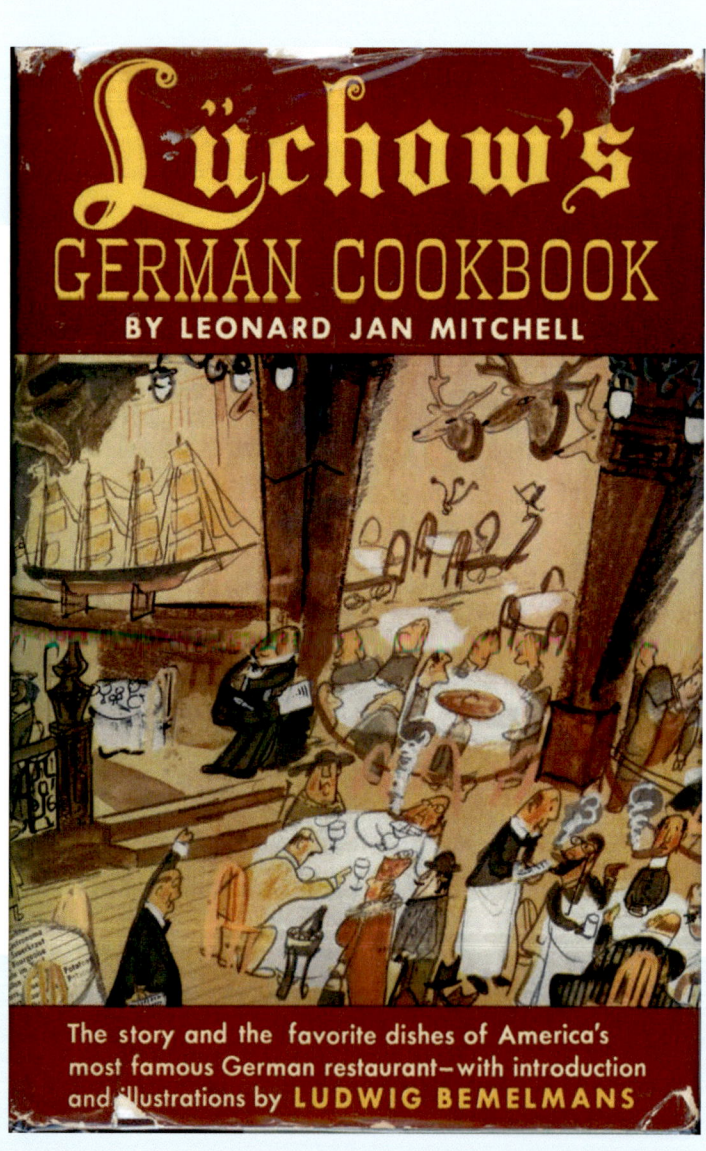

Illustration by Ludwig Bemelmans

PAMELA KURE GROGAN

CHAPTER TEN
Jovial Ghosts of Dining

Before today's glossy color food presentations, cartoon and sketch art could suggest taste emotions

MY COOKBOOK PASSION

CHAPTER TEN
Jovial Ghosts of Dining

At Christmas they had a marvelous tall tree in one of the rooms decorated with traditional German ornaments and a toy train that ran around the base. The Weiner Schnitzel was fantastic, the home fries uncopyable, white asparagus, but the best thing was the German pancake for dessert. Huge, the size of a large pizza and baked in the oven, slathered in cinnamon sugar and lemon juice with lingonberries. You could have it flambéed, so of course that meant you were the center of attention."

Luchow's was founded by August Guido Luchow, who came to America in 1879. He established his business in a three-story brownstone near Union Square, at that time the center of Manhattan culture and home to the Academy of Music. Luchow's was a musician hang-out with the likes of Enrico Caruso, Richard Strauss, Toscanini and later Cole Porter and Leonard Bernstein, as well as writers like Mencken and Dreiser. Trivia Fact One: William Steinway of piano fame with a $1,500 loan set Luchow up in business. Steinway ate there daily. Fact Two: October, 1913 composer Victor Herbert called the first songwriters summit meeting at Luchow's that would lead to the founding of ASCAP (American Society of Composers, Authors, and Publishers) to protect royalty rights. Fact Three: The song, "Yes Sir, That's My Baby", was written on a Luchow's tablecloth in 1925.

The restaurant moved in 1982 to mid-Manhattan and closed soon after. The old building was fire gutted in 1992 and deteriorated into demolition, and the spot today is a dormitory for New York University with a student café hashing out food. Who there will recall the refrain, "Luchow's is more than a restaurant; it's a way of life"?

POT ROAST WITH POTATO DUMPLINGS
Sauebraten Mit Kartoffel Klöss

3 lbs. round steak — 1 tbsp salt
1/2 tsp pepper — 2 onions, sliced — 1 carrot sliced — 1 stalk celery, chopped — 4 cloves
4 peppercorns — 1 pint red wine vinegar
2 bay leaves — 2 tbsp kidney fat — 6 tbsp butter — 5 tbsp flour — 1 tbsp sugar — 8 or 10 gingersnaps, crushed — Potato or Bread Dumplings (see recipe)

CHAPTER TEN
Jovial Ghosts of Dining

Wipe steak with damp cloth; season with salt and pepper. Place in earthen, glass, or enamelware bowl. Combine onions, carrot, celery, cloves, peppercorns, vinegar, and bay leaves and 2 1/2 pints water, or enough to cover meat. Cover and put in refrigerator 4 days. On fifth day remove from refrigerator, drain meat, sauté in kidney fat and 1 tablespoon butter in enamelware, glass or earthenware utensil, until seared on all sides. Add marinade liquid and bring to boil, then lower heat and let simmer about 3 hours.

Melt remaining 5 tablespoons butter in a pan. Stir flour smoothly into it. Add sugar, blend, and let brown to nice dark color. Add to simmering meat mixture. Cover and continue cooking until meat is tender, about 1 hour longer. Remove meat to a warmed serving platter. Stir crushed gingersnaps into the pot juices and cook until thickened. Put the special sauerbraten gravy over meat. Serves 6 or more.

Dumplings are one of the particular glories of the German cuisine. We consider them, along with noodles, as an accompaniment without which many dishes on our menu would seem incomplete.

POTATO DUMPLINGS
Kartoffel Klösse

3 pounds (9) medium-size potatoes - 3 egg yolks, beaten - 3 tablespoons cornstarch - 3 tablespoons raw farina or Cream of Wheat - 1/2 teaspoon pepper - 1/4 teaspoon grated nutmeg - 1 1/2 teaspoons salt - 1 cup toasted or fried white bread cubes - Flour - 1 1/2 quarts boiling salted water - (1 1/2 teaspoons salt)

Scrub potatoes. Boil in salted water until just soft enough to mash. Drain and mash smoothly. Add egg yolks, cornstarch, cereal, pepper, salt, and nutmeg. Beat well; shape into dumplings; place few bread cubes in center of each. (It is a good idea to shape 1 dumpling first, and if it does not hold together while cooking, beat a little flour into dumpling mixture before shaping remainder.) Roll each dumpling lightly in flour. Cook in rapidly boiling salted water 15 to 20 minutes. Remove cooked dumplings from water; serve hot. Makes 12 or more dumplings, serve 6 to 8.

NOTE: Any leftover dumplings may be cut in half, sautéed in butter, and used as garnish on a meat or salad platter.

CHAPTER TEN
Jovial Ghosts of Dining

Cooking à la Longchamps

Good Food – No Nonsense

Longchamps' executive chef, Ernest Imhof, and I [Jan Mitchell] have chosen with the greatest care the easily prepared soup recipes that follow. We promise any one of them will be fine fare, especially if served in a lidded marmite bowl that holds the heat, accompanied by a crusty loaf of toasted garlic, cheese, or herbed bread.

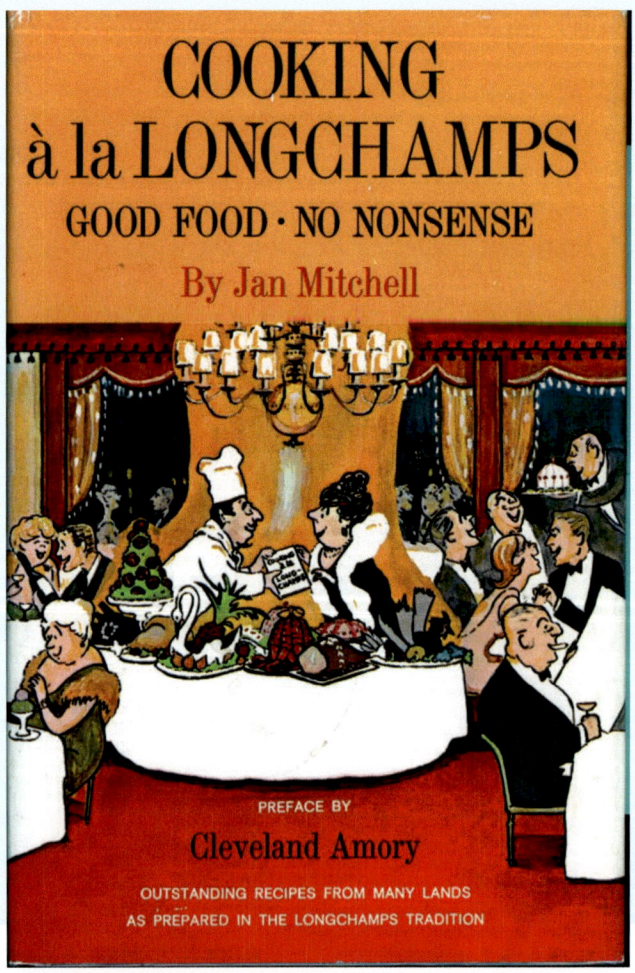

OLD-FASHIONED CREAM OF CHICKEN SOUP

1/2 c. butter – 1 onion, chopped fine – 2 leeks, white part only, chopped fine – 1 small bay leaf – 1 stalk celery, chopped fine – 1/2 c. flour – 1 tspn salt – Dash white pepper – 2 qts. Chicken broth, canned or homemade – 1 c. light cream – 2 egg yolks – 1/2 c. cooked diced chicken – 1/4 c. cooked rice – 1/4 c. cooked diced celery

Heat butter in a saucepan. Stir in onion, leeks, bay leaf, celery; cook over a low heat, stirring frequently, for about 10 minutes. Do not allow to brown. Add flour and salt and pepper; blend well. Pour in broth, cook to a boil, stirring continuously, then reduce heat and simmer gently for 1 1/2 to 2 hours.

Strain into another saucepan and heat to a boil. Heat cream until a film shines on the surface; beat egg yolks lightly. Gradually beat cream into egg yolks, then add mixture to soup. Heat through but don't boil or soup will curdle. Just before serving, stir in cooked chicken, rice and celery. Serves 6 to 8.

CHAPTER TEN
Jovial Ghosts of Dining

Swiss-born and European-trained restaurateur Jan Mitchell bought Luchow's in 1950 and likewise owned the Longchamps restaurant chain. Guests remember Mitchell greeting people at the front door of Luchow's and he maintained the atmosphere of *Gemutlichkeit* ('comfortable geniality') with traditions brought back of original German delicacies to the menu and revived the festivals such as Christmas with venison, goose and wine. A Viennese orchestra entertained diners with Herbert music and Strauss waltzes. Don't forget lunch with a good stein of beer 'down where the Würzburger flows'.

Mitchell authored both **Luchow's German Cookbook** (1952) and **Cooking à la Longchamps** (1964). I have no corporate or news clipping history to tell you what happened to Longchamps? I do believe Mr. Mitchell went on to enjoy himself in the New York art collecting world becoming a patron at the Museum of Modern Art.

Did You Know?
The Forward to **Cooking à la Longchamps** is written by animal activist Cleveland Amory who served as the youngest editor at the *Saturday Evening Post*. A co-founder of the U.S. Humane Society, ten years later he would write a book that is said to have started the anti- hunting movement in America. Not something hearty German eaters would necessarily approve of.

Note the artwork in **Luchow's German Cookbook**. Does it look familiar to parents? The illustrator is Ludwig Bemelmans (1898-1962), famous for his series of 'Madeline' children books. *"In an old house in Paris, that was covered with vines, lived twelve little girls in two straight lines... the smallest one was Madeline."* His "Central Park," a mural on the walls of the Carlyle Hotel's Bemelman's Bar in New York City, is his only remaining artwork on display to the public

CHAPTER TEN
Jovial Ghosts of Dining

**The Antiquarian Sleuth
Always on the Hunt**

Las Vegas Book Festival Poster

Author meets Author. Obtaining a signed cookbook from David Lebovitz while in Paris. I support cookbook authors whenever I meet them.

PAMELA KURE GROGAN

CHAPTER TEN
Jovial Ghosts of Dining

Editor/husband Stephen standing in rare book room at Shakespeare & Co., Paris. He also got a buzz descending into the Abbey Bookstore and browsing book stalls along the Seine.

Learning my croissant skills at La Cuisine Paris; took several baking courses. Great experience, and of course the cuisine around the city was fantastic! The rest of European restaurant travel pretty cool, too.

Browsing a book store in capital city Ljubljana, Slovenia. I was in town researching family history in the government archives. I bought several books while on a European tour where when home used a computer to translate the recipes.

MY COOKBOOK PASSION

CHAPTER ELEVEN
SUPER 'AMERICAN' CHEFS & CULTURAL NOSTALGIA

PAMELA KURE GROGAN

CHAPTER ELEVEN
SUPER 'AMERICAN' CHEFS & Cultural Nostalgia

I want to focus on two chefs who not only owned famous restaurants but as immigrants to the New World achieved the 'American Dream' and shared their good fortune with many
George Mardikian-- Omar Khayyam's

- First edition, 1944, inscribed month of release to movie gossip columnist, Louella Parsons

- A change in book cover for the sixth printing, 1952. Inscribed, *'To the best cook in the family, Love, George.'*

- Omar Khayyam's in San Francisco displayed a very extensive photo wall of celebrity customers. Eleanor Roosevelt gave the compliment 'with good wishes and gratitude for such delicious food.' (Original photo in the Mardikian family archives. Printed with permission)

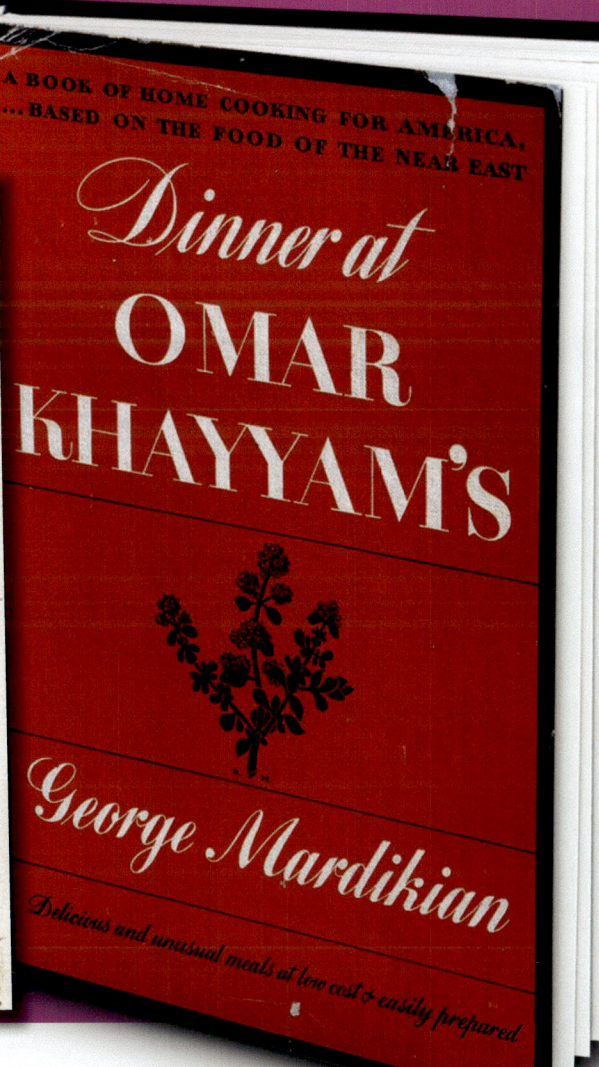

MY COOKBOOK PASSION

CHAPTER ELEVEN
SUPER 'AMERICAN' CHEFS & Cultural Nostalgia

George Mardikian, Armenian restauranteur, wrote: *"You who have been born in America. I wish I could make you understand what it is like not to be an American – not to have been an American all your life – and then suddenly with the words of a judge in flowing robes to be one, for that moment and forever after. One moment, you belong with your fathers to a million dead yesterdays – the next you belong with America to a million unborn tomorrows."*

George Mardikian fled the genocide against Armenians, escaped from prison camp, and made his way to the U.S. in 1922. His first job in America was washing dishes in a cafeteria. Later he became a steward aboard an ocean liner; and from there moved into learning the talents of a chef. He continued to seek out employment that improved his cooking skills. In 1932 he opened Omar Khayyam's in Fresno, California, with his most famous Omar Khayyam's restaurant located in San Francisco. During World War II he offered his talents as an expert to make soldier's food more palatable—honored with presidential commendations for his work. Mardikian's success let him branch out into successful real estate and radio station investments, but his main endeavors meant helping others. Described as a 'Super American' he received the nation's highest civilian award, **The Medal of Freedom.** The book, **Song of America,** is his autobiography.

Side note: **Omar Khayyám** (1048-1123) is Persian not Armenian. A mathematician and astronomer he is famous for his poem of a thousand quatrains (four lines each) called **'Rubáiyát'**. We food romantics often quote the first lines:

Here with a Loaf of Bread beneath the Bough,
A Flash of Wine, a Book of Verse – and Thou
Beside me singing in the Wilderness

In George Mardikian's establishment, one of his favorite framed quotes of Khayyám:

The Moving finger writes: and, having writ,
Moves on: nor all thy Piety nor Wit
Shall lure it back to cancel half a Line

"A Book of Home Cooking for America—based on the food of the Near East." The Forward to **Dinner at Omar Khayyam's** is written by his fellow Fresno Armenian, author William Saroyan. The first edition copy I have, 1944, is inscribed the month of the book's release to: *Louella Parsons, The First Lady of the Movieland,*

CHAPTER ELEVEN
SUPER 'AMERICAN' CHEFS & Cultural Nostalgia

Gastronomically yours, George Mardikian. His publicist in an enclosed memo writes: 'Watch for a *Collier's* piece about Mardikian, issue of October 18. Story is 'Omar Had a Little Lamb.' Good P.R. breeds strong book sales, meaning for a collector, years later plentiful copies exist.

Mix well with meat 1 raw egg, the vegetables, rice, and seasonings. Make into balls the size of walnuts. Roll in flour and gradually drop into boiling, seasoned broth. When all are in, cook until the rice is tender. Then beat the 2 remaining eggs with the lemon juice until very light and fluffy. Pour some broth over this mixture, whipping constantly to keep a creamy mixture. Return this to the broth and meat balls. Stir quickly and serve at once in deep soup bowls. For variation, use dried or chopped mint in this kufté if you like the flavor.

BOLSAGAN KUFTÉ

This kufté is a favorite of folks around Istanbul. Its difference is that it is a hot, stew-like dish, with the kufté formed into round balls the size of a walnut. They are boiled in meat broth and just before serving the broth is thickened with a lemon-egg mixture. This is without doubt the most popular dish to be found in the Hellenic world.

1 pound ground meat, preferably lamb shoulder – 1/4 cup parsley – 1/2 cupful chopped onions – 1/2 cupful uncooked rice – 3 eggs – juice of 2 lemons tablespoonfuls flour salt and pepper – 1/2 gallon meat broth

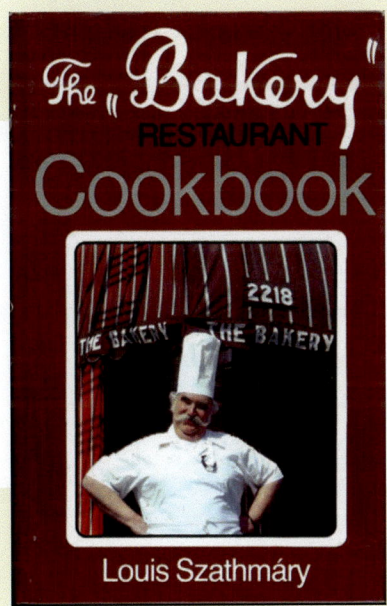
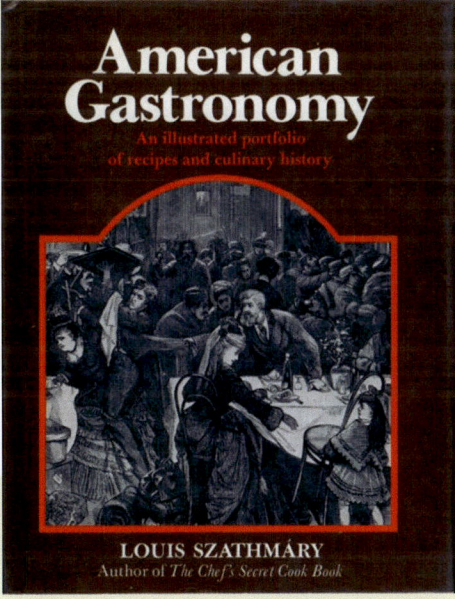

CHAPTER ELEVEN
SUPER 'AMERICAN' CHEFS & Cultural Nostalgia

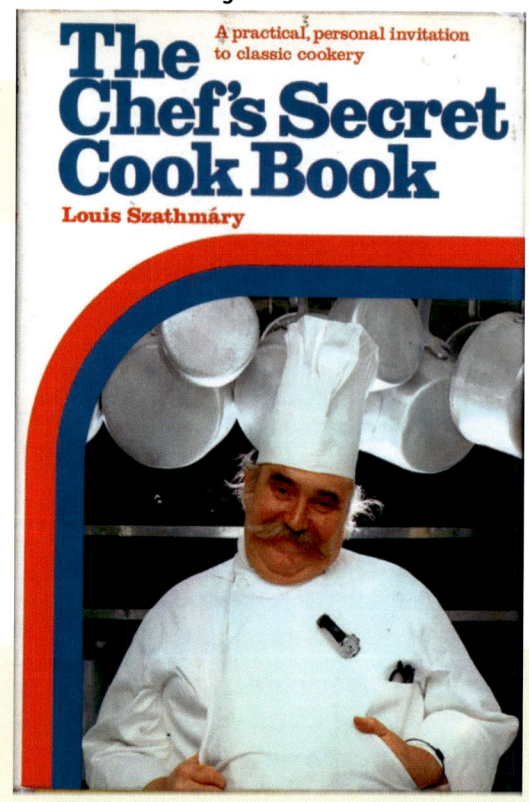

Louis Szathmáry The Bakery

A displaced person in the turmoil aftermath of World War II, a Hungarian prisoner in both German and Soviet prison camps, Louis Szathmáry, emigrated to the U.S. in 1951. One of his earliest jobs he served as personal chef to the chairman of RKO Pictures in New York City meeting movers- and- shakers that led to the family of the Armour and Company meat packing family where he became a consultant, then manager of new product development. In that transition of tastes where we entered the frozen food world, Szathmáry pioneered 'flash frozen' foods for Stouffers.

In 1962 he opened *The Bakery Restaurant* on Chicago's Near North Side. An immediate success, the most well-known entrée item created, Beef Wellington. *Holiday and Town and Country* Magazines named *The Bakery* one of the country's Top 100 restaurants. Among his many honors included election to the Culinary Hall of Fame. He holds a special place among chefs as he was instrumental in moving up executive chefs from their lower classification as 'service' to a 'professional' title in the U.S. Department of Labor official rankings.

CHAPTER ELEVEN
SUPER 'AMERICAN' CHEFS & Cultural Nostalgia

In the world of cookbooks and culinary history he excelled. He authored seven cookbooks, served as the editor over the massive 15 volume *Cookery Americana*, an encyclopedia by Arno Press. His cookbook, **The Chef's Secret Cook Book**, made *New York Times* Best Seller's list.

Did You Know?

Chef Szathmáry's legacy was his massive collection of over 400,000 culinary items of cookbooks, manuscripts, menus, ephemera all related to cooking going back five centuries. During his lifetime he contributed many of these documents to various educational institutions with the understanding that students would have easy access. His primary beneficiary was Johnson & Wales University in Providence, Rhode Island, one of the largest schools devoted to the food and service industry.

POACHED SALMON IN CHAMPAGNE SAUCE

8 salmon steaks, 5 oz. each
4 tbsp butter – 1 tbsp flour – 1 tbsp cornstarch – 1 tsp sugar – 1/8 tsp mace – salt and pepper to taste
1 c. half-and-half – 1 c. dry champagne or dry white wine – 1 egg yolk – 8 slices black truffle or 4 black olives (optional)

1. In a shallow dish, poach the salmon steaks in simmering, lightly salted water for 6 to 8 minutes, depending on their thickness. Remove them carefully with a wide spatula to a warm serving platter.

2. Melt the butter in a saucepan. In a bowl, mix the flour, cornstarch, sugar, mace, salt, and pepper. Slowly stir in the half-and-half, mixing until the mixture is completely free of lumps.

3. Pour this mixture into the warm butter and stir until it starts to bubble. Immediately remove from the fire and stir in the champagne or wine, reserving 3 tbsp. of the champagne.

4. When the champagne is completely mixed into the sauce, put the sauce back on low heat and stir until it boils again. Remove and set it in a warm place, and let it stand until serving time.

5. Just before serving, mix the reserved champagne with the egg yolk. Spoon a little of the hot sauce into the yolk-champagne mixture. Stir it and then pour slowly into the sauce. Spoon the sauce over the salmon. Decorate with truffles or halved olives; serve immediately. Serves 8.

CHEF'S SECRET: The mace enhances the champagne flavor but too much of it would spoil the sauce, so be very careful when using it.

The egg yolk will give the desirable faint yellow hue to the sauce. If for any reason you want to omit it, replace it by adding 1 tsp. more cornstarch and one drop of yellow food coloring to the sauce. Of course, the starch is added with the other dry ingredients.

If you must use an ordinary white wine instead of champagne, add a few drops of lemon juice or orange juice and 2 to 3 tbsp. ginger ale or club soda to it before stirring the wine into the sauce. – **The Chef's Secret Cook Book**

ROAST LEG OF LAMB TURKISH STYLE

2 tablespoons salt
1 small boneless leg of lamb, 3 to 4 pounds
teaspoon whole black peppercorns
1 cup chopped onion, including skin
2 bay leaves, broken into pieces
1 cup chopped carrots
1 teaspoon fennel leaves
1 cup chopped celery
1 teaspoon oregano
1 teaspoon marjoram
1/4 teaspoon garlic salt (not garlic powder)

CHAPTER ELEVEN
SUPER 'AMERICAN' CHEFS & Cultural Nostalgia

1. Preheat oven to 425° F. In a mortar or in the bottom of a strong wooden salad bowl, crush together all spices until no large pieces are recognizable, except perhaps some bay leaf.

2. Rub the whole surface of the boneless leg of lamb with the spice mixture; then roll and tie the leg.

3. Distribute in a roasting pan the onion, carrots, and celery and place the leg of lamb on the vegetables. Add enough water to have about an inch in the bottom of the pan. Roast, turning every 10 minutes, for approximately 1 hour, or until a good meat thermometer registers 120° for rare, 130° medium, 150° well-done, in the thickest part of the leg. Remove lamb and set it on a serving platter.

4. Press the vegetables through a fine sieve along with the liquid from the roasting pan. Skim off the fat. Serve the gravy as is or, if you prefer, thicken with 1 teaspoon cornstarch dissolved in 1/4 cup cold water. Serve it with Rice Pilaf.

CHEF'S SECRET: Don't start to slice the lamb for at least 30 minutes after removing it from the oven.

If your butcher sells already deboned, tied, ready-to-roast legs of lamb, prepare the spice mixture a day ahead. Bring it to the butcher and ask him to rub the inside before he ties it; or take a chance: untie the leg at home and tie it again after rubbing the meat with the spice mixture.

Around the Mediterranean this dish is often served with fresh chopped mint leaves sprinkled on the lamb after it is sliced. – **The Chef's New Secret Cookbook**

Cultural Nostalgia

The Mother of all Italian Restaurants can be claimed by *Mother Leone's* in New York. Louisa Leona (1873-1944) cooked meals for her husband and his business associates. One time she prepared a meal for fifty opera guests when famed singer Enrico Caruso, smitten by the good food, suggested she open her own restaurant. In 1906, her restaurant, Mamma Leone's, opened next to her husband's wine shop. The dinner place held only twenty seats and a full meal sold for fifty cents! At the height of her success, there were eight dining rooms, serving 1,200 people. Their busiest nights happened after an Army- Notre Dame football game at Yankee stadium when they served 6,000 dinners, turning away many more customers. As Gene tells the story, one of their craziest nights, occurred when Liberace showed up with his dinner party. Not enough room in a private corner he had to sit with his friends out in the main dining room, and the place became so swamped with fans, that waiters surrounded the table to let him finish his meal (and we know he liked good food!).

There were east and west coast Mother Leone's locations. In 1959, the main restaurant and name were sold to a restaurant syndicate. I think this is the same corporate group who bought the Luchow's brand. By 1994, Mother Leone's had disappeared from the scene.

CHAPTER ELEVEN
SUPER 'AMERICAN' CHEFS & Cultural Nostalgia

Leone's Italian Cookbook *(1967)* by Gene Leone seeks to capture the restaurant remembrances and provides the recipes for the reader to capture the Italian kitchen smells from his Mother's best dishes. The book's Forward was written by former President Dwight D. Eisenhower.

ANTIPASTO: MOZZARELLA IN CARROZZA (FROM SOUTHERN ITALY)

12 slices of white bread, crusts trimmed, 2 large eggs beaten in bowl – 1/2 c. milk – 6 slices mozzarella cheese, 1/4 inch thick – Flour – 6 thin slices of chicken or prosciutto – 1/2 c. olive oil – 2 tbsp fresh creamery butter – Tiny pinch of finely ground black Pepper

Cut slices of bread into halves and dip into eggs, then into milk. Dust the cheese with a tiny bit of flour. Place a half slice of cheese and a half slice of chicken or prosciutto between 2 half slices of bread. Pin with food picks. Place oil and butter in a skillet and heat well. Place sandwiches in skillet. Cook until light brown, turn, and cook until light brown on the other side and cheese begins to melt. To serve, spoon a little of the hot oil over the sandwich and grind fresh pepper on top. Serve on the antipasto or as an entrée. Serves 4 to 6.

PAMELA KURE GROGAN

CHAPTER ELEVEN
SUPER 'AMERICAN' CHEFS & Cultural Nostalgia

CHICKEN CACCIATORA

George M. Cohan occasionally came to Mother's for spaghetti with meat sauce and chicken cacciatore. On Mother's thirty-second anniversary, he came to her party and sang and danced "Give My Regards to Broadway," with our own Sir Owen Jones accompanying him at the piano.

2 fresh spring chickens (2 1/4 lbs each) – 1/4 c. olive oil – 2 oz. salt pork diced – 1/4 c. butter – 1/2 onions, peeled, diced – 2 chicken livers and 2 gizzards, chopped fine – 2 garlic cloves, mashed – 1 tsp fresh rosemary – 10 fresh parsley sprigs, leaves only – 1 1/2 tsp freshly ground pepper – 1/4 tsp salt – 4 medium-sized ripe tomatoes or 2 c. canned peeled plum tomatoes, chopped – 1 tsp tomato pasted

Cut each chicken into 4 pieces. Combine oil, salt pork and butter in a good-sized pot; heat. Add onions and brown slowly. Add the chicken pieces and chopped livers and gizzards and brown for 10 minutes. Chop garlic, rosemary and parsley together and add to the chicken along with the pepper and salt; stir well. Cook for 5 minutes. Add tomatoes and tomato paste and cook slowly for about 30 minutes, or until done. Check for cooking and salt. Do not overcook. This chicken is delicious with freshly cooked spaghettini on the same plate, with sauce spooned over all. Serves 4.

Alice's Restaurant

The restaurant owned by Alice came first, the 18 minute song next ("Alice's Restaurant Masacree") then the 1969 movie of the same name, 'Alice's Restaurant.' The counterculture anti-war, anti-draft talking blues song by singer-songwriter Arlo Guthrie became a hit song inspired by a true story when Arlo and a friend were arrested by Officer Obie for littering garbage on Thanksgiving Day.

Alice May Brock in 1964 borrowed money from her mother and bought an empty church in Great Barrington, Massachusetts where she and her husband lived (the famed Thanksgiving dinner of the song actually held here) with the real restaurant down the road six miles and down an alley in Stockbridge. The restaurant business only lasted a year for Alice before divorce interrupted the venture. Over time she would own 3 restaurants.

CHAPTER ELEVEN
SUPER 'AMERICAN' CHEFS & Cultural Nostalgia

This is very unusual and really fantastically good. My granma used to make it a lot.

MY GRANMA'S BEET JAM

4 pounds of real beets – 3 pounds of sugar – 3 lemons (juice and grated rind) – 2 ounces of ginger root – 1/2 pound of almonds or walnuts

Wash and peel the beets. Put them through a meat grinder, or grate them. Barely cover them with water and cook them slowly until they are tender. Add the sugar, the ginger (cut up fine), the lemon juice and lemon rind. Cook until thick and clear (at least an hour) Add the chopped nuts.
This stuff keeps. Give some to your friends—it's really something else.

PAMELA KURE GROGAN

CHAPTER ELEVEN
SUPER 'AMERICAN' CHEFS & Cultural Nostalgia

Where are they now?
Alice Brock has retired and is fighting health issues. I wish her well. After her 1976 autobiography, *My Life as a Restaurant,* in 2004 she illustrated a children's book, **Mooses Come Walking**, written by Arlo Guthrie. Alice has her own fun book, **How to Massage a Cat**. Books are well drawn and make great children (and cat owner) gifts. For this writing her artwork, featured here, fits perfect to my own whimsical attitude. Thanks, Alice. As my Husband Stephen sings, *'You can get anything you want at Alice's Restaurant—excepting Alice."*

Spaghetti Dinner with 2 Forks I by Alice Brock (of Alice's Restaurant fame). In author's collection

CHAPTER TWELVE
Bottoms Up

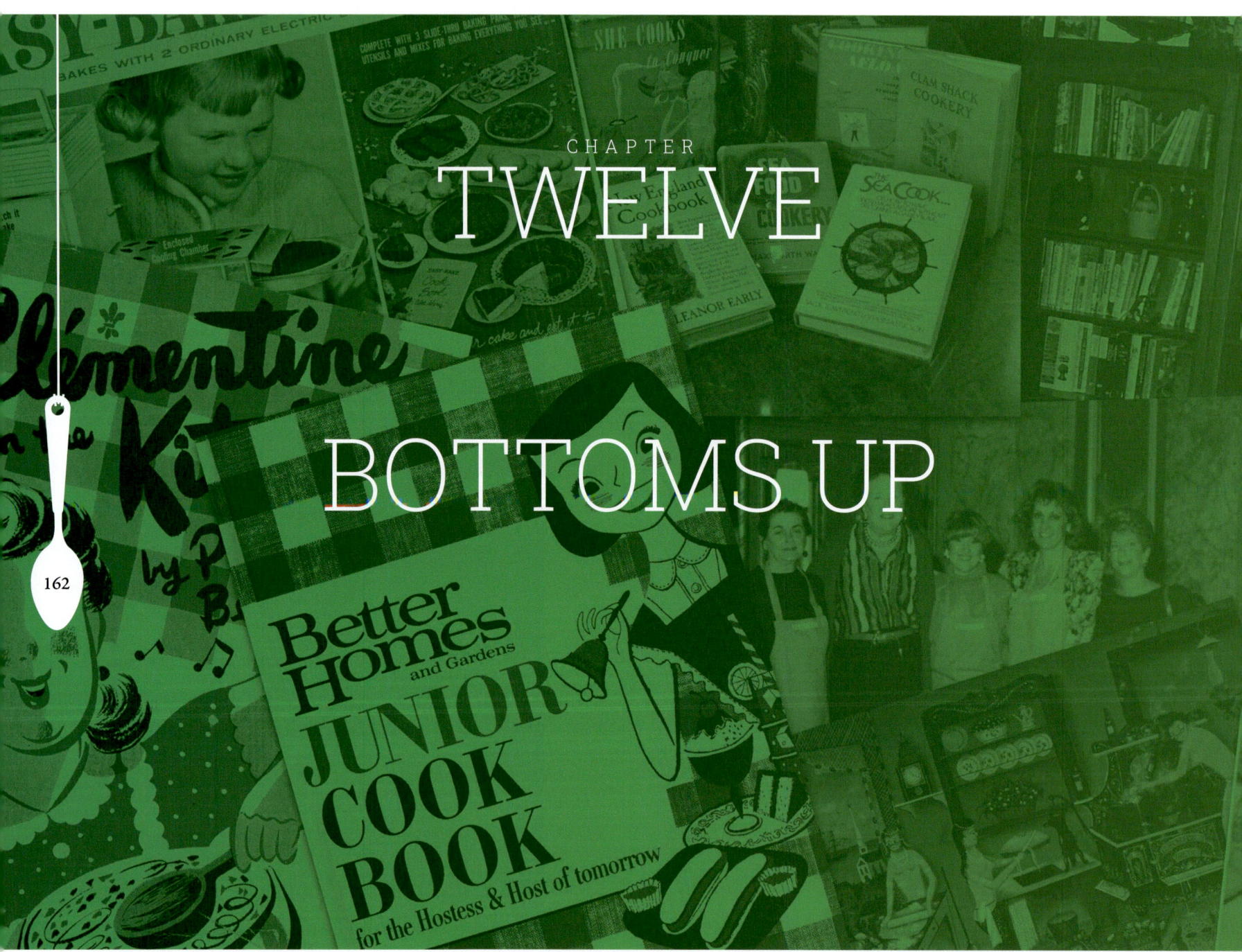

CHAPTER TWELVE

BOTTOMS UP

PAMELA KURE GROGAN

CHAPTER TWELVE
Bottoms Up

"Dost thou think, because thou art virtuous, there shall be no more cakes and ale?" — William Shakespeare, **Twelfth Night**

Our cocktail and wine books have their own bookcase within arm's grasp to the bartender and his mixer setups. The artwork, "The Happy Couple" is an original acrylic by international artist Yuri Kutzenov. My husband commissioned the painting for an anniversary reflecting our mutual hobbies, cat in apron holding a sauce pan, dog with reading glasses and book.

MY COOKBOOK PASSION

CHAPTER TWELVE
Bottoms Up

Dry Years
"Prohibition is better than no liquor at all."
Will Rogers

In the midst of Prohibition the demand for drink basics found a thirsty market. My book is a seventh printing, the first being published in 1927, and it is actually a modern update of a more ancient history published in 1862 by (honorary 'Professor') Jerry Thomas, considered to be the father of the cocktail. His book, **'The Bar-Tender's Guide or How To Mix All Kinds of Plain and Fancy Drinks,** last printed in 1887. An 1886 copy recently sold for over $500. Professor Thomas is remembered today as the creator of the drink, *Tom and Jerry*, and in past days most famous for his flaming *Blue Blazer*.

[Editor's Note: Yes, the cookbook recipe artistry of past eras was usually preceded by a mellowing cocktail., before and after. And the art of wine pairing, not just for the table, but first to the chef's palate in testing that special ingredient. This chapter is designed to encourage themed retro 'cocktail parties' ...with snacks.]

TOM AND JERRY
Use punch bowl for the mixture

Five pounds of sugar. – One and one-half teaspoonful of ground cinnamon. – Twelve eggs – One-half teaspoonful ground cloves – One half small glass of – One-half teaspoonful ground allspice

Beat the whites of the eggs to stiff froth, and the yolks until they are as thin as water, then mix together and add the spice and rum, thicken with sugar until the mixture attains the consistency of light batter.

To deal out Tom and Jerry to customers: Take a small bar glass, and one tablespoonful of the above mixture, add one wineglass of brandy, and fill the glass with boiling water; grate a little nutmeg on top.

PAMELA KURE GROGAN

CHAPTER TWELVE
Bottoms Up

Adepts at the bar, in serving Tom and Jerry, sometimes adopt a mixture of one-half brandy, one-fourth Jamaican rum, and one-fourth Santa Cruz rum, instead of brandy plain. This compound is usually mixed and kept in the bottle and wineglassful is used to each tumbler of Tom and Jerry.

FYI. A teaspoonful of cream of tartar, or about as much carbonate of soda as you can get on a dime, will prevent the sugar from settling to the bottom of the mixture.
This drink is sometimes called *Copenhagen,* and sometimes *Jerry Thomas.*

Strawberry Grape Float
Mix two tablespoonfuls of strawberry syrup, one tablespoonful of orange syrup, and one tablespoonful of vanilla syrup. Fill a glass one fourth full of cracked ice, pour over the syrup and add soda water. Then pour in carefully one tablespoonful of grape juice so that it floats on top, and add a spoonful of whipped cream

[Here is how you are suppose to obtain the strawberry syrup] Dissolve two pounds of sugar in one pint of water in a porcelain kettle. Boil and skim until clear Mash ripe strawberries and strain through a jelly bag. Put the syrup over the fire again, and boil rapidly until a ball is formed in cold water, then add two pints and a half of the strawberry juice. Let it once more come to a boil, skim, and seal in sterilized jars. [Rather, just buy a sno-cone.]   Note: There is an entire chapter on 'Invalid Drinks'.

Professor Jerry Thomas mixing

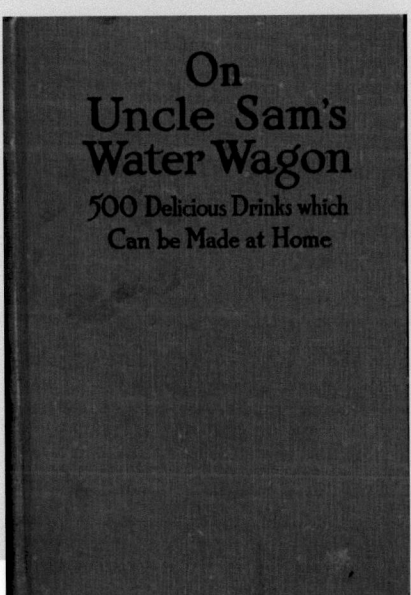

Published in 1919, anticipating Prohibition, the Forward states: *It is the aim of this little book to present a collection of some hundreds of recipes, for making in the home delicious, appetizing, and wholesome drinks, free from alcoholic taint.*

MY COOKBOOK PASSION

CHAPTER TWELVE
Bottoms Up

IMITATION OLD TOM LONDON GIN

Dissolve in 1 quart 95 per cent alcohol, 1 drachm [dram] oil of coriander, 1 drachm oil of cedar, 1/2 drachm oil of bitter almonds, 1/2 drachm oil of angelica, and 1/2 drachm oil of sweet fennel; add it to 40 gallons French spirit 10 above proof, with 1 pint orange-flower water, 1 quart syrup and 1 drachm oil of juniper dissolved in sufficient 95 per cent alcohol to be clear.

Please don't try this at home, alone, multiplying quantities and using your bathtub

Remember 'bathtub gin'? This is the book, published in 1928, that touts 'how to make home-made drinks, cordials, wines, etc.' I bought the book for the name and its 'flapper' cover art. A subtitle to further sell the book, 'includes eleven famous cocktails of the most exclusive club of New York as served before the war when mixing drinks was an art.' The actual famous cocktail recipes are barely two pages of mediocrity. The how-to's are interesting.

PAMELA KURE GROGAN

The Classics

"When men drink, then they are rich and successful and win lawsuits and are happy and help their friends. Quickly, bring me a beaker of wine, so that I may wet my mind and say something clever." — Aristophanes

Now that we have dispensed with several of the mixing oddities Prohibition produced, let's with all speed hasten past that era. I want to regain the world of the bon vivants, those who knew how to live well, epicureans at fashionable tables, witty of current events, draped in black tuxes and elegant evening gowns. Their drink mixing books of the 1930's reflected such atmosphere and for collectors are the ones to pursue for your collection. Here's what I am talking about, from the book's first page: "In Memory of certain gentlemen of other days, who made of drinking one of the pleasures of life—not one of its evils; who achieved content, long ere capacity was reached or overtaxed; and who, whatever they drank, proved able to carry it, keep their heads and remain gentlemen, even in their cups."

The background is to tell stories and supply cocktail recipes from the famous Big Brass Rail where people stood for drinks when the Waldorf bar first opened in 1897. Published in 1931 this was a nostalgic book time reflecting on the demolition of the Old Waldorf. The stories include the times when George Boldt served as General Manager. The first 'Gin Rickey' was conceived and poured at the bar. Many drinks christened: 'Chanticleer' named for a Broadway play opening; 'Dorlando' after a marathon runner in the 1908 Olympics; 'Roosevelt Sour' for Colonel Theodore Roosevelt who probably never even tasted the name-sake concoction.

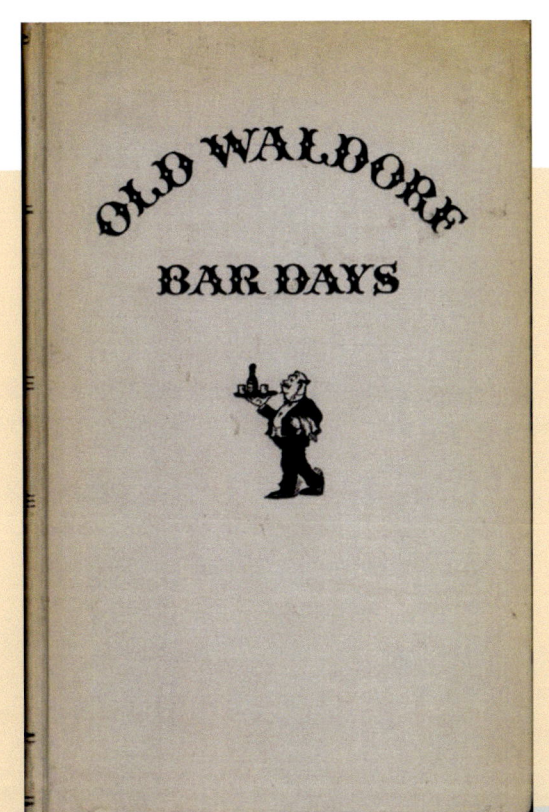

JERSEY FLASHLIGHT

One ingredient was what is now synonymous with "Jersey Lightning," though the term "flashlight" may have been suggested by the flame.

Two lumps Sugar – One dash Angostura Bitters – One piece Lemon Peel – One jigger Apple – Whiskey

Fill with hot Water; ignite the whole Mix while blazing

CHARLIE CHAPLIN

One-third Lime Juice One-third Sloe Gin – One-third Apricot Brandy

MY COOKBOOK PASSION

CHAPTER TWELVE
Bottoms Up

One of the most sought after bar books, the **Savoy Cocktail Book**, 1930, drink recipes compiled by Harry Craddock, is as famous for its art deco design by Gilbert Rumbold. Harry Craddock**,** one of the most famous barmen of the London scene in the 1920's and 1930's, came from the United States during Prohibition. In the Savoy he worked in the American Bar. He is given credit for inventing the *White Lady* and popularizing the **Dry Martini.** His cocktail book remains in print today.

Collector's Corner: *Touted as 'Greatest Book on Drinks',* Savoy Cocktail Book, "This Cocktail was created by Harry Craddock for the Leap Year celebrations at the Savoy Hotel, London, on February 29th, 1928. It is said to have been responsible for more proposals than any other cocktail that has ever been mixed." depending on condition, for first edition, can go for between $US 2,000-$9,000.

LEAP YEAR COCKTAIL

1 Dash Lemon Juice – 2/3 Gin, 1/6 Grand Marnier, 1/6 Italian Vermouth – Shake well and serve in cocktail glass––Squeeze lemon peel on top.

PAMELA KURE GROGAN

CHAPTER TWELVE
Bottoms Up

Savoy Cocktail Book -- Art Deco illustrations throughout by Gilbert Rumbold

MY COOKBOOK PASSION

CHAPTER TWELVE
Bottoms Up

Another Classic

If London had its American barkeep Harry Craddock, Paris offered up Frank Meier, steward and bartender at the art deco Cambon Bar in the Ritz Hotel. If there are mixologist stars of the day, Frank Meier, with his center parted hair and pince- nez, can take the grand bow. Arriving after World War I he served faithfully until his death in 1947. It is said he could mix from memory 300 cocktails using only 13 liquors. Among the striking drinks attributed to his pourings were the Side Car, Monkey Gland, and Corpse Reviver #1.

The book I own is a rare limited edition created for his special patrons and friends, published in 1936. As here, to create degrees of rarity, 26 copies were limited by alphabet designation, 300 copies printed on hand- made paper, with the remaining 700 printed on Cream Vellum paper. My copy is #726.

Bees' Knees-- In shaker: the juice of one-quarter Lemon, a teaspoon of Honey, one-half glass [one-ounce] of Gin; shake well and serve.

Talk about smart cross marketing. On your next cruise (in 1936) ask for Frank Meier's personalized cocktails created just for the Atlantic crossing [See next page]

CHAPTER TWELVE
Bottoms Up

SS Manhattan
- *In shaker: a dash of Benedictine, half Orange juice, half Bourbon Whiskey; shake well and serve.*

How to Mix Drinks by Bill Edwards, 1936. Nothing deep, just drinks. Pages holed and tied with heavy string. I assume to hang on a peg at your home bar.

SIBBY'S SPECIAL

5 parts Jamaica Rum – 1 1/2 parts Dry Gin – 3/4 part Italian Vermouth – 3/4 part French Vermouth – 1/2 part Cointreau – 1 part Lime Juice – 2 parts Lime Syrup D'orgeat – A few drops of Absinthe per cocktail

Did you know?
Absinthe, which is an anise (licorice) flavored liquor, is making a comeback in the world of cocktails. Until recently it had been banned in the U.S. (since 1912) because it supposedly contained a concentrated chemical drug that could lead to psychoactive intensity (of hallucinogenic qualities). Nowadays that concern has been distilled out. Absinthe is a green colored potent drink, 70-80% alcohol, nicknamed the 'Green Fairy'. There is a whole ritual in the pouring and use requiring a special spoon, diluting with water and sugar. In the 19th and 20th century it was a big turn-on in the artist and writers circles of France, and as you see in the early 20th century bar books used quite a bit in cocktail mixing and no one complained, unless of hangovers. Pre-1915 bottles of Absinthe (before being banned) go as collectors' items for thousands of dollars.

We return to **Volume II of The Gentleman's Companion by Charles H. Baker, Jr.** (See page 62 Vol I) or as he aptly puts it, and remember I like his wit writing style, "BEING AN EXOTIC DRINKING BOOK, or, around the world with jigger, beaker and flask."

AN ABSINTHE COCKTAIL
As Mixed for Us by an itinerant Russian Prince on the Occasion of Our Usual Morning Pilgrimage to Harry's American Bar, which is in Paris

During several weeks domicile in Hotel Daunou over Ciro's across the Rue Daunou, we often groped to Harry when visibly withering on the vine—seeking aid and comfort. On this special occasion a Russian gentleman spied our ambulant corpse, took pity, bowed Harry aside in his spotless white coat, and in a small frappe shaker compounded the following life saver. We advocate putting it in The Mixer for a jiffy with finely cracked ice.

This is an excellent appetizer and tonic. Twist bit of peel to insure getting oil on surface of drink. Must be very cold. Absinthe, 1 1/2 jiggers – Orange & Angostura bitters, dash each Anis or anisette, dash – White of egg, 1 tsp – Water, 1/2 jigger – Twist of lime or lemon peel Sugar or gomme syrup, 1/2 tsp or less

CHAPTER TWELVE
Bottoms Up

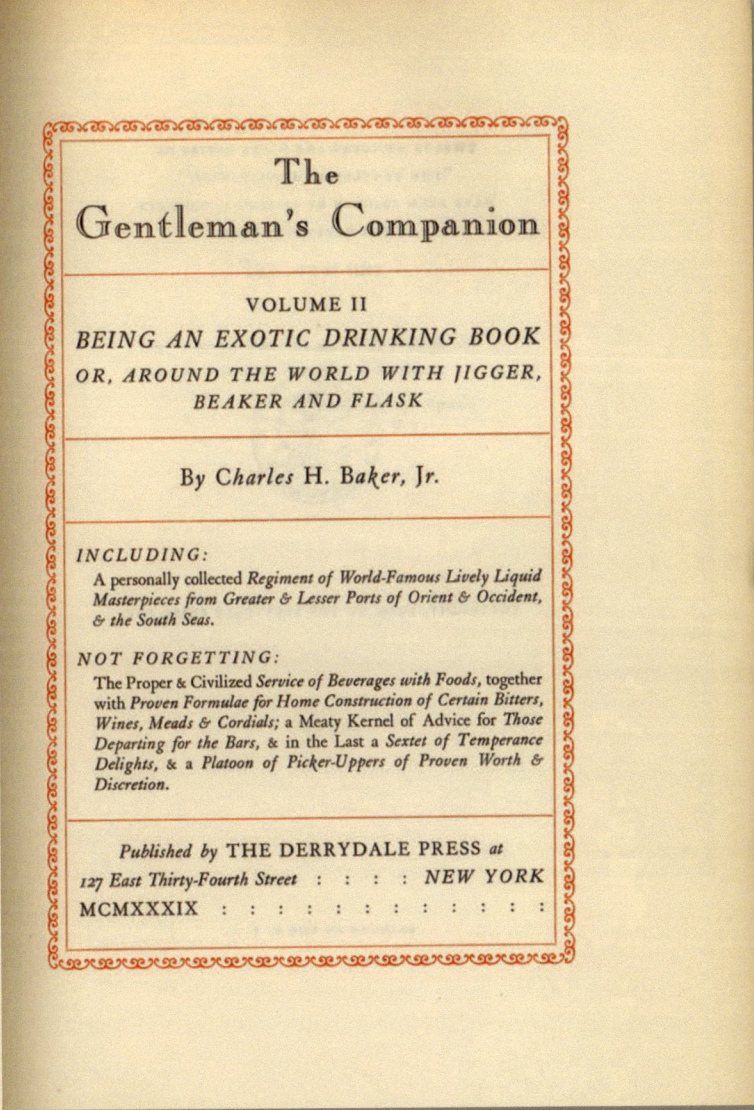

And like Charles Baker, we can follow Crosby Gaige cavorting through several decades enjoying the good life. His *Ladies Companion* cocktail guide (see page 52 is a humorous romp and all our old friends show up to offer drink or food recipes: James Beard, Dr. Charles Browne, Lucius Beebe (**Stork Club Bar Book**), Gene Cavallero (**Colony Restaurant**), to name a few.

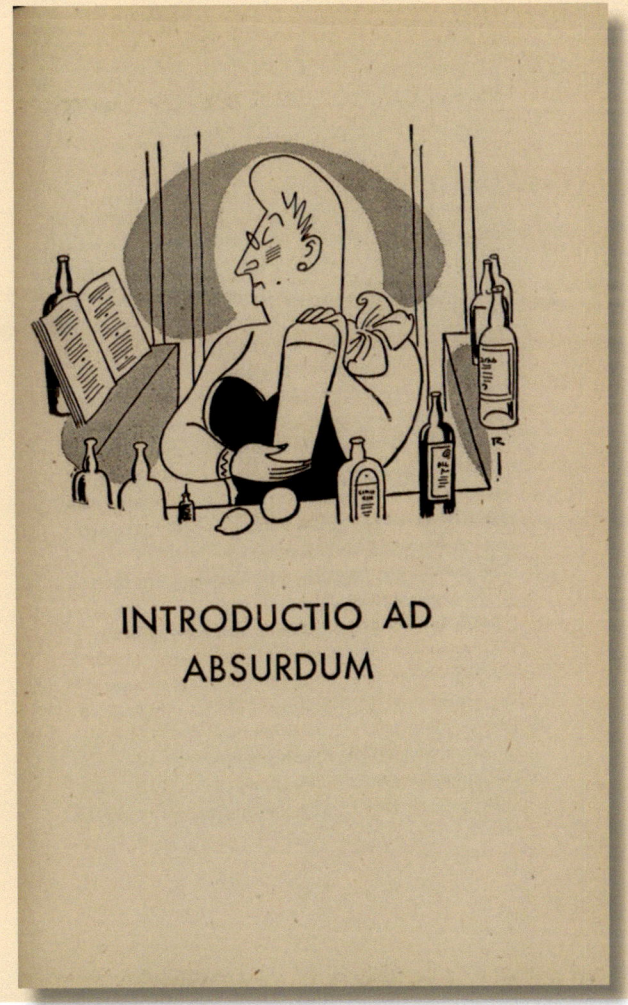

Again, I recommend reading Baker's two volumes if just for the pleasure of his world travels. Many of his food and drink recipes are now found as menu staples in today's haute cuisine 5 Stars.

OKOLEHAO PUNCH

Offered by Charles Rochester, Manager, Hotel Lexington, New York

1 1/2 ounces of Gin – 1 1/2 ounces of Coconut Milk – 3/4 ounce Lemon Juice Dash of in recipe below (Dowager) Curaçao – 1 teaspoon sugar

Shake a few minutes and serve in a coconut shell with a little crushed ice.

THE DOWAGER DUCHESS (FOR 6)

Place the rind of 1 Orange, a teaspoon of Peach Preserve, a large Apricot and its crushed kernel in the bottom of a shaker. Add 2 jiggers of Brandy and 1 teaspoon of Kirsch. Let this soak for a couple of hours. Then add: 1 jigger White Wine – 2 jiggers Dry Gin 2 jiggers French Vermouth

Fill shaker with ice. Shake and strain into cocktail glasses.

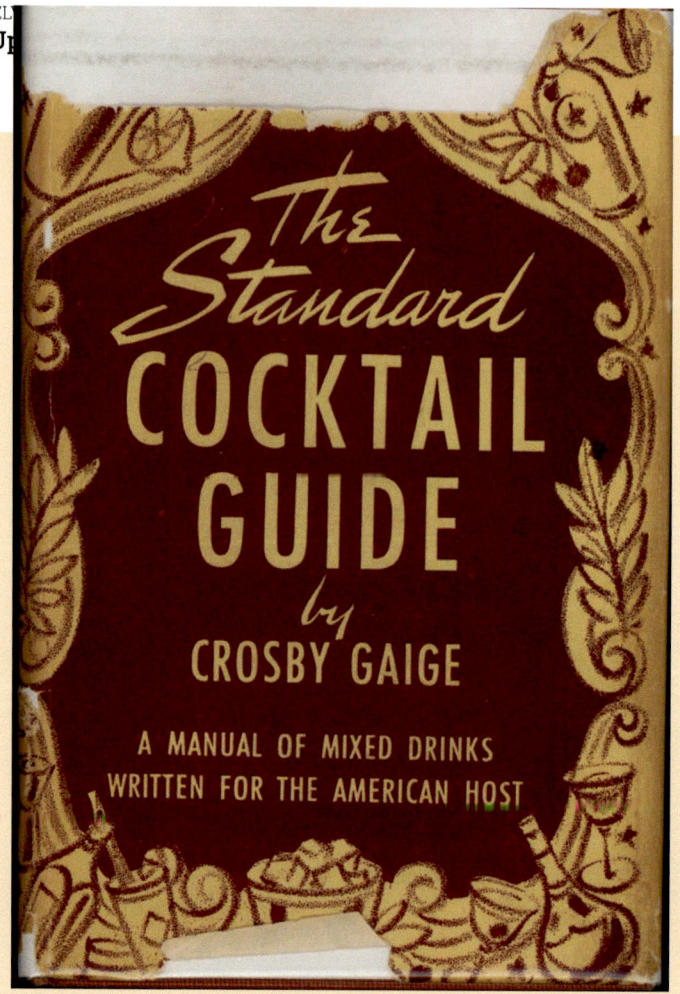

[Taste testing all the ingredients I learn:1 jigger equivalent to 1 1/2 ounces; Vermouth (Vermuth) in the old days was considered of two varieties: Italian being sweet, and French, sec, dry; Kirsch or Kirschwasser, a wild cherry liquor..spg]

Crosby Gaige's **"The Standard Cocktail Guide"** (Barrows, page 80) is more a straight forward manual and considering all the cocktail recipes I may reproduce, it is interesting to note, beyond the hard core, what the well stocked bar of 1944 included to create various libations:

PAMELA KURE GROGAN

CHAPTER TWELVE
Bottoms Up

Yellow Chartreuse - Crème de Cacao - Cointreau - Maraschino - Crème de Yvette - Grenadine - Orange Bitters - Orange Curaçao - Dubonnet and Dry Sherry - Crème de Menthe (White and Green) - Benedictine Cherry and Apricot Brandy

Gaige sets forth 'Three Basic Rules for the Good Host'. Simplified they state: (1) Always follow a recipe accurately; (2) Never stir a carbonated water vigorously; and (3) the careful hosts knows his bar glasses. "A Collins is a long, tall drink designed not only as a stimulant but as thirst-quencher. It is tradition that it gets its name from a barman named Collins who labored at the old Astor House in New York." Here is one of Gaige's many selections.

CAPE COD COLLINS

1 jigger Puerto Rican Rum – 1 jigger Cranberry Juice – 1 cup Shaved Ice

Place ingredients in shaker and shake until well mixed and chilled. Fill tall Collins glass half full of shaved ice and pour into mixture. Fill with Soda Water, stir once or twice, and top with Orange slice or Maraschino Cherry, and a sprig of Mint.

The Bars

Lucius Beebe writes: *'The Stork Club's drinking has never been accomplished in the cloistered privacy of old gentleman's clubs; it has been orchestrated to sweet music, illuminated by the heat lightning of photographer's flashes and upholstered in broadcloth and starched linen. It has been drinking in the grand manner, guzzling with a panache of chic and elegance, a hoisting of crystal chalices in the secure knowledge that the wit, beauty, chivalry and wealth of the world were doing the identical thing at adjacent tables, each one a location of distinction and reserved for names that makes news alone. Make no mistake, drinking at the Stork is neither a shy, anonymous nor retiring occupation. It is a public rite and requires stylish gestures and the distant, barely audible accompaniment of French horns.*

Do you hear the French horns calling? I do.'
His way with words I'd let this man write my obituary. In the **Stork Club Bar Book,** Beebe divides up his chapters into "Morning", "Afternoon", and "Evening at the Stork Club." I have no idea why you discuss making Manhattans and Dry Martinis in the morning? On martini variations, he writes of the drink:

CHAPTER TWELVE
Botto

ROSALIND RUSSELL

2/3 jigger Danish Alborg aquavit – 1/3 jigger vermouth or dubonnet Shake or spoon and serve in the same manner as a Martini.

BALTIMORE EGGNOG

1 fresh egg – 1/2 tbsp. fine granulated sugar – 1/4 jigger brandy – 1/4 jigger Jamaica rum – 1/2 pt. fresh milk

Shake well and strain into highball glass. Serve with a grating of nutmeg.

Miss Russell's own comment on this arrangement is: "My father-in-law, Carl Brisson, introduced me to this drink and six months later I married his son!"

Beebe writes of 'Morning at the Stork Club': *"It is in the early watches that the knowing and perceptive barkeep must most closely fill the function of physician and adviser. His clients are in humbled or quiescent mood, usually in search of soft words and consolation. By noontime he may be in requisition as adviser on the race track situation and by nightfall, variously in demand as councilor at love, bail bondsman or bouncer, but in the morning his technique is guided by a strictly bedside manner."*

Further on Beebe makes the statement: *An improvement, as some may think, on the conventional Alexander cocktail is the brainstorm child of Nelson Eddy and he calls it—*

ALEXANDER THE GREAT

1/2 oz. crème de cacao – /2 oz. coffee liqueur – 1/2 fresh cream – 1 1/2 oz vodka

Shake until cold as Siberia. Watch your Steppes, because more than three of these gives the consumer a wolfish appetite.

CHAPTER TWELVE
Bottoms Up

Did You Know?
The Stork Club held the reputation as one of the flashiest New York City nightclubs in the 1930's-1950's, the Café Society scene of power, wealth and glamour stardom. It even had its own television show for five years in the 1950's.

Lucius Beebe (1902-1966) gains my vote as being perhaps the most visible and flashiest of the gourmand bon vivants of Post Prohibition, the temple scribe to the glittered New York society akin to a Truman Capote sort with flamboyant character, in words and in his own fashion statement. We find Beebe writing the Forward to Crosby Gaige's **Cocktail Guide**. He wrote as a society columnist for the New York *Herald Tribune*, his column "This is New York" and his journalistic gossip power rivaled that of tattle wags, Ed Sullivan and Walter Winchell. Actress Tuallah Bankhead, herself an encyclopedia of dry witticisms, once spoke of Beebe: "He must have a great respect for the truth since he very rarely uses it." Beebe is one of those eccentrics destined to have his story in some future bio film drama. Outside living the good life, he and his partner, were excellent photographers and wrote several books together detailing their fascination with the railroads of America, easy to write about when you have your own opulent private rail car from which to view the passing scenery. [He wrote 35 books most homage to the steam era of railroading]

Toot Shor's Restaurant
Here's a book with no recipes at all within. Husband Stephen bought it for me when I was trying to capture that 'atmosphere' of past tense restaurants and nightlife. We've

seen the Colony Restaurant and the Stork Club. Other to-be-seen places would have been the El Morroco, the 21 Club, and Toot Shor's Restaurant, the place for sporting celebrities, where food was 'nuttin' fancy. Famous at Toot's was their large circular bar. It was the favorite hangout of baseball great, Joe DiMaggio. My copy of **Toots** by Bob Considine is autographed by both Considine and Toots, the restaurateur and barman inscribing, "After reading this book I formed the A.A." Considine gained fame as a celebrity biographer but also wrote the war book, "Thirty Seconds Over Tokyo". Coincidentally, reading in another bar book I ran across a Toot's cocktail.

CHAPTER TWELVE
Bottoms Up

CRUM BUM

By Toots Shor, Toots Shor Restaurant, New York City

1 jiggers rye whiskey - 1/2 jigger Triple Sec Dash Peychaud bitters - Place cracked ice in a 6-oz. old-fashioned glass. - Pour liquor over it, add bitters. Stir. Decorate with thin lice lemon.

Libation of Knowledge

Here are three books that I class as learning tools, thick with pages, each in their own way a fount of liquid education. To have one or all of these as the foundation to your collection would be wise.

The American Drink Book (1953) by S. S. Field, signed. The sectional divides of the book define your education: 'Taverns, Tankards and Tallow'; 'The Best-Cellar Book on Wines'; 'A Quicker Liquor Curriculum on Spirits and Beer'; 'The Complete Bartender and the 100 Greatest American Drinks'; and 'Now Your Cooking With Liquor'. I was waiting for the critics to say, 'well, she did not include such-and-such drink, my favorite, so she lacks the savoir fair of the sommelier or the bar keep.' The issue with old drink books is that the bar label names today are not the ingredients used in colonial times up through the 1950's. Modernity defines the faddish. Health and lawsuits decries all colonial habits. A commercial bartender today dare not use a fresh egg in a drink, and to them bitters and absinthe are not essentials in the what's popular restaurant cocktail. Mr. Field provides us his list, *100 of the Greatest American Drinks*, half I can't find in current bar books, and that's only fifty years back! There

PAMELA KURE GROGAN

CHAPTER TWELVE
Bottoms Up

is one however which has stood, pardon the pun, the taste of time: *The Mint Julep*. Several bar books I've presented have multi- variations of the Julep, but here's the one I suggest you enjoy on the veranda. *Nowhere in the bibulous history of man is there evidence that this taste experience has been surpassed*

KENTUCY MINT JULEP

Place a dozen tender young mint sprigs in a bowl with a full teaspoon of powdered sugar. Muddle the mint and sugar gently, bruising the leaves. Add enough water to dissolve the sugar, and muddle some more. Place half the mint leaves and liquid in a pre-chilled 12-ounce tumbler of thin glass, or in a silver tankard. Fill the glass half full of finely crushed ice. Add the remainder of the crushed mint and pack the glass level with ice. Pour in as much Bourbon Whiskey as the glass will take, and stir briskly until frost appears. Bury in shaved ice for at least an hour. When ready to serve, cut away a rim of the surrounding ice with the glass, decorate with sprigs of mint powdered sugar, and serve with short straws. If burial of the drink is impracticable, store in the refrigerator.

Historical narrative and drink recipes sets out the **Esquire Drink Book** (1956), edited by Frederic A. Birmingham. Offered is variety with illustrations by Charmatz.

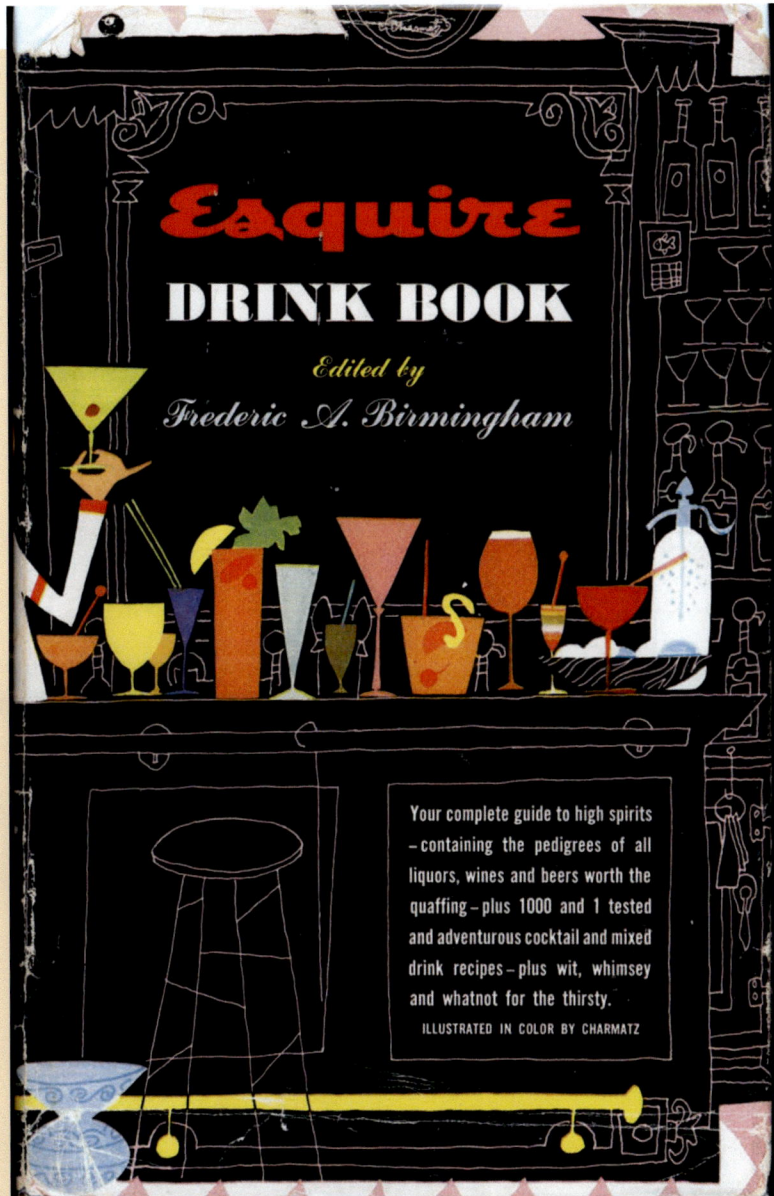

CHAPTER TWELVE
Bottoms Up

The Johnson Delight:
From the campus of Yale University, and served over the bar at Chi Psi Fraternity, where Frederick W. Johnson, extolled by the brothers as "Yale's most qualified sommelier," presides, and has for twenty-one years, comes the J.D.: He serves the lads a deceptively smooth drink which they have rejoiced in ever since a Radcliffe girl had three and beat up her date in public (a Harvard man). **This capsule goes like so: 2/3 Pernod, 1/2 Cointreau, juice of 1/2 lime. Shake well and strain over cracked ice in Old Fashioned glass. Repeat often as desired, facing east. from Esquire Drink Book: party people**

PAMELA KURE GROGAN

CHAPTER TWELVE
Bottoms Up

*Above is the book's cover but next page shows the full **"Bottoms Up"** artwork by Al Dorne (1904-1965). Of course, a Bottoms Up drink would be appropriate here:*

Bottoms Up

byTed Saucier (1896-1970). Ted served four decades as publicist for the Waldorf-Astoria Hotel in New York. Cocktail recipes have been contributed and solicited from famous restaurants and bars from around the world, several we have noted in this chapter. What is the attention-grabber to *Bottoms Up* (1951) are the full page risqué illustrations of beautiful, scantily-clothed women, drawn by twelve well-known artists, including James Montgomery Flagg (of 'Uncle Sam' poster fame).

RUM JUBILEE (FROZEN)
By Gene Leone, Leone Restaurant, New York City

1 oz. Myers rum – 2 scoops orange sherbet – 1/2 scoop chocolate ice cream – 1/2 oz. Myers rum float – 2 dashes Cherry Heering

Mix sherbet, ice cream and rum with spoon. Pour in champagne glass. Add rum float and Cherry Heering.

MY COOKBOOK PASSION

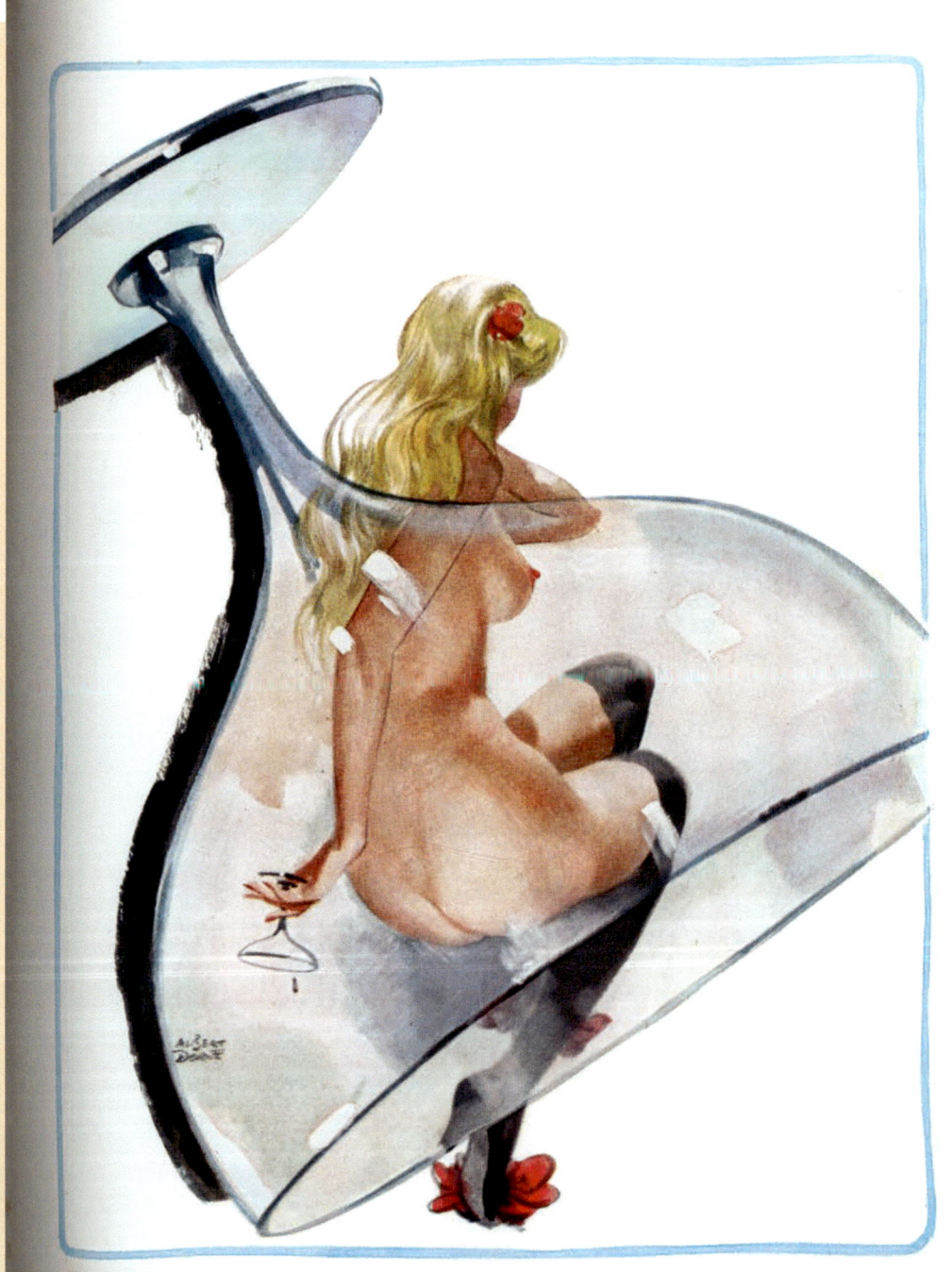

Bottom's Up Cocktail
1 jigger of Coronet brandy; 1/2 jigger curaçao; 1 bar spoon grenadine; 1 bar spoon heavy cream; yolk 1 egg; ice. *Shake well. Strain into Cocktail glass.*

Dorne, an important magazine illustrator, would receive the Horatio Alger Award for his rags-to-riches life, surviving TB and a heart condition to found the Famous Artists Schools. His artwork includes menus for The Stork Club.

Star Mixers

As we have seen elsewhere books with celebrities providing their recipes gains a following. Here are a few as applied to mixology.

CHAPTER TWELVE
Bottoms Up

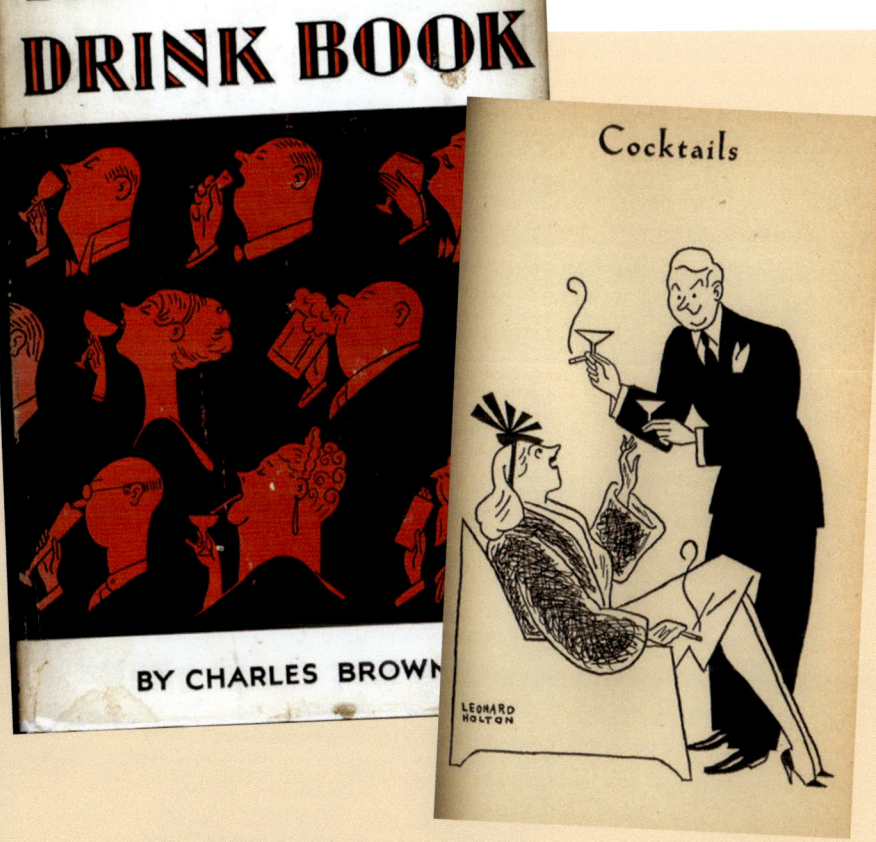

The Formula (courtesy Mr. John Wagner, a citizen of the State in Schuylkill):

Slack 1 pound loaf sugar in a bowl. When dissolved, add 1 quart lemon juice 2 quarts Jamaica rum – 1 quart brandy (cognac) – 1 wineglassful (circa 4 oz.) peach brandy 2 quarts water

Put large lump of ice in the bowl and allow mixture to "brew" for two or more hours, stirring occasionally. More water may be needed, depending upon how rapidly the ice melts. It is better practice to allow the lemon juice and sugar to blend for an hour or so in one container and the liquor and water in another before combining.

What makes a 'wit'? This accolade was bestowed by several critics of Dr. Browne's two books. Let me provide Browne's opening statement to his drink book: *As this book is written only for those who want to drink, there is no reason to discuss the effect of alcohol either on the human system or on the morals of the race. Endless arguments have been advanced by those who favor total abstinence, or the "Drys" as one learned to call them during the ten lean years, to prove that alcohol in any quantity is a poison. Well, what of it? Why argue? At any rate, it is a pleasant poison and certainly slow in its action. Many of us have had grandfathers who lived more than nine decades and who were accustomed to take a nip of rum or a bottle of Bass or maybe a dram of spirits daily. They might have lived longer, but who wants a grandfather more than a hundred years old, especially if one be his residuary legatee?*

This is the sequel to **Gun Club Cook Book** (page 80). One of the threads woven through most of the earlier drink books is the use of the punch bowl. Charles Browne at this time was the President of the Gourmet Society of New Jersey, so this story tracks.

FISH HOUSE PUNCH

Fish House Punch has been the main specialty of the "State in Schuykill" since this association was founded in 1732. This drink has made countless thousands happy, including George Washington, Lafayette and, later, General Pershing.

MY COOKBOOK PASSION

CHAPTER TWELVE
Bottoms Up

Mystery Author S. S. Van Dine offers the dying a curative libation—'So Red the Nose'

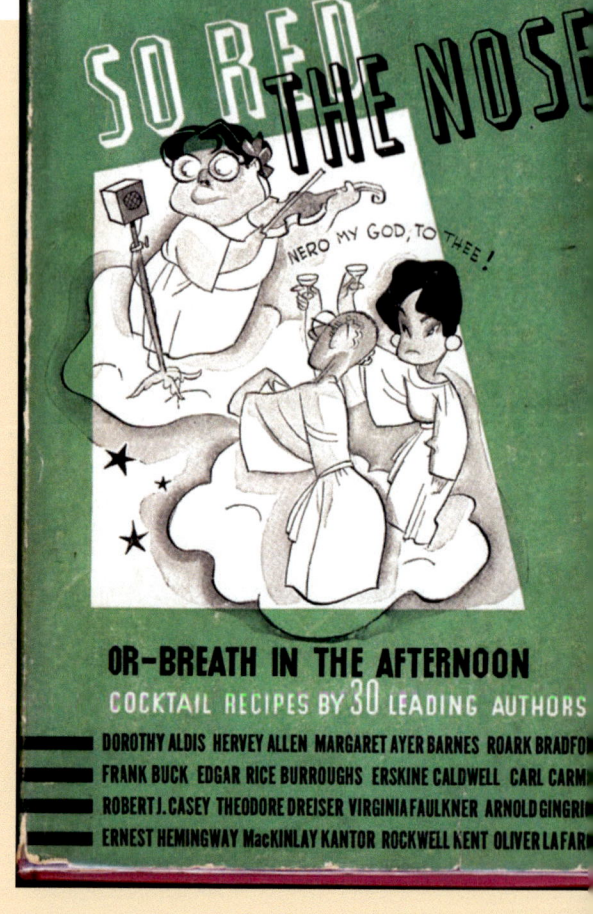

We must forgive Sterling North (1906-1974) and Carl Kroch (1915-1999) for this book. To my read it's just not that good; it's like they might have asked literary stars what their favorite drinks were, and whether they responded or not, created cute and pithy pandering stories about them, and borrowed drinks from other sources. Both had entrée to approach the literati. North served as literary editor for the NY World Telegram and later the NY Sun. Kroch, a legendary bookseller.

The cocktails in *"So Red the Nose—or Breath in the Afternoon"* are named after a featured author's book, such as in 'Ernest Hemingway's *Death in the Afternoon* Cocktail.' Made with our friend Absinthe and champagne, North/Kroch write: "After six of these cocktails, *The Sun Also Rises*." Other well known authors of 1935 included: Edgar Rice Burroughs, Erskine Caldwell, Theodore Dreiser, S.S. Van Dine, Alexander Woolcott, among others. What saves the book as I see it are the caricatures of Roy Nelson, a talented artist viewed in many magazines most predominately in "Esquire".

Beyond this effort, Mr. North goes forward into life as free-lance writer and does much better. His book *Midnight & Jeremiah* in 1947 becomes a Disney movie, *So Dear To My Heart*. He's most remembered for his 1963 best-seller, *Rascal*, a coming-of-age story with a pet raccoon.

Mr. Kroch in his lifetime created one of the largest privately owned bookstore chains in the country, Kroch's & Brentano's. In 1952 he opened in Chicago, Super Book Mart, touted as the 'world's largest bookstore. In 1991 he contributed the principal gift of $10 million to Cornell University to the Carl A. Kroch Library for rare manuscripts.

PAMELA KURE GROGAN

CHAPTER TWELVE
Bottoms Up

SNACKS

HOT CRABMEAT CANAPÉS

12 ounces crabmeat – 1 cup broth or water – Salt and pepper – 2 ounces grated Parmesan cheese – 3 tablespoons butter – 2 ounces grated Swiss cheese – 1 small onion, minced fine – Toast squares – 2 tablespoons flour

Season crabmeat with salt and pepper to taste. Melt 2 tablespoons butter in saucepan. Add onion and sauté gently until cooked. Add 1 tablespoon flour and stir constantly for 2 minutes. Add broth or water and crabmeat and let cook slowly for 15 minutes, stirring occasionally. Turn mixture into a bowl and let cool. Place 1 tablespoon butter in a pan and blend in 1 tablespoon flour; add the cheese, mix well and turn out to cool. Spread the toast squares with the crabmeat mixture. Roll the cheese into tiny balls and place one in the center of each canapé. Place under broiler until lightly browned, about 5 minutes.

CHAPTER TWELVE
Bottoms Up

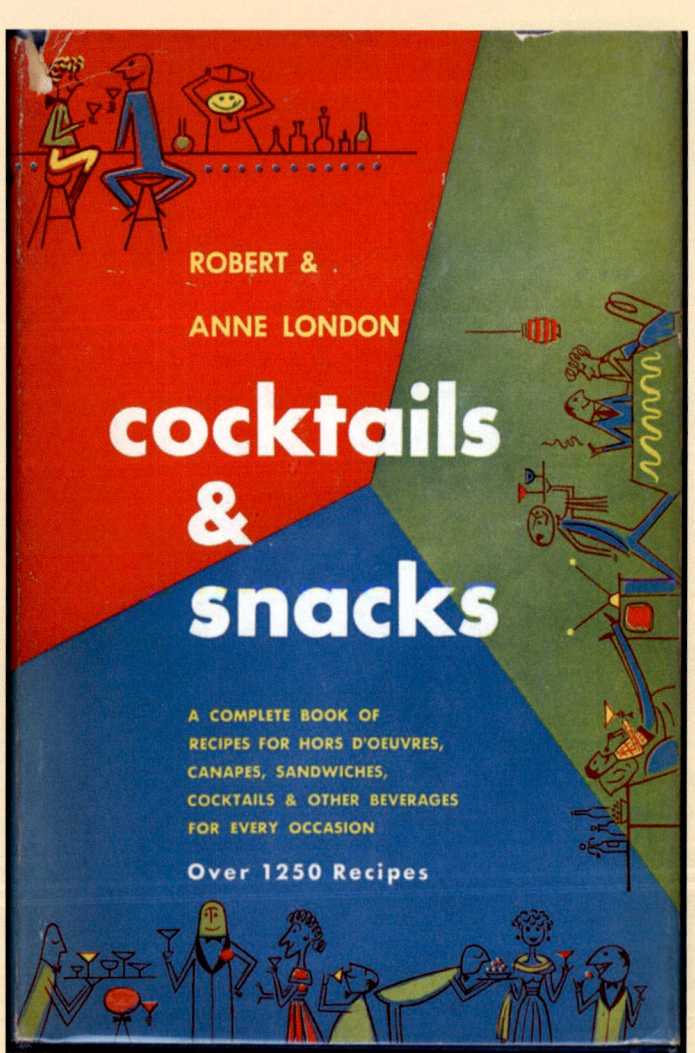

(Cocktails & Snacks, Robert & Anne, London, 1953, over 1250 recipes

PAMELA KURE GROGAN

CHAPTER TWELVE
Bottoms Up

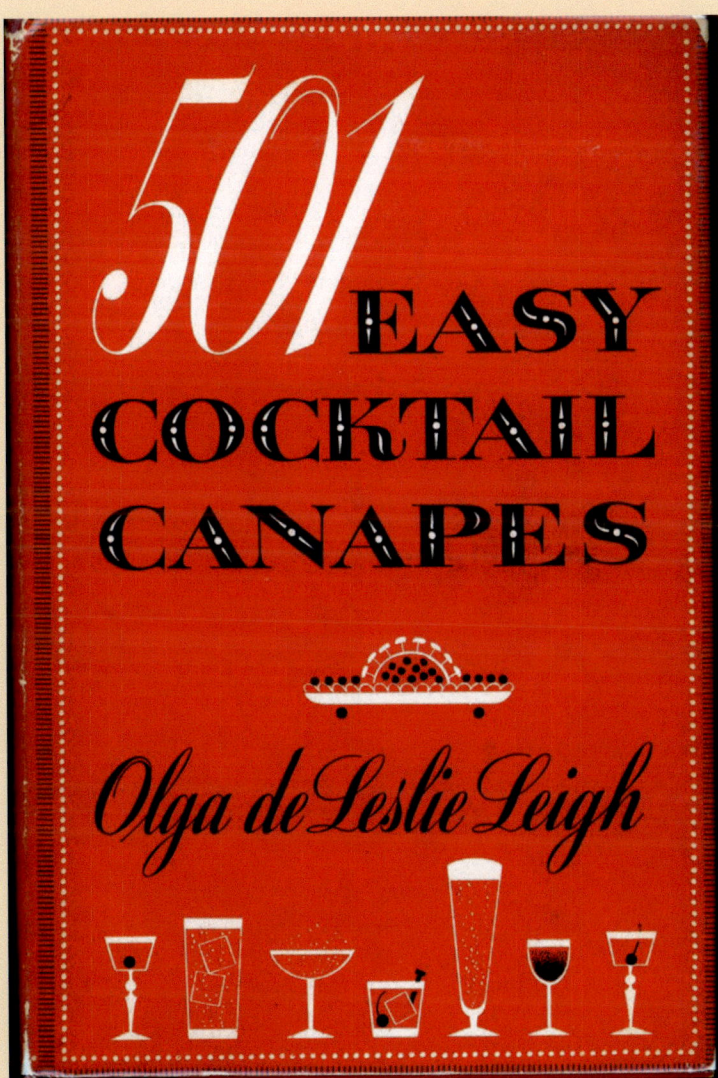

TOAST

Anyone can make toast, but few people know how to preserve its crispness. After the toast is done, it should be stacked on end, never piled up. If you pile it, or cover it with a napkin or cover of any sort, it will become soggy and tough in no time. (**Tipple & Snack,** compiled by Dexter Mason, 1931; he also wrote **The Art of Drinking**)

HAM AND MUSHROOM SNACKS

Blend 1 cup ground cooked ham with 2 tablespoons chopped chutney. Moisten with a little chutney syrup. Fill sautéed mushroom caps with this mixture. Garnish each portion with grated Parmesan cheese. Makes 38-40 snacks. (**501 Easy Cocktail Canapés** by Olga de Leslie Leigh, 1953)

CABBAGE FOR A KING

From your grocer get a large green cabbage completed with outer leaves and into the hollowed center of this sink a can of Sterno. Stick cocktail sausages on little metal skewers—the new Smokey Links cut in bite-size pieces are also good. These are then stuck into the cabbage. Light the Sterno, and let your guests toast their own. (**Cocktail Companions** by Marian Courtney, 1954)

MY COOKBOOK PASSION

CHAPTER THIRTEEN
Entertainment is Fun!

The hostess must be like the duck calm and unruffled on the surface, and paddling like hell underneath.
Anonymous

Circa late 1950's-- Entertainment Committee on clean up patrol. A staged photo op for the local newspaper promoting the good deeds of their favorite social charity. Husband Stephen's mother on far left.

We quickly realize that cooking does not stand alone, on the same presumption that we should not dine alone. More than one at dinner is the makings of a good party, and by your dish prepared for such an occasion, you have become the 'entertainer.'

CHAPTER THIRTEEN
Entertainment is Fun!

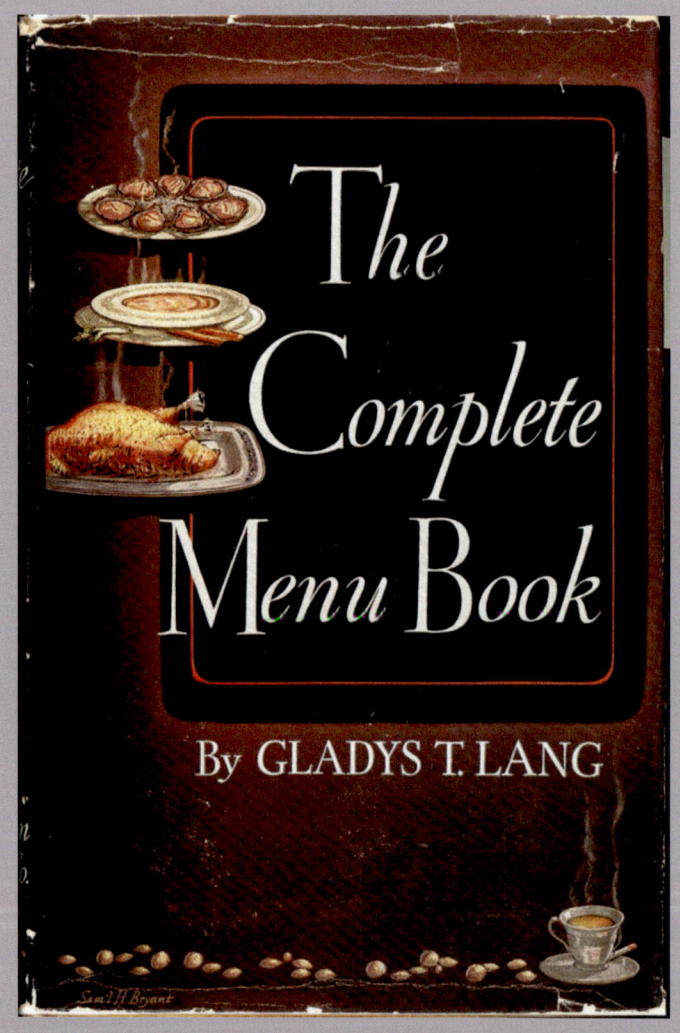

Famed U.S. Educator John Erskine (1879-1951) wrote in his essay, *The Complete Life*, "Since flavoring and the mixture of flavors is the essence of cooking, we can't get far by preparing only separate and unrelated dishes. **The Complete Menu Book** (1939) by Gladys T. Lang has given me many ideas about meals planned as a whole." Gladys sets out various menus, and the recipes therein, very simple instructions. I'll give examples from several different menu presentations, and my tease is that you will want to see how all the other dishes are created.

Menu: *Mock Egg Canapé, Fish Mousse with Lobster Sauce Wilted Cucumbers - Asparagus - Toasted English Muffins, Coffee - Pineapple Ice - Cream Chantilly - Pecan Puffs*

Recipe:
WILTED CUCUMBERS

Peel and slice cucumbers very thin and cover with ice water and salt. Let stand for a few hours, then drain and wipe dry. Cover with a highly seasoned French dressing and place in refrigerator for several hours and serve with dressing in side dishes.

CHAPTER THIRTEEN
Entertainment is Fun!

Menu: *Strawberry Juice Cocktail - Pea Timbale Ring with Shrimp and Mushrooms, Cucumber Salad, Hot Biscuits Coffee, Coconut Pudding*

Recipe:
PEA TIMBALE RING

Rub through a sieve on quart of peas cooked in a small amount of water with a pinch of soda and two tablespoons of sugar. (Canned peas may be used.) Drain and rub through a sieve. Make a thick cream sauce using four tablespoons of butter, two tablespoons of flour, and a cup of milk, one and a half teaspoons of salt, a little pepper, and a few drops of onion juice. Mix this with two cups of pea pulp and add four beaten eggs. Turn into a well-buttered ring mold, place in a pan of water, cover with oiled paper, and bake slowly until firm, about an hour. Unmold on heated platter and fill center with shrimps and mushrooms.

Menu: *Bunch of Grapes, Salad, Frog Legs Poluette,- Italian Fried Cucumbers - Toasted French Loaf, Peach Icebox Pudding*

Recipe:
FROG LEGS, POULETTE

Salt and pepper sixteen small frog legs, roll in flour and brown lightly in one half cup of melted butter. When colored, add one half cup of sherry and cook covered for ten minutes. Prepare two cups of rich cream sauce, pour gradually over the frog legs, and serve immediately on a heated platter, garnished with toast points, dipped in melted butter, then in minced parsley.

[Lang's earlier books included: **Choice Menus for Luncheons and Dinners** (1930), **More Menus for Luncheon and Dinners** (1933)]

Can you see it all coming together? The recipe leads to the dish, the menu sets the dinner, and with entertaining the ambiance of the room is essential to total success of the event. Modern interior decorating and the name of Dorothy Draper (1889-1969) are synonymous. She was a pioneer, revolutionizing design, inventing the style "Modern Baroque." The words *brash* and *bodacious* speak to her talent. Her signature designs were splashy colors. When allowed she relished playing with public spaces. Look around. The 'Draper Touch', furniture and interiors, exists today in many classic hotels, including one we visited previously, The Greenbrier in White Sulphur Springs, West Virginia.

CHAPTER THIRTEEN
Entertainment is Fun!

Following on her best seller, **Decorating is Fun** (1939), in **Entertaining is Fun, How to be a Popular Hostess** (1941) she paints a broad brush stroke of advice. When it comes to food she leans heavily on a researched bibliography at book's end. In her "Dinner Parties" chapter, she writes *"The secret of all good cooking can be written: flavor first ... If you want to add something quite different do this with a really good (and, alas! this means rich sauce). Beurre anchois, for instance, which does something unforgettable to plain broiled halibut or cod. (Cream together unsalted butter and anchovy paste and spread this on the hot fish before serving it.) "Why not learn at least three or four fine sauces and how to make these down to perfection? The three might be hollandaise (to be used on fish and on certain vegetables); béchamel (a very rich white sauce); and béarnaise (delicious on beef); or Newburg sauce. You may want one sweet sauce for puddings. Perhaps a wine sauce... Try a béarnaise sauce on hamburgers!"*

Who did Dorothy Draper consider her food mentors? **The Boston Cooking School Cook-Book** by Fannie Farmer ("With this book in one hand and a well stocked pantry you can face any domestic crisis which involves feeding people with perfect equanimity.") **Elsie De Wolfe's Recipes for Successful Dining** [Drape]. **June Platt's Party Cook Book**. **America's Cook Book**, compiled by Herald Tribune Home Institute.

Sidenote: Dorothy Draper gives research credit to several cooking publications by the newspaper *Herald Tribune*. Not surprising therefore the Forward to **Entertaining is Fun!** is written by Eloise Davison, food writer and Director of the Home Institute at the *Herald Tribune*. Eloise herself would be a contributor to the 1958 **House & Garden's Cook book** which boasted such luminaries as James Beard, Helen Evans Brown, Charlotte Turgeon, and Myra Waldo.

Trivia: Illustrator Hilary Knight wondered what Eloise Davison would look like as a child when he originally sketched the six year old *Eloise* of the Plaza. Eloise, the storybook child, was the inspiration and alter ego creation of actress-singer Kay Thompson--a timeless ingénue and worthy of her own story but not here.

Collector's Corner: 'Entertaining is Fun' is hard to find in 1941 dust jacket. Book reprinted in 2004.

Similar to Dorothy Draper, another pioneering professional interior decorator, even more famous as a female bon vivant and raconteur is **Elsie de Wolfe** (1865-1950). Going

CHAPTER THIRTEEN
Entertainment is Fun!

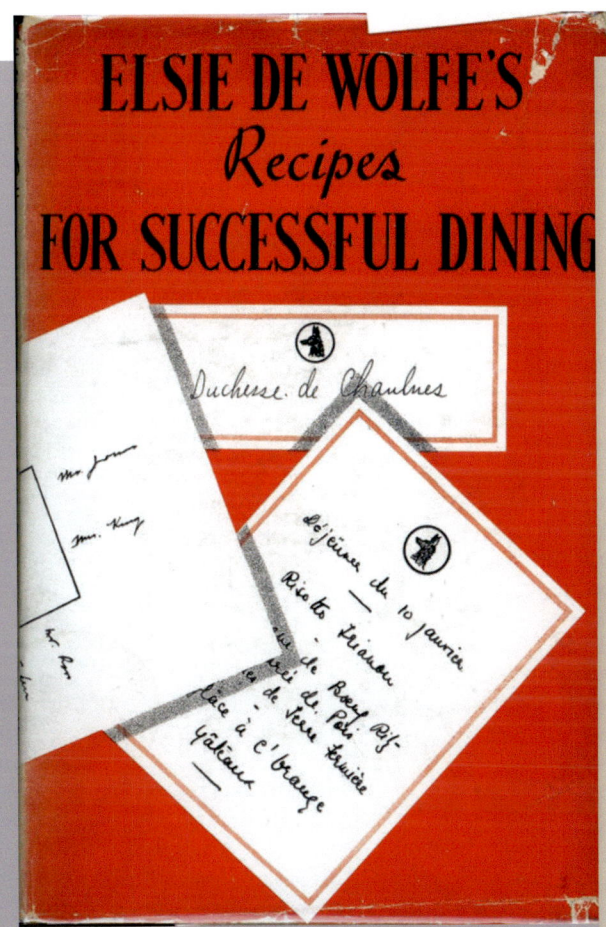

THE KITCHEN AT THE PARIS APARTMENT

from a mediocre actress to a fair show producer she gained interest in how plays were staged, the craft of set design. In 1913 she authored the influential **The House in Good Taste** becoming the quintessential grande dame of home decoration. "It is the personality of the mistress that the home expresses. Men are forever guests in our homes, no matter how much happiness they may find there." Publicity followed her and when in 1926 after a life time companionship with one of the first female theatrical agents, Elisabeth Marbury (1856-1933), she married platonically into a family crest and thereafter the press knew her as Lady Mendl. In 1935, Paris fashion experts named her the best-dressed woman in the world. Her autobiography in 1935 at age seventy let the world know she exercised daily in yoga, standing on her head. She scandalized diplomats when at a gala ball she entered doing handsprings while dressed as a Moulin Rouge dancer. That incident was enough to have her enter a Cole Porter lyric you might recognize: *'When you hear that Lady Mendl, standing up--Now turns a handspring landing up— On her toes—Anything goes!'*

Elsie De Wolfe 's **Recipes For Successful Dining** (1941), a small book, at a mere 102 pages, is a rare and expensive book to acquire. Elsie writes: "This is not a cookery book at all. It is rather a selection of dishes known and unknown—

MY Cookbook Passion

CHAPTER THIRTEEN
Entertainment is Fun!

the result of many years of traveling in many lands and in many out-of-the-way places; of making friends with interesting and interested maîtres d'hôtels; of amusing adventures, instructive in many ways that were not culinary and better than any lesson in geography I have ever had in school. It is a book, I hope, that may prove of aid to the distracted hostess."

Parthenon, she exclaimed, "It's beige—my favorite color!" Named as one of "The 100 Influential Women of all *Time*" and in design circles feted as "12 Legendary Women Who Defined the Art of Style."

MARBURY ROLLS
(Recipe by Miss Elisabeth Marbury, New York)

Take very fresh sandwich bread. Cut in very thin slices and butter. Fry bacon and chop fine. Then put a little roll of the bacon in the middle of each slice, sprinkle with grated Parmesan cheese, and finely chopped parsley. Also sprinkle with a generous quantity of paprika and a very small dash of cayenne pepper. Roll like a cigarette and hold together with a wooden toothpick. Put on a tin platter and grill in the oven until nicely browned, and serve hot.

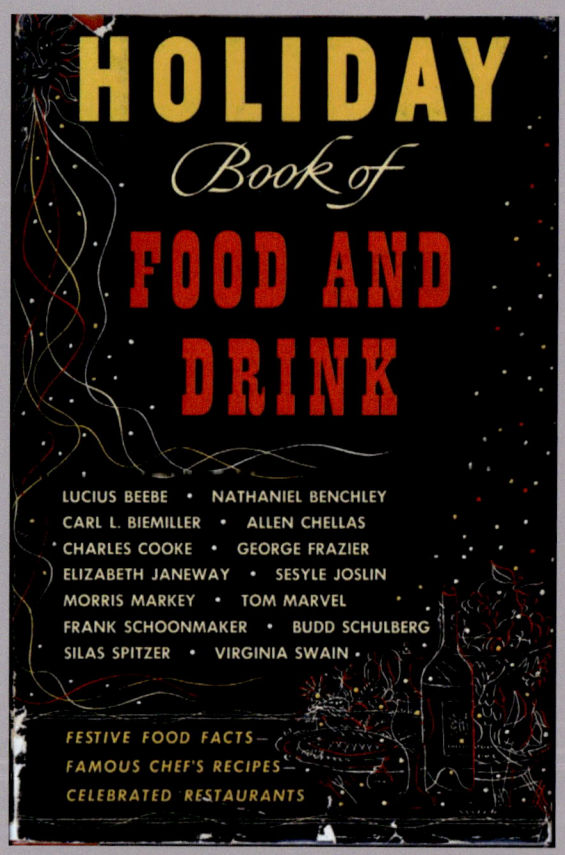

Sidenote: Elsie De Wolfe as the eccentric, covered antique footstools with leopard spotted chintzes, one of the first fashionable, elderly women to streak her hair blue, and embroidered taffeta pillows with her motto: "Never complain, never explain." Upon seeing the Greek

Editor Ted Patrick of Holiday Magazine (a Curtis Publishing subsidiary) brings together twenty popular authors of the year (1952) in compilation stories. As he writes, 'by the happiest coincidences, life's fundamental necessity is

CHAPTER T...
Entertainme...s Fu...

also one of life's supreme pleasures: Food." We run across our bon vivant friend, Lucius Beebe reminiscing about Chicago's 'fabulous' Pump Room and his many eatery stops at San Francisco's Trader Vic's. Budd Schulberg (author of **What Makes Sammy Run**) puts us behind the scene at Chasen's restaurant in Beverly Hills.

Morris Markey's article: "Chef at the St. Regis" provides the background to the successful career of Joseph Castaybert, Chef de Cuisine.

"Tell me," I said, "have you a particular theory or a particular philosophy about cooking?"

He thought for some moments, a little frown of concentration upon his face.

Finally he said, *"I think you could call me the enemy of heavy sauce, the sauce that is made with too much flour and thickening, the enemy of too much of any kind of sauce. I do not think they are good for the dish. I do not think they are good for the stomach."*

Then he was eager to explain exactly what he meant: *"Of course, in the French school of cooking, sauce is essential. But it should be used for the purpose it is meant for, to bring out the flavor of the dish, to heighten the natural flavors, not to disguise the lack of flavors. Nothing is so bad as a little slice of tasteless fowl or meat or fish, drowned under a big wave of sauce. Mon Dieu!"*

A recipe from M. Castaybert:
LE FAISAN SOVAROFF
For two. (Designed for pheasant, but guinea hen will serve.)

Stuff the pheasant (or guinea hen) with diced cooked goose liver and diced truffles, mixed. Canned truffles should always be peeled before using. Cook in casserole with its own juices and gravy, add one glass of Maderia or sherry to which more diced truffles have been added.

When nearly done, close casserole completely with pie paste. Leave in the warming oven for ten to fifteen minutes before serving.

Sadie Lady
Arriving in 1938 at the Centennial Club, a woman's club in Nashville, Tennessee, Sadie Le Sueur served as executive secretary and primary hostess. The Club founded after the 1897 Tennessee centennial celebration, supported municipal reform and city beautification. These two books (**Recipes and Party Plans**, 1958, Parthenon Press and **Holiday and Party Cook book**, 1959, Hearthside Press) were the result of her tenure, the little knowledge I have of her career. Mrs. Le Sueur wrote: *'Since notable speakers are part of the program of the club I serve, we have entertained countless celebrities, and many of the recipes in this book*

CHAPTER THIRTEEN
Entertainment is Fun!

have received their accolade. The letters they have sent me have been heart-warming...A letter came from the editor of a national magazine, who wanted the recipe for the sweet potato ring with caramel topping which he had eaten at the club." So, without delay:

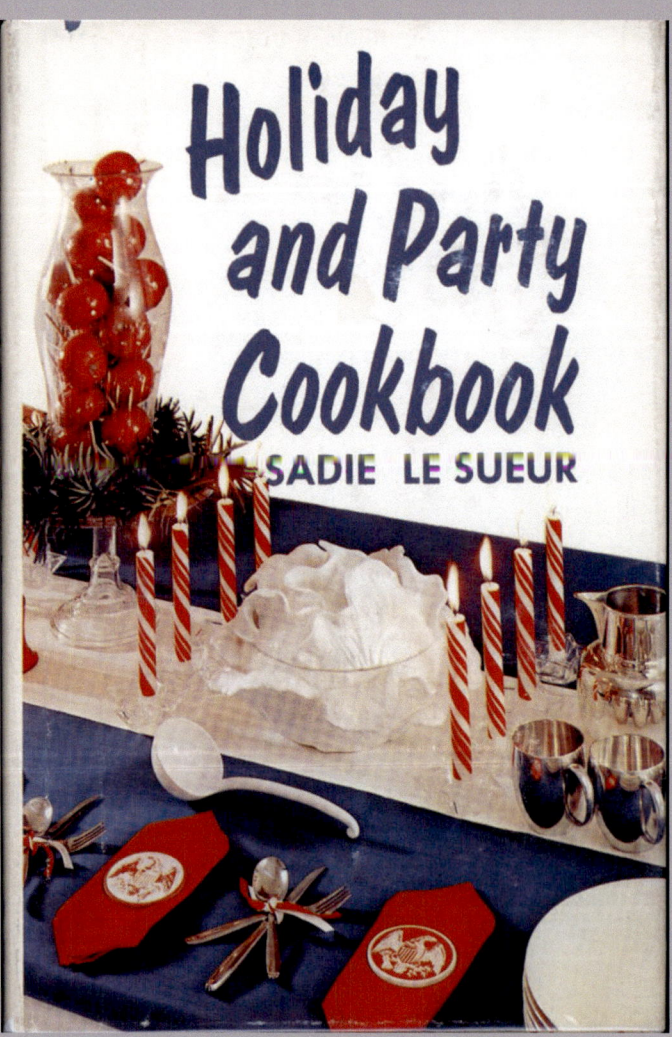

PAMELA KURE GROGAN

CHAPTER THIRTEEN
Entertainment is F

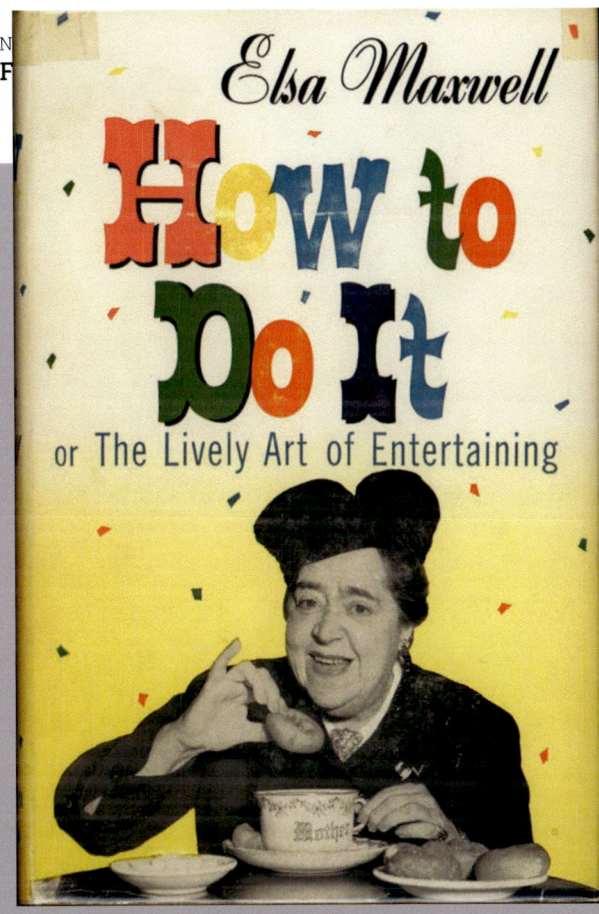

SWEET POTATOES WITH CARAMEL SAUCE

4 large sweet potatoes – 1/2 cup sugar – 1/2 cup of milk – 1/8 teaspoon cinnamon
1 tablespoon butter – 1/8 teaspoon salt

Boil potatoes, skin, run through a ricer; cream potatoes by adding milk and butter; add sugar, salt and cinnamon; pile roughly around the edges of a large flat casserole; run in the oven to brown lightly; when ready to serve, pour "Caramel Sauce" in the center of casserole. Serves 8.

CARAMEL SAUCE

1 cup sugar – 1/2 cup cream
1/2 cup butter – 1/2 teaspoon vanilla

Melt butter and sugar in iron skillet; cook until a deep tan; lower heat, add cream slowly; cook two minutes after adding cream; add vanilla.

"Giving parties is a trivial avocation, but it pays the dues for my union card in humanity."

At the end she defined herself: "not bad, for a short, fat, homely piano player from Keokuk, Iowa, with no money or background, who decided to become a legend and did just that." **Elsa Maxwell** (1883-1963), the consummate party giver and to her math, threw over 2,000 parties, all shapes and sizes. She invented the 'scavenger hunt' a popular craze in the 1930's. Her book, **How To Do It, or the Lively Art of Entertaining** (1957), is more a biographical tour de force of name dropping. Only Elsa could get away with it, because the stories true or truth stretched, personify her character.

MY COOKBOOK PASSION

CHAPTER THIRTEEN
Entertainment is Fun!

"While Jack Barrymore and I were standing on the hill watching the raging fires that had sprung up after the earthquake [San Francisco 1906], Jack London, the writer, and George Sterling, the poet came along. They told me I was insane to do lunch at the St. Francis with Enrico Caruso."

Her way with food is equally a showpiece. "A consommé that Diana Vreeland serves as a first course at dinner is a savory legacy from the recipe collection of Elsie de Wolfe, at whose house I first tasted it. The sweetbreads, with *salade Parisienne*, makes an excellent main course at luncheon." I'll presently pass on the whole recipe of *Sweetbreads Lyonnaise* and let epicureans with continental tastes search out the dish.

Rather, I like this: "The Pavillon may not be the only restaurant in New York that serves *Billibilli*, but I doubt that Henri Soulé's recipe for it could be matched anywhere. This soup was a great favorite of the Aga Khan's, who liked to serve it as a preliminary course to one of his curry dinners.

BILLIBILLI
(6 servings)

Place the following ingredients in a large saucepan: 3 pounds of fresh, cleaned mussels, 1 onion and 3 shallots (chopped), 3 parsley branches, 2 tablespoons butter, 1 pint dry white wine, and 1 quart heavy cream. Add salt and pepper and a dash of cayenne. Cook for 10 minutes and strain through cheesecloth. Serve very hot with cheese straws.

Advertising pamphlet featuring Elsa Maxwell, known as 'The Hostess With The Mostess'. The product? The very modern 1952 Universal Cook-a-matic, waffle iron and reversible griddle.

KURE GROGAN

CHAPTER THIRTEEN
Entertainment is Fun!

What I gleaned from her entertaining style, reading Elsa's stories of the invited who's who and costumes, is that fun parties are rare in present day society. And I mean fun, not just cocktails and conversation. She writes: "At one large party I gave, I wondered how I would get the guests to mix and become acquainted, as many of them did not know each other and would tend to gather into small groups. I hit on what turned out to be just the thing. Behind a large screen in the corner of the room I placed a swarm of bees that I had borrowed from one of my friends in the country. They were in a screened box, of course, and their busy humming was loud enough to get everyone wondering and asking his neighbor what it could be." Husband Stephen, to rid an ending party of dawdling guests, would have let the winged stingers loose.

The play on words, **My Favorite Things** is a take-off on Dorothy Roger's husband's song of the same title, written with Oscar Hammerstein II, for their musical hit, "The Sound of Music". Richard Rogers (1902-1979), one of two people to have received in his lifetime the Grammy, Tony, Oscar, Emmy awards and a Pulitzer Prize. Dorothy married Richard in 1930 and gaining experience of years on the road running households, found her book published in 1964. "I am a domestic creature, and this is a personal book about the things I love." In the 1930's she ran a home decorating and repair business called Repairs, Inc. In 1945, she invented 'Johnny Mop', a toilet bowl cleaner, still used today by custodians and domestic goddesses.
In her chapter, "Menus with a Sense of Balance (and Recipes), Summer Lunch 16": [Next page recipe.]

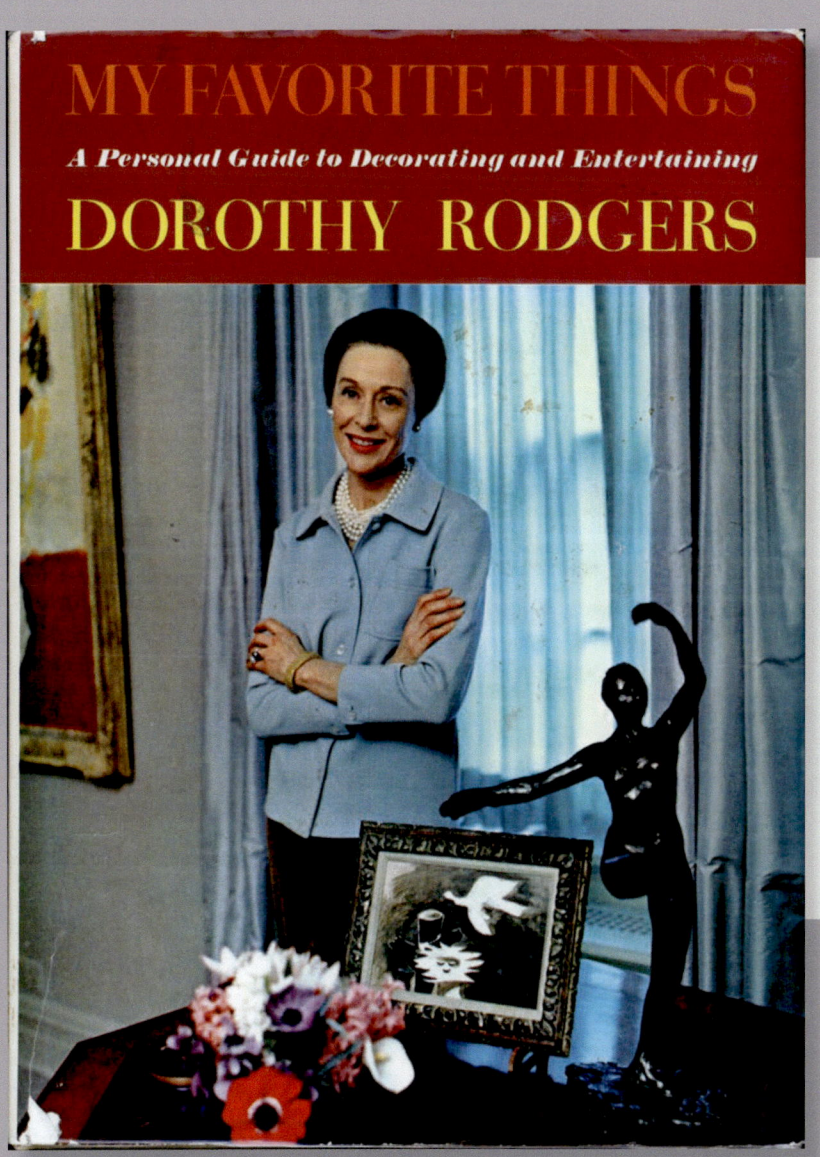

MY COOKBOOK PASSION

CHAPTER THIRTEEN
Entertainment is Fun!

Summer Soup Plus
Salmon Mousse, Curried mayonnaise, Cold leeks vinaigrette sauce, Creamed lime ice

SUMMER SOUP
(Serves 8)

1 ½ lbs shrimp – 1 medium cucumber – 1 ½ tablespoons of fresh dill or 3/4 teaspoon of dried dill weed – 1 ½ teaspoons salt – 1 ½ granulated sugar – 2 ¼ teaspoons prepared mustard – 1 ½ quarts buttermilk

Cook shrimp, remove shells, devein and cut into small bits. Peel and dice a medium-sized Cucumber. Cook 1 ½ lbs. Cut fine 1 ½ tablespoons Mix together 1 ½ teaspoons salt, 1 ½ teaspoons granulated sugar and 2 ¼ teaspoons prepared mustard. Stir this into 1 ½ quarts buttermilk. Add the shrimp, cucumbers and dill. Chill thoroughly before serving in chilled bouillon cups.

I like tie-ins, coincidences, where the world is smaller than we think. In her Chapter **Parlor Games and Other Diversions,** Dorothy Rogers wrote: *"Elsa Maxwell's parties were huge and elaborate and always had a theme. Today costume parties have a faintly forced New Year's Eve air to me, but we all loved Elsa's. We took great pains with our get-ups and always had make- up men put on the finishing touches. I still have a picture taken at one of Elsa's 'Come as Somebody Else' parties in 1929, just after Dick and I announced our engagement. In it, Jules Glaenzer, George Gerswhin, Justine Johnson and Dick look startling like the four Marx Brothers. Jules was Chico; George, a remarkable Groucho; Dick was Zeppo; and with the wig and horn she borrowed from Harpo—you'd certainly never guess that Justine was one of the world's most beautiful women."*

1946 excerpt from fundraising letter signed *Elsa Maxwell*. In Author's collection. *I am coming to Chicago to put on a party—the Chicago Opera Ball in the Chicago Opera House ...and I want it to be my most fabulous party...I've assisted in the organization of balls at Covent Garden in London, long before the war, at the Paris Grand Opera and at the Metropolitan Opera House in New York. And now we're going to top them all here at your Chicago Opera!*

CHAPTER THIRTEEN
Entertainment is Fun!

1935-- Philanthropist and financier William Rhinelander Stewart (left), Elsa Maxwell, and composer/songwriter Cole Porter

Entertaining ends here on a high note: *a treasure chest of delectable recipes*. We now meet Mildred O. Knopf (next page), and we will meet her book introducer, June Platt in a future sequel where Platt opines: *"As one writer of cook books speaking of another's, I can think of no greater tribute to pay than to say I wish I had written it."* I would endorse that sentiment. **The Perfect Hostess** (1950), 653 recipes, 16 chapters, presents a class act of food choices. I best like how Mrs. Knopf makes the dedication to the 'nostalgic past'.

MY COOKBOOK PASSION

CHAPTER THIRTEEN
Entertainment is Fun!

Mildred K. writes, *"This book would scarcely be complete without special mention of my mother's fabulous cook, Marie Agress...Some years before she came to America, Marie worked as a young apprentice in Kaiser Franz Josef's palace kitchens at Schoenbrunn in Austria... Marie left Austria [a sad story of lost romance], and it was at the Immigration Bureau at Ellis Island that my mother took the forlorn young woman home with her. There she stayed for twenty- five years, caring nothing for the world, caring only passionately for her cooking and for the kitchen realm over which she reigned supreme."*

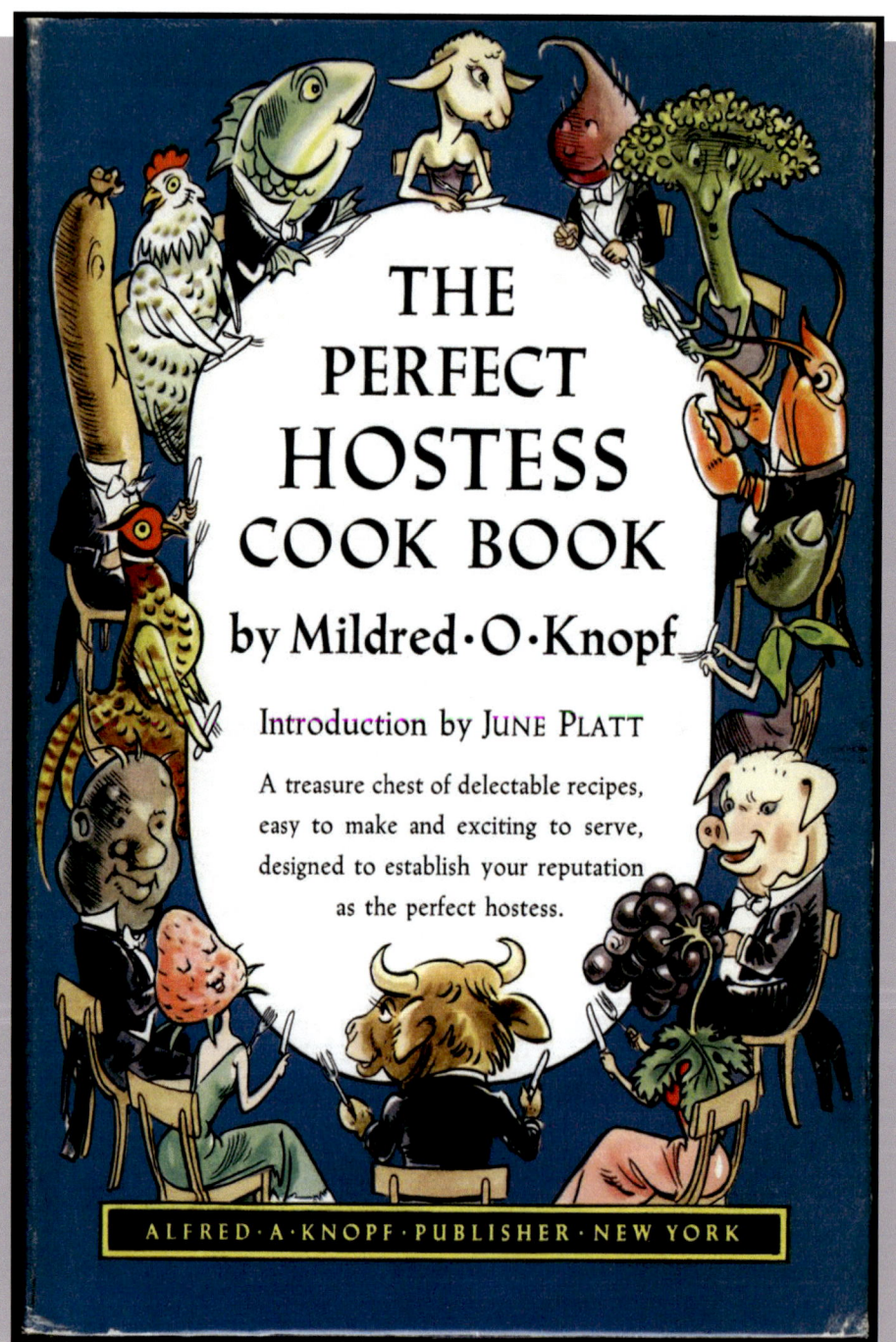

PAMELA KURE GROGAN

CHAPTER THIRTEEN
Entertainment is Fun!

SWEDISH MEAT BALLS

1/2 lb. pork – 1/2 lb. beef – 1/2 lb. veal – Salt – pepper – pinch of nutmeg – 2 medium sliced onions, 2 oz butter – 1 c. milk – 3/4 c. beer – 3 eggs – 2 pieces zwieback – Spaghetti and Spaghetti Sauce

FIRST Have your butcher put 1/2 pound pork, 1/2 pound beef. And 1/2 pound veal through his meat-grinder twice. Add salt, pepper, and pinch of nutmeg

SECOND Lightly fry 2 medium-sliced onions in 2 ounces butter. Add to meat.

THIRD Combine 1 cup milk with 3/4 cup beer and 3 beaten eggs. Soak 2 pieces of zwieback in this liquid and add to meat, mixing thoroughly.

FOURTH Shape meat balls with the help of teaspoon. Let them stand half an hour. Then drop them in the skillet in which the onions were cooked and fry lightly on both sides. Serve with Spaghetti and Spaghetti Sauce.

WINE FROTH SAUCE

1/3 c. sugar – 1 c. white wine or sherry – 3 egg yolks – 1 tbsp lemon juice – 2 egg whites

FIRST Dissolve 1/3 cup sugar in a double boiler with 1 cup white wine and 1 tablespoon lemon juice. Add 3 egg yolks. Beat with a wire whisk until smooth and thick.

SECOND Beat 2 egg whites until stiff. Remove the top of the double boiler from the stove, fold in the whites, and continue to beat with the wire whisk until thick and very foamy.

NOTE Marie liked to serve this wonderful light, winy sauce with: Christmas Plum Pudding, Apple Charlotte, or Apple Dumplings.

CHAPTER THIRTEEN
Entertainment is Fun!

Facsimile of the last luncheon menu aboard the RMS Titanic, signed later in life by Millvina Dean, the youngest passenger at 10 weeks old when rescued in 1912 after the ship foundered, hitting an iceberg. She passed away in 2009. In author's collection.

PAMELA KURE GROGAN

CHAPTER THIRTEEN
Entertainment is Fun!

Perhaps the height of entertaining would have been First Class pampering aboard one of the Queens of the Sea. The entryway in our home is called the Lord Nelson Gallery with original English seafaring prints, one a formal pose of Lord Horatio Nelson, dated 1798 while still alive, commemorating the Battle of the Nile. Located here also are framed sets of original knives and forks, and postcards, from the earlier ocean liners, RMS Queen Mary and RMS Queen Elizabeth.

MY COOKBOOK PASSION

CHAPTER FOURTEEN
SOCIAL STUDIES

PAMELA KURE GROGAN

CHAPTER FOURTEEN
Social Studies

Instead of my writing pages of sociological comment, philosophical observations, and personal opinions, it is best to let the book covers show America, for better or worse, as its people trudge out of the past into the future, and in the process change not only their eating habits but go through an enlightening of social ethics and mores. Debates might arise. Are we stepping too quickly to ultimate political correctness? Government control of our tables? Vaccine passports to enter a restaurant? Fois Gras is banned in select cities. Veal is targete d. The French, who eat horse meat as an acceptable meal without a second thought, can't import from U.S. processing plants, as legislative pressure has shut down that industry. Vegetarian cookbooks rise and fall to their latest fads. Free range and organic branding have caused a surge of new wave health-ecco food stores. Societies evolve, hopefully for the good of all. So, with a crystal ball of cookbooks, let's see if the past hints at the future.

No better place to watch an evolution, correct that, a Movement is in Black Americana cooking. *Miss Minerva's Cookbook* by Emma Speed Sampson (1931), part of a popular Miss Minerva series in Negro dialect. 12 children books, written between 1909 and 1939, Sampson (1868-1947) would become a well known children's writer, even ghosting writing under the pseudonym of Nell Speed (*The Carter Girls* and *Tucker Twins* series) and Edith Van Dyne. The latter nom de plume was for several books in the *Aunt Jane's Nieces* series, the earlier book subjects created by Frank Baum of Wizard of Oz fame, who, in turn, commercially exploited a young adult theme to ride the popularity on the 'Little Women' success of Louisa May Alcott.

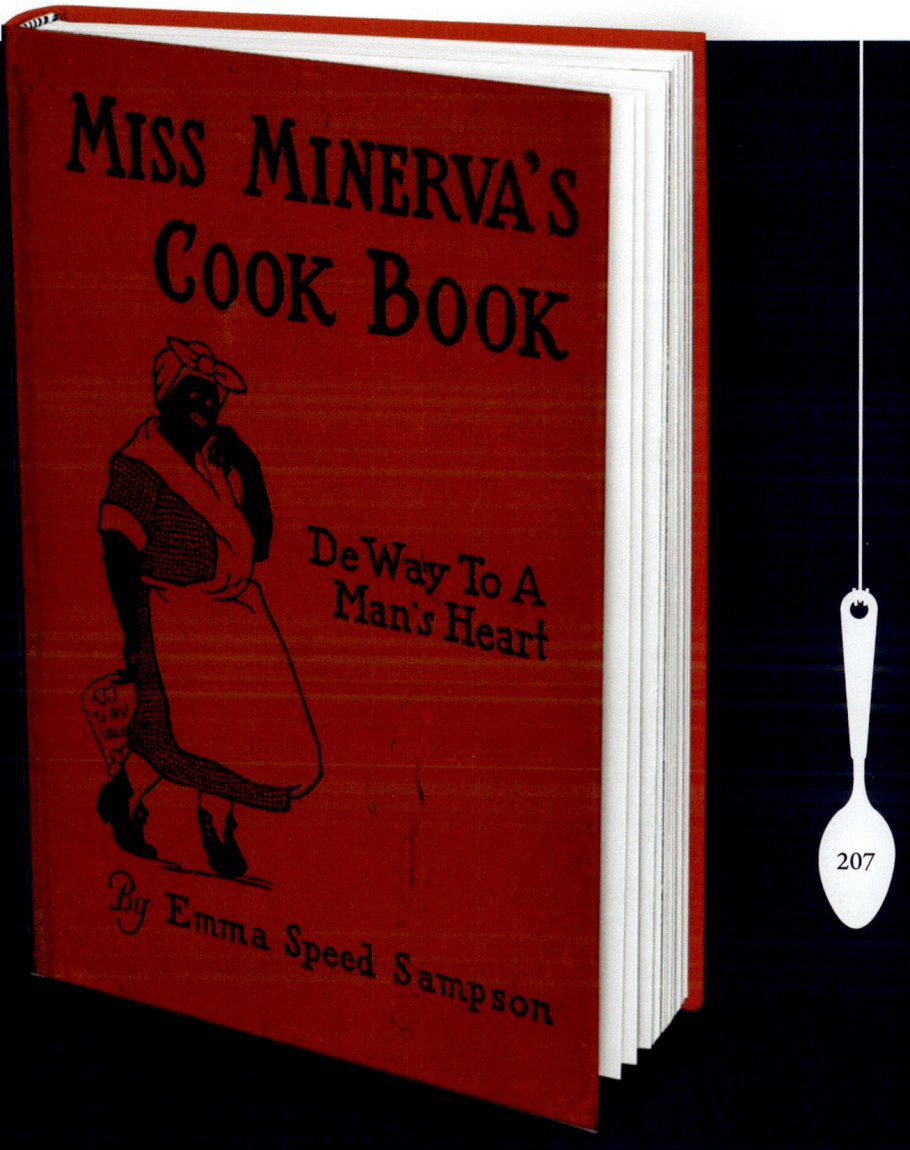

CHAPTER FOURTEEN
Social Studies

Whether an example of sentimental Southern humor fiction or empowering Jim Crow servitude, or both, with the debate continuing, Sampson, a white woman, wrote this cookbook to sell, the buying public sharing in any national, collective remorse (the book written in Virginia, published in Illinois). Sampson wrote: "Cooking is never a task to me. I really like to do it—that is, if someone else washes the pots and pans. I think a cook, after having gone through the throes of making, say a chicken pie, should no more have to 'keel the pot' than Othello should be expected to make up the bed after smothering Desdemona..."

Miss Minerva rests today in the subconscious. When President Clinton issued a Thanksgiving proclamation without any mention of food, a Richmond, Virginia newspaper editorialized that the whole proclamation should have been replaced with one of Miss Minerva's thanksgiving prayers: "Dear Lord, make us able--to eat everything at this end of the table."

Rebecca Pudding

I ain't never knowed how come this here puddin' was named after Miss Rebecca an' what's mo I aint never got settled in my min' whether this here Miss Rebecca air the one what was allus gittin' her pixture took a-standin' by the well. Be that as it may, it air a toothsome puddin'.

You puts in yo' double biler three cups an' a half er milk an' lets it come ter a good scald. Now take half a cuper cawn starch, half a cuper sugar an' a good pinch er slat an' moisten all with half a cuper col' milk an' then stir it inter yo' scalded milk an' let it cook some twenty minutes. Keep a-stirrin' now an' then so's it won't lump. When it gets smooth an' thick take it off the stove an' add a cup er grated cocanut an' a teas poon er bugnilla. Then fold in the whites er three airs which you air whupped up as light as a cloud.

It ain't gonter hurt none if you mold this here puddi n' in a ring mold an' then when you turn it out it mought 'ze mble a well curbin'. S ar ve i t wi th whupped cram, seasoned an' sweetened an' flecked over plentiful with a nice quince jelly.

Collector's Corner: Collecting historic Black Americana has grown in popularity. African-Americans are the main collectors desiring the sense of heritage, or perhaps as a poignant reminder of how a majority could misconstrue the culture of a minority, and be so wrong. People likewise collect to make great deals and see values rise. **Miss Minerva's Cook Book** is quite rare depending on book jacket condition. My copy is signed.

Progress to full rights in slow steps.

The publisher's promo back cover states: "This extremely charming brown-skinned little woman who has written **A DATE WITH A DISH** brings a wealth of experience as well as a natural bent to her subject." Published in 1948 and touted as the first true 'American Negro Cookbook' De Knight came with strong credentials, college graduate in home economics, 'collected thousands of recipes from Negro sources', and most important at the time of publication was the Cooking Editor of *Ebony* Magazine, writing a monthly column, 'A Date With A Dish'. Reprinted in 1962 with multiple

PAMELA KURE GROGAN

CHAPTER FOURTEEN
Social Studies

re-printings, revised in 1978 by Johnson Publishing. Original forward by Gertrude Blair, who would co-author **Jewish Festival Cookbook,** 1954. She writes: "There is the savor of good living in every page of this book...that puts magic into cooking."

De Knight's boss, John H. Johnston, set as his credo in founding his magazine: "We wanted to give Blacks a new sense of somebodiness, a new sense of self-respect. We wanted to tell them who they were and what they could do. We believed then--and we believe now--that Blacks needed positive images to fulfill their potentialities." Freda De Knight sets her own culinary voice: "It is a fallacy, long disproved, that Negro cooks, chefs, caterers and housewives can adapt themselves only to the standard Southern dishes, such as fried chicken, greens, corn pone, hot breads, and so forth. Like other Americans living in various sections of the country they have naturally shown a desire to branch out in all directions and become versatile in the preparation of any dish, whether it be Spanish in origin, Italian, French, Balinese, or East Indian."

Though she wrote about universal skills, I truly enjoy the Southern recipes, culled from her travels.

My book, **A Date With A Dish,** inscribed by author De Knight to Mary Margaret McBride (1899-1976) pioneer radio show host. McBride wrote **Encyclopedia of Cooking** (1959, 1350 pages, Homemakers Research Institute). Working in radio and television for over 30 years, plus a syndicated columnist, at the height of her career she reached 5-7 million nightly listeners. While at NBC, on her 15th Anniversary celebration in 1949 she filled the 75,000 seat Yankee Stadium.

MY COOKBOOK PASSION

CHAPTER FOURTEEN
Social Studies

ROAST TURKEY WITH PEANUT BUTTER

10-12 lb. turkey – 1 tbsp. paprika – 1 tbsp. flour – 1 tsp. celery salt – 1/2 cup peanut butter – 1/2 cup milk or cream – 1 tbsp. salt (enough to make a medium paste) 1 tsp. pepper

Mix flour, salt, pepper, paprika, celery salt and peanut butter into a paste. Blend in cream or milk.

Wash, clean and stuff bird. Place in roasting pan. Spread paste over entire bird, covering well. Add 1 cup water in pan. Place in moderate oven, 400º F., for 3 hours, basting every 30 minutes and turning at least twice to brown on all sides. One cup stock can be substituted for 1 cup of water. Allow ¾ pound per person.

CRAB AND TOMATO BISQUE

1 cup flaked crabmeat – 2 tbsps. flour – 3 tbsps. Butter – 2 cups milk – 1/2 tsp. salt – 1/2 tsp. season-all – 1 cup tomato juice pinch sugar dash red pepper – dash garlic salt – 1/2 cup chives, chopped

Melt butter. Add flour and blend. Add milk gradually. Cook until thick. Add seasonings and crabmeat. Heat tomato juice and sugar. Add gradually into crab mixture.

Sprinkle chives on top of each serving. Serves 6-- Lobster may be used instead of crabmeat.

Equal to De Knight's compilation of many gathered recipes is the thinner spiral bound, **The Historical Cookbook of the American Negro** (1958), presented by The National Council of Negro Women. Brief snippets of the historic perspective to the Movement with recipes contributed from the many multi-state councils. A worthy read, the booklet is rarely found in good condition.

CHAPTER FOURTEEN
Social Studies

BRUSSEL SPROUTS WITH PAPRIKA SOUR CREAM

1 quart brussel sprouts – 1/4 tsp salt
1/2 c. sour cream – Dash white pepper – 1/3 c. mayonnaise
1/2 tsp paprika – 2 tsp lemon juice

Cook brussel sprouts until crisp, tender. Drain. Serve with the following: paprika, sour cream sauce: combine liquids and other ingredients mixing thoroughly; heat and serve over sprouts.

TWO IN ONE PRUNE RULE
To Honor Carter G. Woodson Take a package of prunes, wash carefully and place in a jar with enough water to cover. Add two thin slices of lemon or a teaspoon of lemon juice. Cover tightly and place in the refrigerator.

After two days, the prunes will be plump and so delicious. Serve four at a time with your favorite dry cereal and milk or cream. For the two-in-one trick, remove prunes from jar as you need them with a fork. Remaining in the jar will be Prune Juice Supreme.

MY COOKBOOK PASSION

CHAPTER FOURTEEN
Social Studies

Sidenote: Carter G. Woodson (1875-1950), Father of Black History, founder of the Association for the Study of Negro Life and History. Dr. Woodson (Ph.D. in History, Harvard, 1912) established Associated Publishers for furthering African-American publications; he help to establish "National Negro History Week."

"Many of us will remember going to Dr. Woodson's office and sitting beside his desk while he ate dry prunes (which he offered his guests at meal time) and 'lectured' us for being derelict in imparting salient knowledge to our children, and having no sense of history! We loved him for thus disturbing us to an awareness of things vital."

NEED I SAY MORE? WOMEN LIBERATION

Streamlined meals. 'We are emancipated and can live our own lives.'

The Working Girl Must Eat by Hazel Young. 1938.

Menus with working plans for cooking efficiency. **The Working Girl's Own Cook Book** by Hazel Young. 1948. She also wrote **Better Meals for Less Money** (1940)

'If I can show you how to cook like an angel and only have one saucepan to wash up that would be different, wouldn't it?' **The Reluctant Cook** by Ethelind Fearon. 1953. Part of Home Entertaining Series, London published, where she wrote several books on jellies, herbs, as well as **The Reluctant Gardener** and **The Reluctant Hostess.**

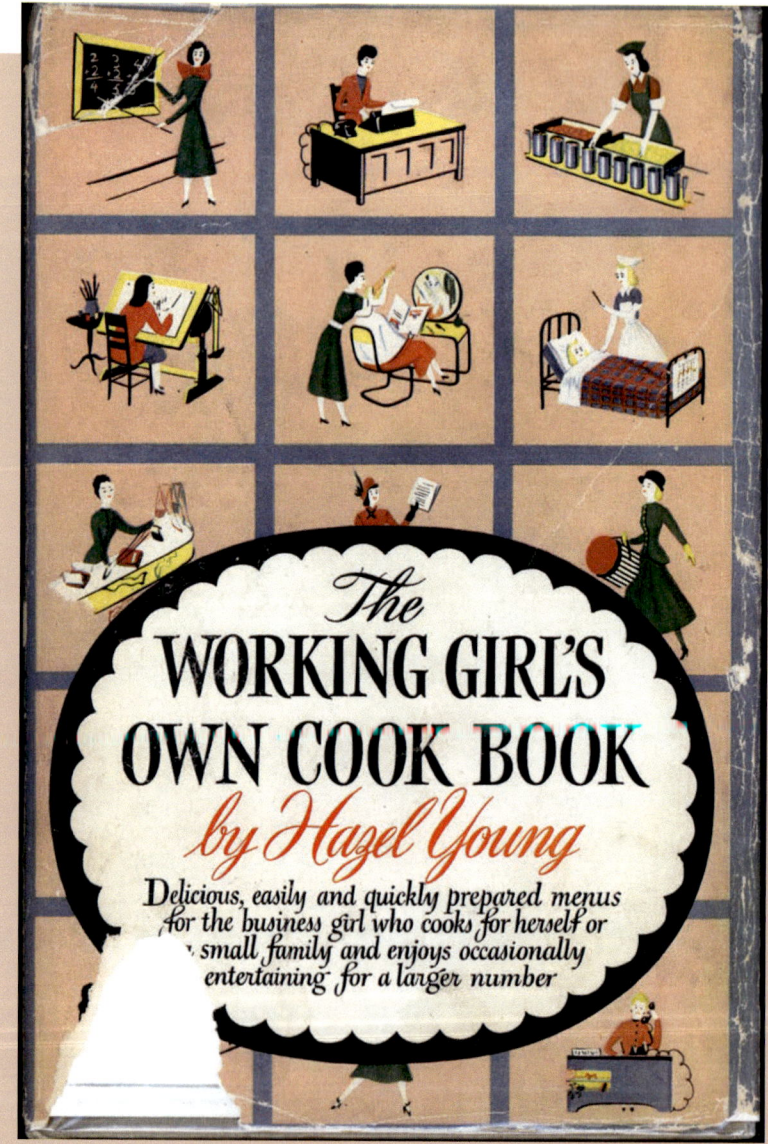

The Liberated Cook and hostess of the 1970's should be able to pick up the telephone and ask anyone in for a meal on a moment's notice. The Liberated Cook Book by Arlene Cardozo. 1972.

CHAPTER FOURTEEN
Social Studies

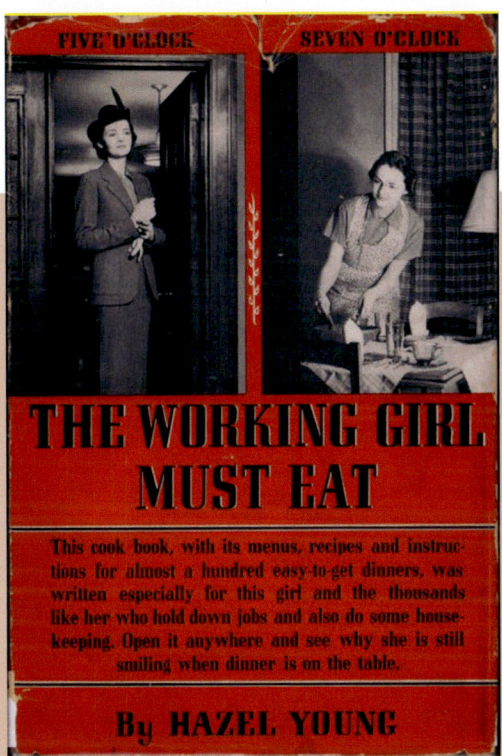

MY COOKBOOK PASSION

CHAPTER FOURTEEN
Social Studies

Who Says I can't sneak 'Sex' into this Book?
The loves of most people are but the results of good dinners.
CHAMFORT

'Any home economist can tell you it's bad form to cook without clothes on, even if you do use an apron.'

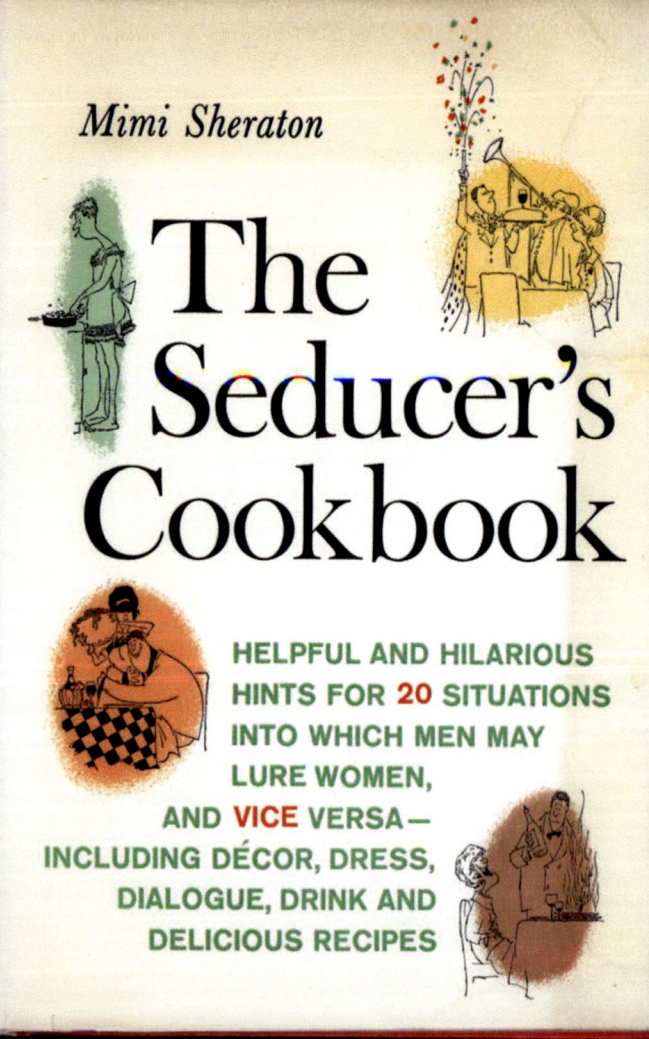

... when she takes something off, you do likewise ...

The Seducer's Cookbook by Mimi Sheraton. 1962. We have run into Mimi before (page 141). Fifty plus years later she is one of the foremost food writer-critics in the country. Still a good read (seductive foodie hints are timeless) with funny illustrations by Paul Coker.

Meal seduction becomes clinical. Historic orgies and debauchery, foods as aphrodisiacs, small wonder most recipes are French! Chapters include: 'Progressive Regeneration of Energies', 'Perfumes of Love', and 'Digestive and Regenerative Properties of Chocolate'. **Cuisine D'Amour, A Cook Book for Lovers,** compiled by Charles F. Heartman. 1952. Author, a well known bibliophile, like myself, a collector of books.

PAMELA KURE GROGAN

CHAPTER FOURTEEN
Social Studies

prone writer, feuded on and off with D. H. Lawrence (**Lady Chatterly's Lover** fame). Douglas wrote witty travel books, made Capri a must-see place, and was a friend of food writer, Elizabeth David. Most famous novel, **South Wind.** Author and friend Graham Greene writes the introduction. Rare in London published version. Reprinted today in mass paperback.

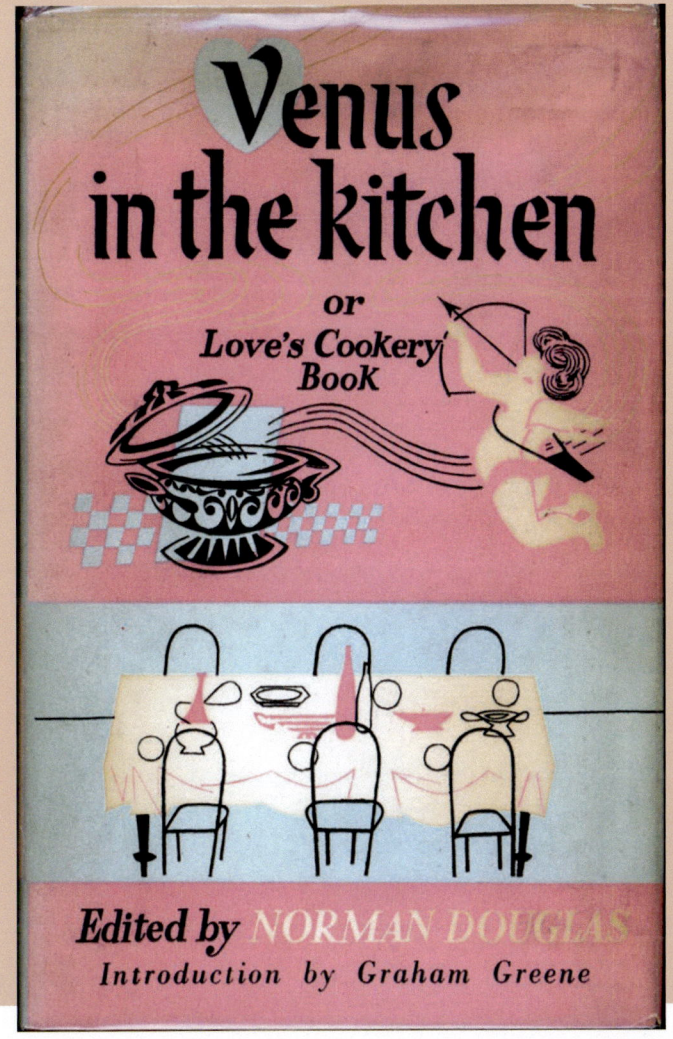

"Aromatic herbs and aphrodisiac recipes judiciously used in the preparation of meals, renew weakened organisms; they bring back to life exhausted feelings, and permit man to enjoy for a long time 'those endowments of strength so dear.'" The Squire of Baudricourt

Styled literary recipes. **Venus in the Kitchen or Love's Cookery Book** by Norman Douglass. 1952. Written under the pseudonym of Pilaff Bey, and published in London, posthumously. Douglass, a controversial, sexually scandal

MY COOKBOOK PASSION

CHAPTER FOURTEEN
Social Studies

SORBETS AU CHAMPAGNE (Champagne Sherbet.)
Steep in one and a half pints of sugar syrup, the sections of a whole orange and that of half a lemon; add half a bottle of Champagne wine , the juice of four oranges and that of a lemon; mix the whole, pass through a sieve, add again a half bottle of Champagne . Serve in glasses. **Cuisine D'Amour** - Charles F. Heartman

RICE WITH SHRIMPS
Chop very fine a branch of celery, a small carrot, half an onion, a clove of garlic, and put all in a pan with a small piece of butter and half a spoonful of olive oil and fry till brown. Have ready half a pound of shelled shrimps. Take half of the m and let them fry with the above ingredients for a few minutes, season with pepper and salt, and go on adding hot water little by little till you have put enough for cooking in it one pound of rice. Let the water boil at least a quarter of an hour.

Pass through a sieve , seeing that the meat of the shrimps goes well through. When passed, put it in a sauce pan over the fire, and when boiling add one pound of rice and a piece of butter. Let the rice absorb the liquid. If it becomes too dry before being cooked, add a little hot water, but the rice must not be too moist. When nearly cooked, add the other half of the shrimps, mix well, and serve with grated Parmesan cheese. **Venus in the Kitchen** - Norman Douglas.

Cookbooks as Barometers of Change
I am indebted here to Sherrie A. Inness who edited, **Disco Divas, "Women and Popular Culture in the 1970's"** (2003— University of Pennsylvania Press). What intrigued me was her own written chapter, **"Impress a New Love with Your Culinary Prowess": Gender Lessons in Swinging Singles' Cookbooks.** As she writes, "For the first time, being single was trendy and hip, and the media wanted to profit from this situation. One genre that rushed to address the needs of single people was the singles' cookbook."

PAMELA KURE GROGAN

CHAPTER FOURTEEN
Social Studies

Inness further elucidated: "[Singles' Cookbooks] helped create new ideas about the relationship between men, women, and food. They demonstrated to men and women that cooking to seduce a member of the opposite sex was acceptable, especially when in pursuit of a mate. The books helped spread the notion that gourmet cooking was a way to make a cook, whether male or female, appear more worldly. In these ways, these cookbooks suggested ways to change who did the cooking and for whom they cooked."

Non-subtle male authors seeking cleverness had a field day with this 'literary school':

The Naked Chef: A Survival Plan for the Single Man (1978) by Len O'Dell - **How to Eat Well and Stay Single** (1974) by Nigel Napier-Andrews - **The Single Man's Guide to Fun and Games Cookbook** (1977) by Julian G. Richter - **The Single Chef's Cookbook** (1970) by Sandy Lesberg - **The Cookbook for Swinging Singles** (1976) by Sandy Lesberg - **Suddenly Single: A Survival Kit for the Single Man** (1973) by Edwin Greenblatt - **Pots and Pans** (1974) by Donald Kilbourn

Kilbourn wrote: "Throw your wife or girlfriend out of the kitchen and pack her off to her mother for the day. She'll probably threaten to go there, anyway, once she realizes that you intend to solve all these womanly mysteries on your own."

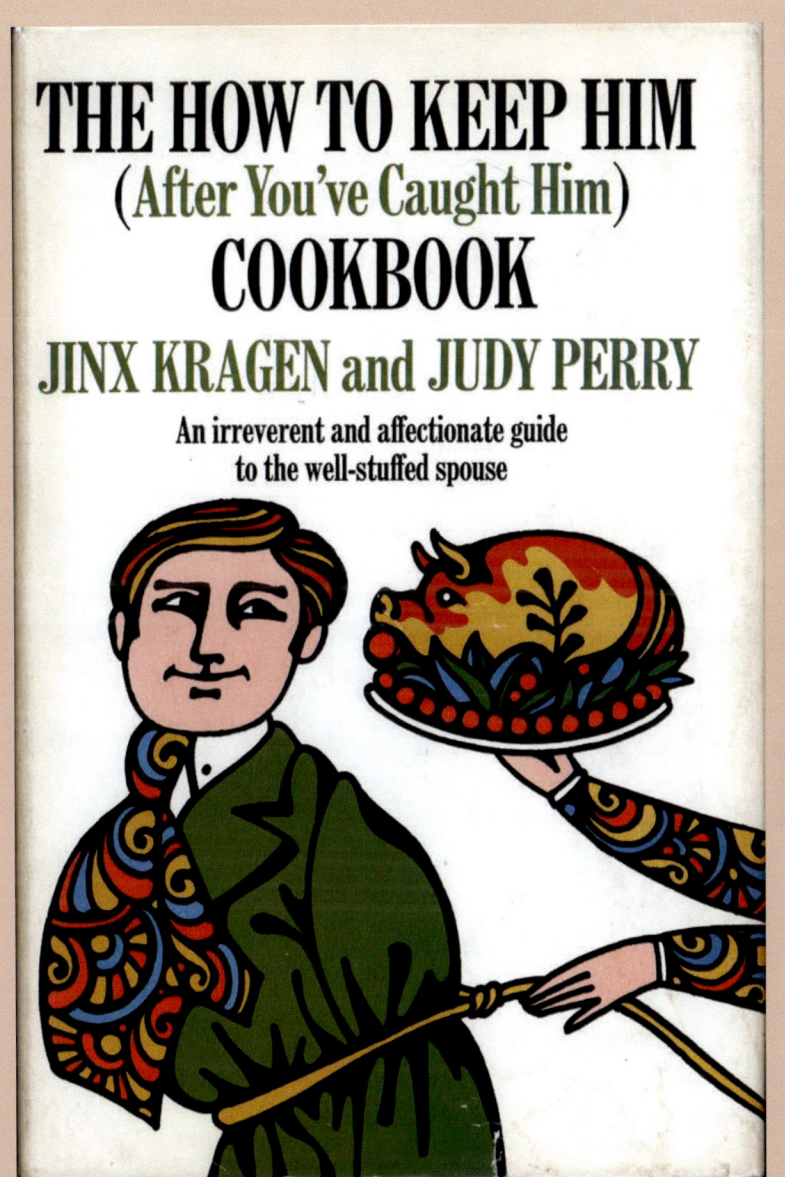

1968

MY COOKBOOK PASSION

CHAPTER FOURTEEN
Social Studies

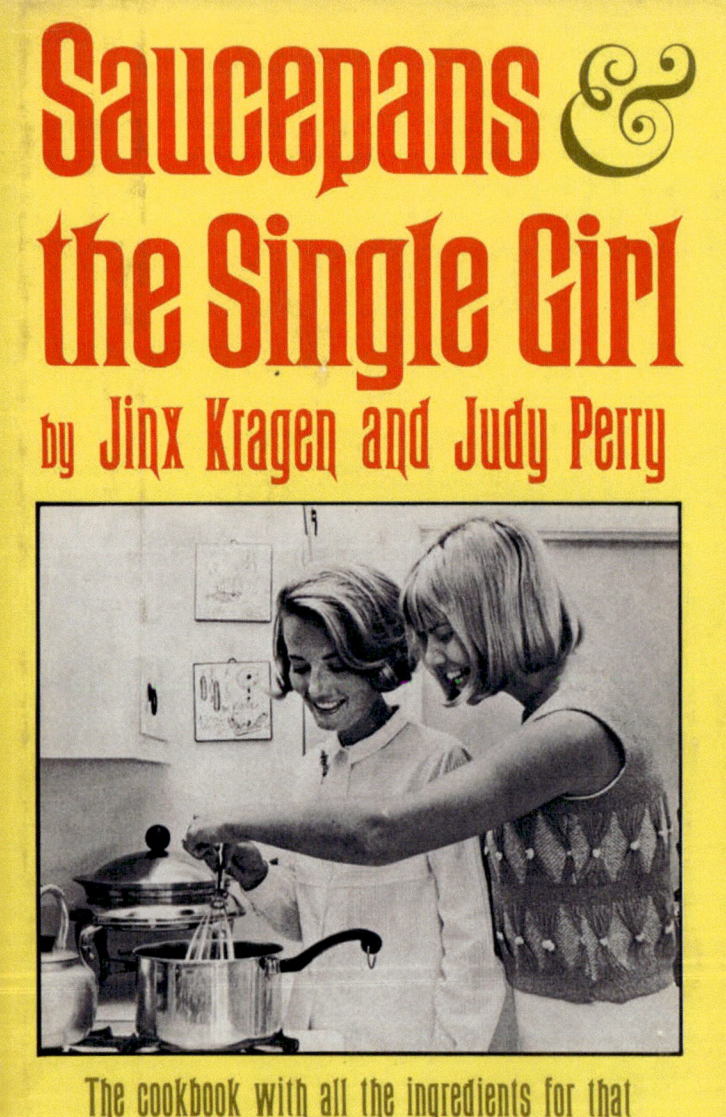

'Ingredients for that light-hearted leap from filing cabinet to flambé.' **Saucepans & the Single Girl** by Jinx Kragen and Judy Perry. 1965 (Doubleday & Company) followed by **The How to Keep Him Cookbook,** 1968, Doubleday. 'Nothing sends a girl into a tizzy as fast the realization that she must cook dinner for a man.' Former Stanford room-mates, attractive California girls, with time on their hands, thought up the idea on the beaches of Malibu. Recipe ingredients use pre- packaged products as a single girl might. Book went paperback in 1968. This book fit the gender themes of the day, similar to the male (no hurry to settle down) bachelor book—**Life, Loves and Meatloaf** (1964) by Carl Randall. His premise: "The greatest American man-trap is the steak dinner."

What Can I Say? At the time Food and Drink Editor of *Esquire* Magazine, Robert H. Loeb tries to put his 1950's sexual chauvinism into racy turns of 'wolf guidance' phrases, or give young women helpful tips at not being placed 'on a shelf by twenty'. These are picture books, with cooking-dating instructions, basic line art, no museum masterpieces here. **Wolf in Chef's Clothing** has its humorous moments. Later in life he would see the error of his ways, publishing in 1977 **Breaking the Sex-Role Barrier**, advice on not letting male stereotypes of women block their worth and accomplishments. But here, one acquires only to capture the unique, like a Polaroid snapshot of eras thankfully forever gone.

PAMELA KURE GROGAN

CHAPTER FOURTEEN
Social Studies

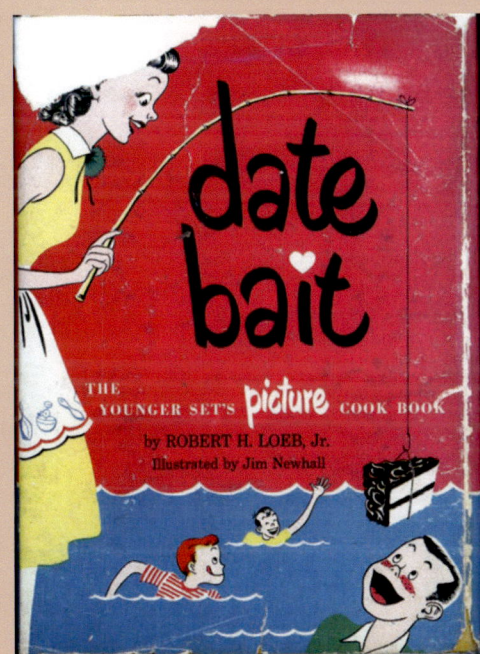
1952

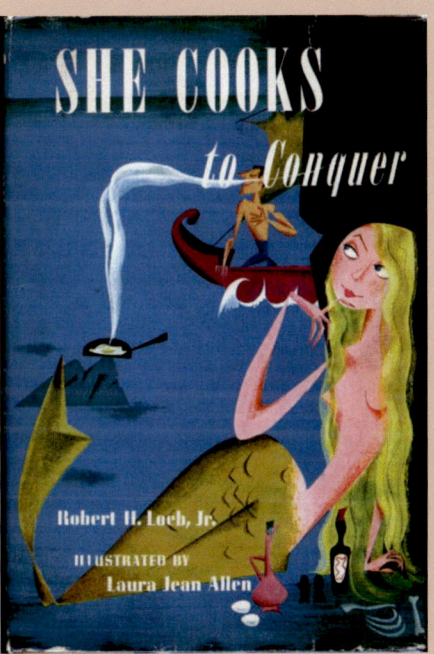
1952

1950

Author of **Wolf in Chef's Clothing,** offers what menus to prepare by grading the women he is dating and cooking for. "Here are four $10 specials graded for type: menu #1 – If she's the athletic type—long, lean, and limbsome, who prefers a game of tennis to a shot of 3-star Henness (ey): [serve] tomato juice a l'ocean—mignon et béarnaise—baked potatoes—salad Roquefort."(published by Wilcox & Follett).

MY COOKBOOK PASSION

CHAPTER FOURTEEN
Social Studies

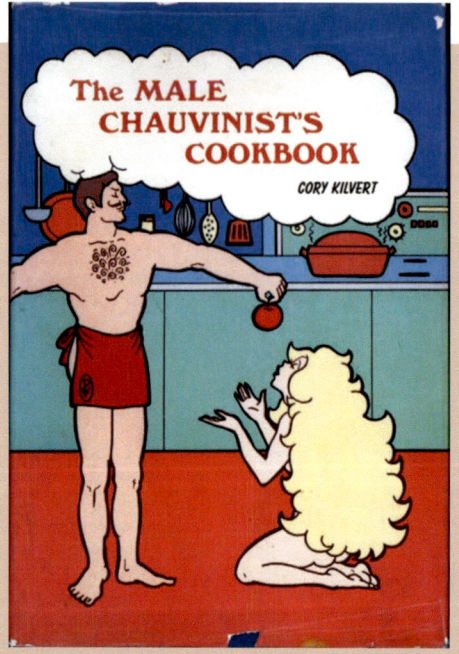

1974 (Winchester Press)

1965 (Sherbourne Press) First Edition, no dust jacket [Campy cartoons by David Costain]

Of course: **Oyster Salad** (for two, of course)Oysters fresh (1/2 pint) or canned whole (1 8-ounce can) Lettuce, iceberg, Mayonnaise, Lemons, Parsley, White wine vinegar, dill (dried) **If you have fresh oysters, cook them in one cup of simmering water for 5 minutes. If you have canned, drain them. Mix together 1/4 cup mayonnaise and 1 tablespoon white vinegar and 1/4 teaspoon of dill. Arrange lettuce on each plate and divide oysters between them. Pour the mayonnaise and wine vinegar mixture over the oysters, and put the plates in the refrigerator to chill. When you are ready to serve, garnish each plate with a lemon wedge and some parsley.**

Dedication: *To all members of the stronger sex. May this book ease and hasten your triumphs –in the kitchen as well as elsewhere.*-- **The Male Chauvinist's Cookbook**

It is fitting I end the transformation of working women post WWII, moving past the 'free love generation,' to now take notice of the tremor of cultural awareness where the maturing sexual revolution prepares to slam into the political feminist movement. No greater proponent of bringing women uninhibited with little subtlety into the kitchen was Helen Gurley Brown (1922-2012). For 32 years she was editor-in-chief of *Cosmopolitan* Magazine. A secretary-to-publisher success story she transformed a stuffy, highbrow magazine into the mantra of the working single girl, that within these pages 'sex, love, and money' were yours to obtain without remorse, and thus invented 'The Cosmos Girls'. In the book world, she produced nearly a dozen sex-advice tomes including **Sex and the Single Girl** in 1962 which as a best-seller became a movie hit and vehicle for star Natalie Wood. Helen was married to successful film

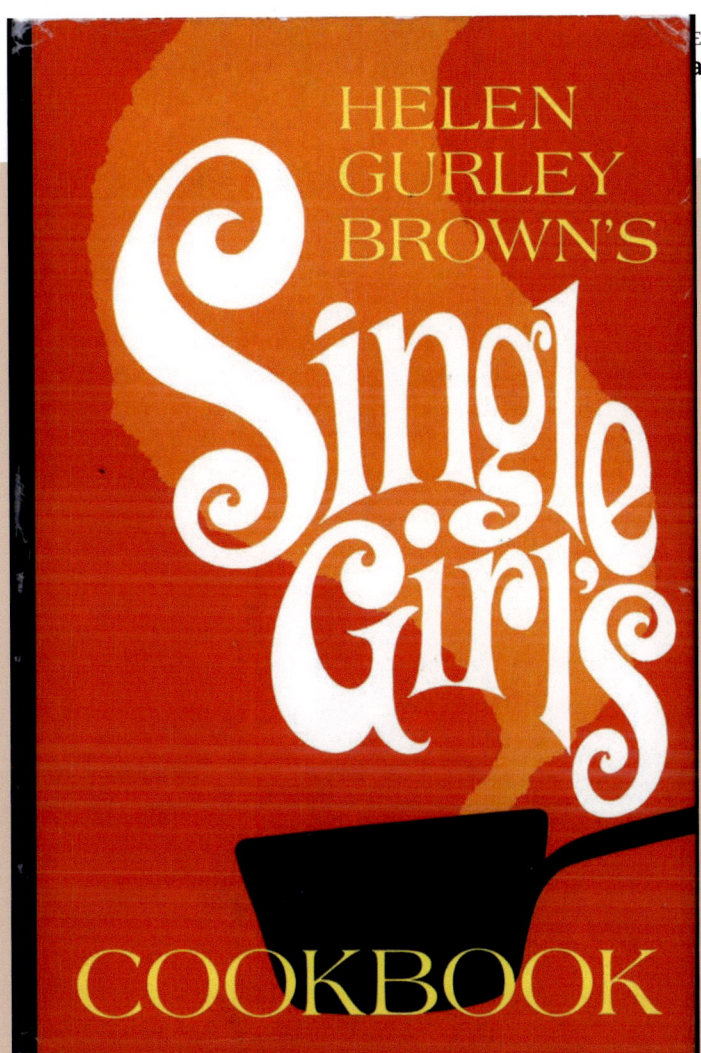

Helen Gurley Brown wrote: "You want to be a good cook not only because it's creative but because cooking is a way to please friends and solidify lovers…Well, to accomplish this, your cooking must have a little style—yes, a little chic". She has witty chapters like "Oh, god, he's brought me his fish!" And five chapters covering menus and meals for affairs. Phase I –(You aren't lovers yet), Phase II (You're in Love), Phase III (He's acting funny and you must win him back), Phase IV (Enough Already!) and Phase V (Goodbye Forever, Thank God!). Here she prepares menu creations designed to 'frighten' him to leave. Yes, food prep can be calculating: "But I made these for you, darling…you always loved my cooking…What you have to do is put together foods that are sure to offend your man."

Bored Hors-d'Oeuvres

1 package (10 cent size) potato chips, left open overnight to get soggy
1 small package corn puffs, left open overnight to get limp
1 can Vienna sausages, cutting into 1-inch lengths, not rinsed, dumped into a saucer 1 box stale popcorn, carefully hoarded from the movie you went to the night before with somebody else

"Any other revolting but essentially edible things you find in the icebox are appropriate, such as: dried-out cheese cubes, the last of the can of deviled ham or tuna, 2 black olives, and 1 green one, hidden in the bottoms of their jars for weeks, etc., etc. Be imaginative! A hard-cooked egg, still warm, cut into quarters and served naked is utterly loathsome."

and theatre producer, David Brown (*Jaws*, *Driving Miss Daisy* and for fans of food romance, *Chocolat* (2000). Yes, I do have a large collection of food-related movies, about twenty quality titles, classics to me, and never tired in watching them.

Meanwhile, **After Sex and the Office** (1965) came her **Single Girl's Cookbook** (1969, published by Bernard Geis Associates) with the 1st Section title, *"How to Sneak Up On A Kitchen and Cook Something"* and Chapter 1: *"Come fry with me"*.

MY COOKBOOK PASSION

CHAPTER FIFTEEN
Tradition

CHAPTER
FIFTEEN

TRADITION

PAMELA KURE GROGAN

CHAPTER FIFTEEN
Tradition

We all grow up with the weight of history on us. Our ancestors dwell in the attics of our brains as they do in the spiraling chains of knowledge hidden in every cell of our bodies.
Shirley Abbott, author

Austrian Cooking by Ann Knox. 1953. Revised edition 1960. Published by Spring Books, London,

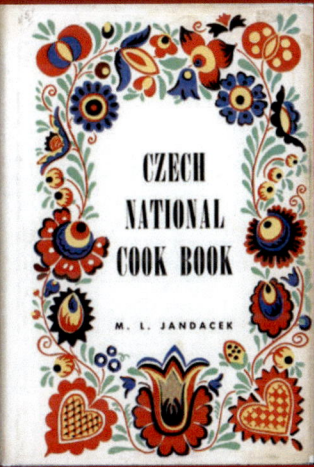

Czech National Cook Book by M. L. Jandacek. 1961.

Hungarian Cookery by Lilla Deeley. Illustrated by L. Farkas and Z. Pohárnok. 1938

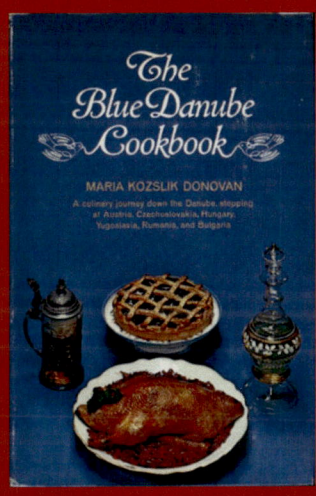

The Blue Danube Cookbook by Maria Kozlik Donovan, 1967. I like this book as it takes in the cuisines as the water way courses through six European countries. Maria, an Australian diplomat's wife, authored Continental Cookery in Australia (1955), *The Far Eastern Epicure* (1958), and *Astrology in the Kitchen* (1972), 'to please the palate as well as the planets'. Her Blue Danube is not to be confused with *The Blue Danube Cookbook*, self-published in spiral the same year, by Max Knight, republished in 1979 as *The Original Blue Danube Cookbook*.

CHAPTER FIFTEEN
Tradition

To appreciate an older cookbook one must realize the collected recipes were not test tube created in a corporate kitchen. Their genesis came from handwritten recollections, passed down through families for generations. An heirloom recipe should be honored like a postcard from a dear departed friend or relative, asking that we remember them by appreciating their thoughts and creative touch. A cookbook of a hundred recipes sings as a choir of immortality.

Laid on thick perhaps, but I believe it; a **passion** knowing that when in the kitchen, kindred spirits whisper tales of good times through special meals I am allowed to bring to life. And somewhere up the family tree the cooks of my Kure-Taskay ancestral branch once mixed wonderful ingredients and where several of their favorite recipes surely found a home in the books within this chapter.

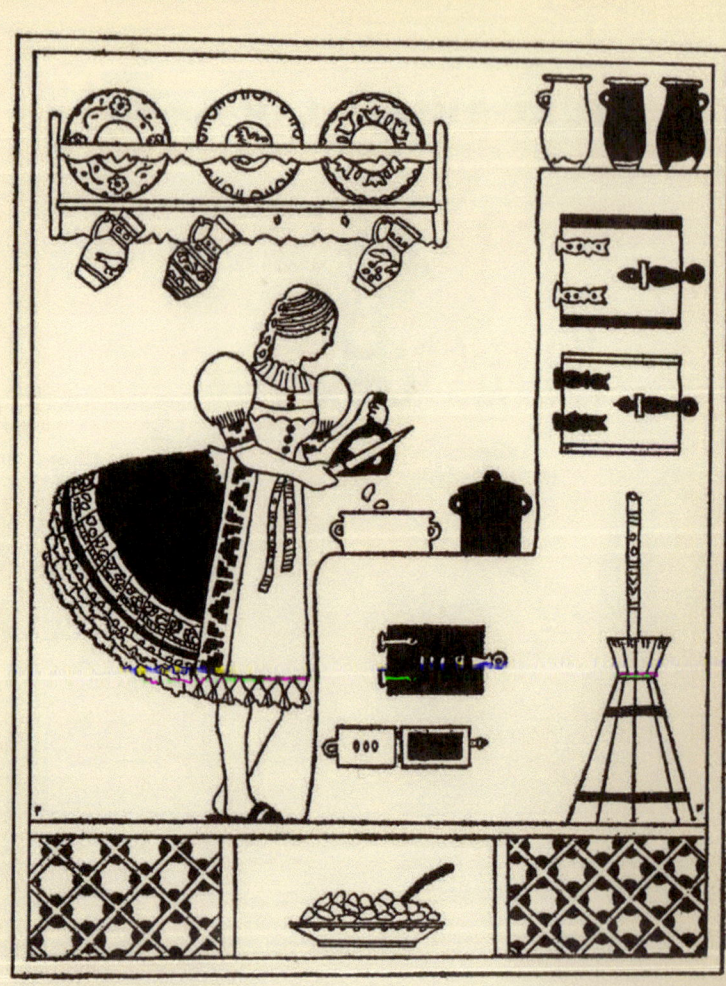

PAMELA KURE GROGAN

CHAPTER FIFTEEN
Tradition

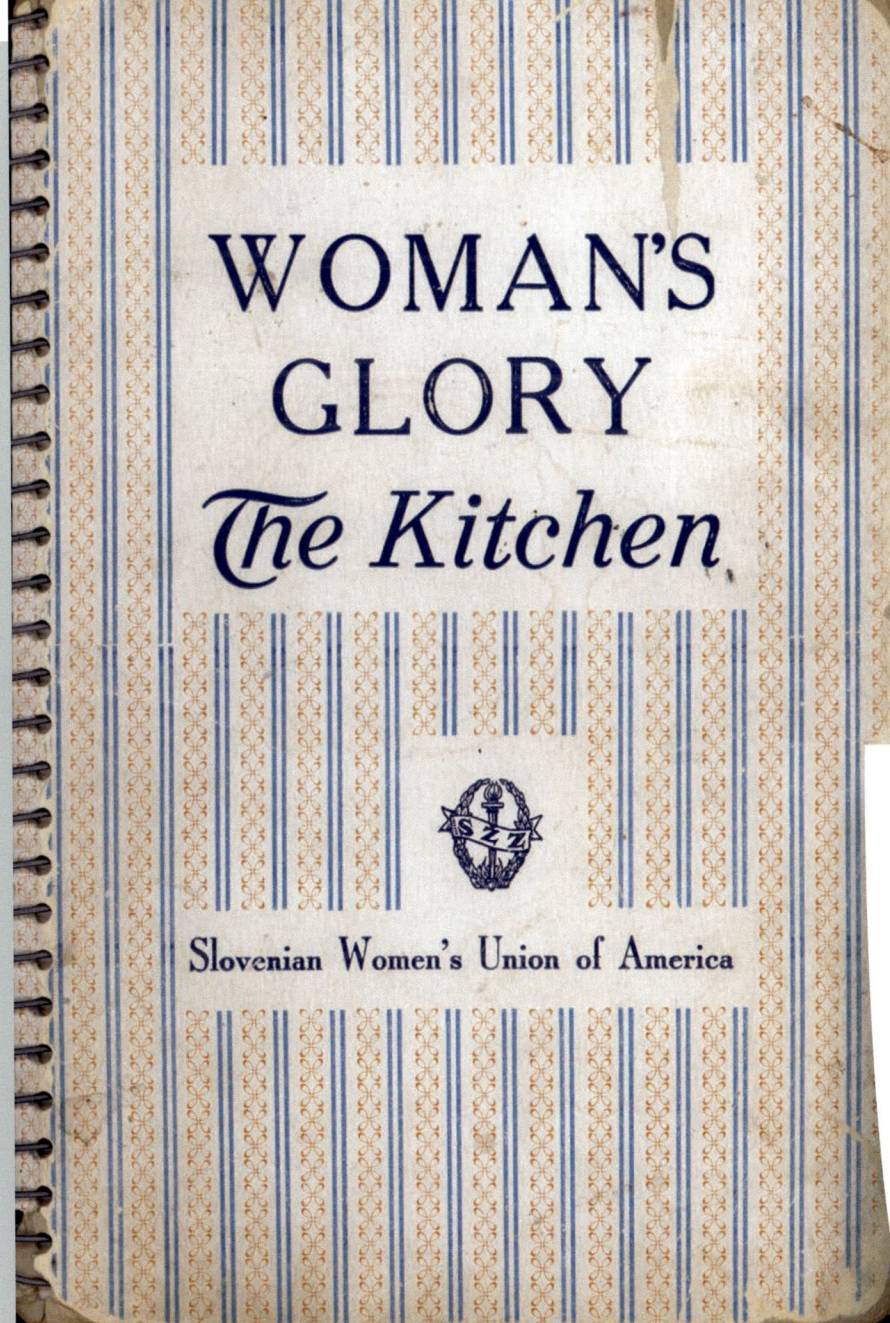

Woman's Glory—The Kitchen, presented by the Slovenian Women's Union of America. Spiral Bound, 1951. Many of the recipes contributed by Miss Frances Jancer of La Salle, Illinois, a columnist in the Zarja-The Dawn, the organization's magazine.

ŠTRUKLJI (ROLLED DUMPLINGS)

There are many different kinds of Struklji. Some may be served as main dishes, while others as side dishes, or as a garnish for soups. Many struklji are cooked like dumplings, and since there is no equivalent for the word "struklji", I have decided upon "rolled dumplings" as a suitable name.

DOUGH FOR ROLLED DUMPLINGS

Ingredients: 1½ – cups flour – 1 egg – 1 tablespoon butter – luke warm water – 1/4 teaspoon salt

Sift flour in mixing bowl, cut in butter and add salt, 1 egg, and enough luke warm water (about 5 or 6 tablespoons) to make dough. Place dough on floured board and knead by hand for about 20 minutes until dough is smooth. Cover dough with warm bowl and let rest for half hour.

MY COOKBOOK PASSION

CHAPTER FIFTEEN
Tradition

CHEESE ROLLED DUMPLINGS

1 pound cottage cheese – teaspoon salt – 1 cup sour Cream – 3 egg yolks – 2 egg whites beaten stiff

Mix together well cottage cheese, sour cream, egg yolks, and salt. Fold in egg whites beaten stiff.

Place dough on cloth-covered table, sprinkled with flour. Roll dough very thin with rolling pin, and spread with cheese filling. Then roll up like potica. Wrap rolled dumplings in a wet cloth. Tie one end with cord, then wind cord around cloth-covered dumplings, progressing toward the other end, and fasten. Place into boiling salt water, to which a teaspoon of sugar has been added, and cook for a half hours. When cooked, untie, unwrap and cut dumplings into pieces about 2 inches long. Top with browned buttered bread crumbs.

The Art of Hungarian Cooking by Paula Pogany Bennet and Velma R. Clark. 1954. Drawings by Willy Pogany. "The zest for good food and wine that is so freely expressed in the folk songs and fiery csárdá of the food-loving Magayars."

PAPRIKA CHICKEN

3-pound fry chicken, disjointed – 2 onions, finely chopped – 3 tablespoons fat – 1 tablespoon paprika – 1 teaspoon salt – 1 cup sour cream – Soft noodles

6 SERVINGS

Wash the chicken well and drain. Brown the onion lightly in the fat; add the paprika and the chicken. Sprinkle with salt. Cover and cook slowly about 1 hour or until tender. Pour the cream over chicken. Heat for a minute only. Serve with freshly boiled soft noodles.

PAMELA KURE GROGAN

CHAPTER FIFTEEN
Tradition

Hungarian paprika, fondly described as "nemes édes [noble and sweet]," has an indescribably richer flavor than Spanish or American paprika. This is due to the alluvial soil in which it thrives. The pods of the Hungarian plant are small and ripen to bright orange-red, a color which is retained through the drying and grinding process...The Hungarian housewife does not sprinkle it on. She measures it by the teaspoon or tablespoon so that meats become a rich reddish-brown, soups have a rosy blush, and vegetables an added zest.

Note: 1/8 teaspoon black pepper may be substituted for the paprika.

CUCUMBERS WITH SOUR CREAM
TEJFÖLÖS UBORKA

4 large cucumbers – 2 teaspoons salt – wine vinegar – teaspoon paprika – 2 tablespoons salad oil – cup heavy sweet or sour cream

6 SERVINGS

Peel the cucumbers and slice thin. Sprinkle with the salt and let stand 15 minutes. Drain and press out the moisture. Add the vinegar and paprika. A few minutes before serving add the salad oil and cream.

Cover a large table (about 50 x 50 inches) with a clean white sheet and sprinkle well with flour to all edges. Place dough in center and roll out round to 1/2 inch thickness, then brush with melted butter. Reach under the dough (palms down) and stretch it gently all around so as to have it as thin as paper and hanging over the edges. Trim thick edges with scissors or sharp knife. Sprinkle melted butter over the dough and gently spread to cover.

Pour cottage cheese filling all over dough and gently spread to cover. With the aid of the sheet turn up the dough on three sides to make it even with the edge of the table and then with the aid of the sheet start to roll the dough over (not to tight), pulling cloth and dough towards you. Grease bottom and side of a 9 x 13 baking pan. Cut strudel into three even rolls, pinch ends to seal and place into baking pan. Brush the tops with butter and bake at 350 degrees for one hour or until golden brown. Cut into slices and serve warm.

GRAMMA KURE'S COTTAGE CHEESE STRUDEL

Dough Recipe – 4 cups flour – 3 tbsp oil – dash of salt – $1^{1/4}$ – $1^{3/4}$ cup warm water Filling Recipe – 3 lbs. cottage cheese – 3 large eggs – $1^{1/4}$ cup sugar – dash of salt

Combine flour, salt and oil in the bowl of an electric mixer. On low speed gradually add the water. Continue to mix on low speed until the dough leaves the side of the bowl. The dough should be soft and smooth. Remove the dough from the bowl, lightly oil the ball of dough and place on a plate, cover with an inverted bowl and let rest for 1/2 hour. Meanwhile prepare filling by mixing all ingredients in a bowl until well blended.

CHAPTER FIFTEEN
Tradition

Many years back, scanning my collection of early *Gourmet* Magazines, I picked up on in different issues various stories of a Russian cook working in a California family household in the 1920's. Recipes offered with each tale. At the same time, back in those days of the 1940's, readers began asking, 'When was there going to be a cookbook about this fun- loving Russian émigré? In 1947, their queries were answered with the publication of **Katish, Our Russian Cook, a novel-plus-cookbook**. The author was Wanda L. Frolov, a well known *Gourmet* columnist who wrote under the pseudonym of Wanda E. Ivanoff. Book's illustrations by Henry J. Stahlhut. The story is warm and fuzzy with reminiscences of childhood.

One of Katish's most famous recipes was her cheesecake. In fact, in an article in 1991, "25 Favorite Desserts," *Gourmet* Magazine featured Katish's Cheesecake as #1 (for some reason less one egg in the recipe?). Here is the recipe exactly as Frolov presented it in 1947.

KATISH'S CHEESE CAKE

Cover the bottom of a spring form mold with 18 pieces of finely crushed zwieback mixed with 1 1/2 tablespoons each of butter and sugar. Then cream 1 cup plus 2 tablespoons of sugar with 4 packages of Philadelphia cream cheese. Add 2 level tablespoons of flour, a pinch of salt, a 1-inch length of vanilla bean finely cut, and the beaten yolks of 4 eggs. Mix well and add 1 cup of sour cream. Fold in 4 stiffly beaten egg whites and put into the crumb-lined pan. Bake in a moderate oven (350°) for about one hour. The crumb crust will be thin and crisp and the cake very light and creamy.

The cheese cake that Bob munched so contentedly was the first we had ever tasted that did not have the regrettable texture of peanut butter. That cake was later to win Katish a proposal of marriage, much to Aunt Martha's chagrin. from **Katish**

MY COOKBOOK PASSION

CHAPTER FIFTEEN
Tradition

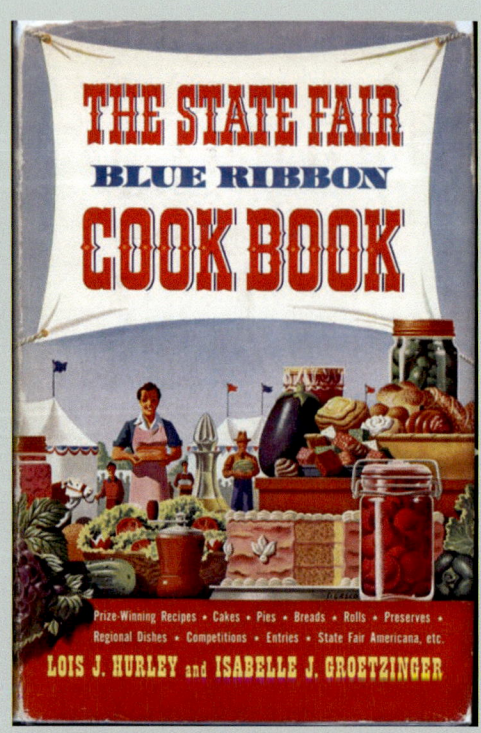

Farmers Markets and State Fairs

Sometimes traditions take our memories back to fun-time community gatherings...corn dogs and cotton candy, and Blue ribbon prize-winning from gardens and fields The **State Fair Blue Ribbon Cookbook** by Lois J. Hurley and Isabelle J. Groetzinger (1950) **Farmers Market Cookbook** by Neill and Fred Beck (1951). Not general farmers' markets but the specific one still there today in Hollywood. Signed.

And then there are political gatherings...history-related traditions **The Congressional Club Cook Book (1961).** Forward by Mrs. John F. Kennedy. Politically correct her recipe is Massachusetts Fish Chowder, her other choice more her style and international, Crème Brulee. Book is signed by Congressman Duruo of Oregon. **The First Congressional Cook Book** was published in 1927.

Collectors Corner: In 1974, Desert Charities, Inc. would produce a fundraiser tribute book for the Eisenhower Medical Center entitled: **Five Star Favorites, Recipes from Friends of Mamie and Ike**. Celebrity contributors. Leather in presentation box. Novice collectors are misled when they say the book is autographed by Mamie, when in fact it is her printed signature.

PAMELA KURE GROGAN

CHAPTER FIFTEEN
Tradition

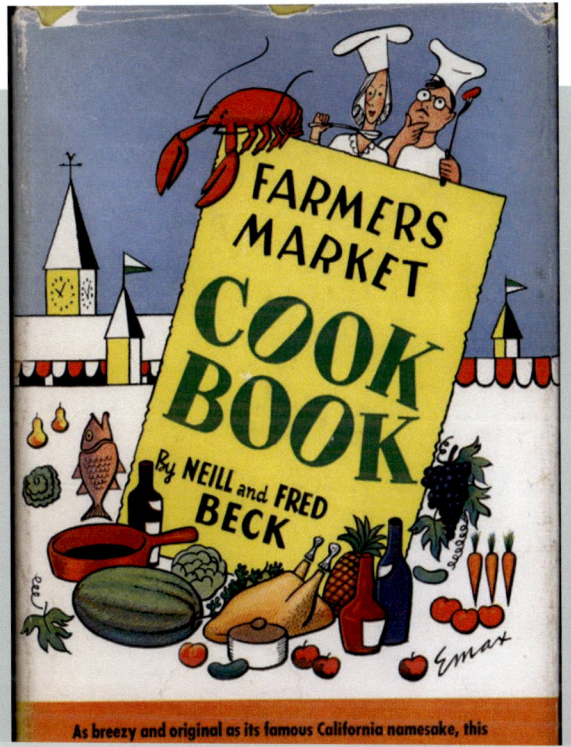

Eat, Drink and be Merry in Maryland, compiled by Frederick Philip Stieff (1932). Vice President of the Stieff Piano Company and a collector of old recipes, many never before published. Emily Post writes the Forward.

"Baltimore...the gastronomic metropolis of the Union. Why don't you put a canvas-back duck on top of the Washington column? Why don't you get that lady off from the Battle Monument and plant a terrapin in her place? Why will you ask for other glories when you have soft crabs?...if you open your mouths to speak nature stops them with a fat oyster or offers a slice of the breast of your divine bird."...

Quote from book by Oliver Wendell Holmes **The Professor at the Breakfast Table**, 1859

COLD CURRY SOUP

1/3 c. butter – 1/4 c. minced onion – 1/4 diced celery – 1/4 c. flour – 1/8 tsp pepper – 1 1/2 tsp curry powder – 1 tsp salt – 1 qt. milk – 2 chicken bouillon cubes – Flaked coconut

Melt butter in saucepan over low heat. Sauté onion and celery in butter until transparent. Blend in seasonings and flour. Add milk, stirring constantly. Cook until smooth and thickened. Add bouillon cubes; stir until blended. Chill thoroughly. Pour into chilled bowls and sprinkle with flaked coconut. Makes 6 servings. Mrs. Dwight D. Eisenhower, wife of former President of the United States—The Congressional Cookbook

CHAPTER FIFTEEN
Tradition

The Connecticut Cookbook, compiled by the Westport Woman's Club (1943). This is a wartime book, "when even the best cook's style is cramped by ration coupons and great gaps in the grocer's shelves and the butcher's counter." Illustrators are famed Connecticut artists, one being Southport resident, Harold Gray, of Little Orphan Annie fame. Artist Gray (1894-1968) produced Orphan Annie Christmas Cards annually from 1920's thru 1960's.

Sidenote: How often do we investigate the recipe contributor? So I notice several recipes by contributor Mrs. J.V.N. Dorr (ex., 'Ravioli', 'Sweet French Dressing', and a worksheet on herbs and food applications.) And here is the front cover photograph, "jacket photo taken in her own Connecticut kitchen, is by Nell Dorr." One and the same? More research and the answer is 'yes'. In fact, Nell Becker Dorr (1895-1988) is remembered as a major photographer, specializing after 1954, when her young daughter died, in photographing mothers and daughters, trying to memorialize her own lost child. In 1955 she appeared in the "Family of Man" exhibit at the Museum of Modern Art, presented by Edward Steichen. Her photo contribution: her friend and neighbor, illustrator Tasha Tudor, nursing her son Tom. And what about hubby? Dr. John Van Nostrand Dorr (1872-1962), a successful metallurgical engineer and inventor, began his career as a 16 year old assistant to Thomas Edison!

As the story goes, Nell Dorr complained one night coming home in the rain to their Connecticut home, that the glare from on-coming cars made her momentarily blind, and

PAMELA KURE GROGAN

CHAPTER FIFTEEN
Tradition

ST. MARY'S MANOR

(BUILT in 1820 by Dr. J. Thomas Brome, grandfather of Mrs. J. Spence Howard, on the site of the original grant to Leonard Calvert in 1634 known as Governor's Field. It was the first patent in Maryland. Here the first grist mill was built on this side of the Atlantic, the old mill stones of which now repose on the grounds of St. Mary's Manor.)

PEACH FOAM

Put a cupful of fine peaches, cut into small bits after peeling, into a bowl with half a cup of powdered sugar. Beat for a while with a silver fork, then add the white of one egg well beaten. Beat all together for half an hour. Chill in the refrigerator and serve with cream, either whipped or plain. This is a delicate and tempting dish for an invalid.—*Mr. and Mrs. J. Spence Howard, St. Mary's Manor, St. Mary's County.*

---

her car drifted towards the center line white markings, vulnerable to fatal side-swiping. John Dorr investigated as an inventor might and determined a solid white line on the road shoulder would have a driver correct away from the road's center. Who'd thunk? John and Nell Dorr saved lives. Of course, it took years to convince state governments and their skeptical highway departments, but all came around to accept statistical truth. From recipes to photography to getting you safely down the roadway to your cooking classes. A cookbook can sift out knowledge, as well as measured ingredients.

CHAPTER SIXTEEN
Return to the stars

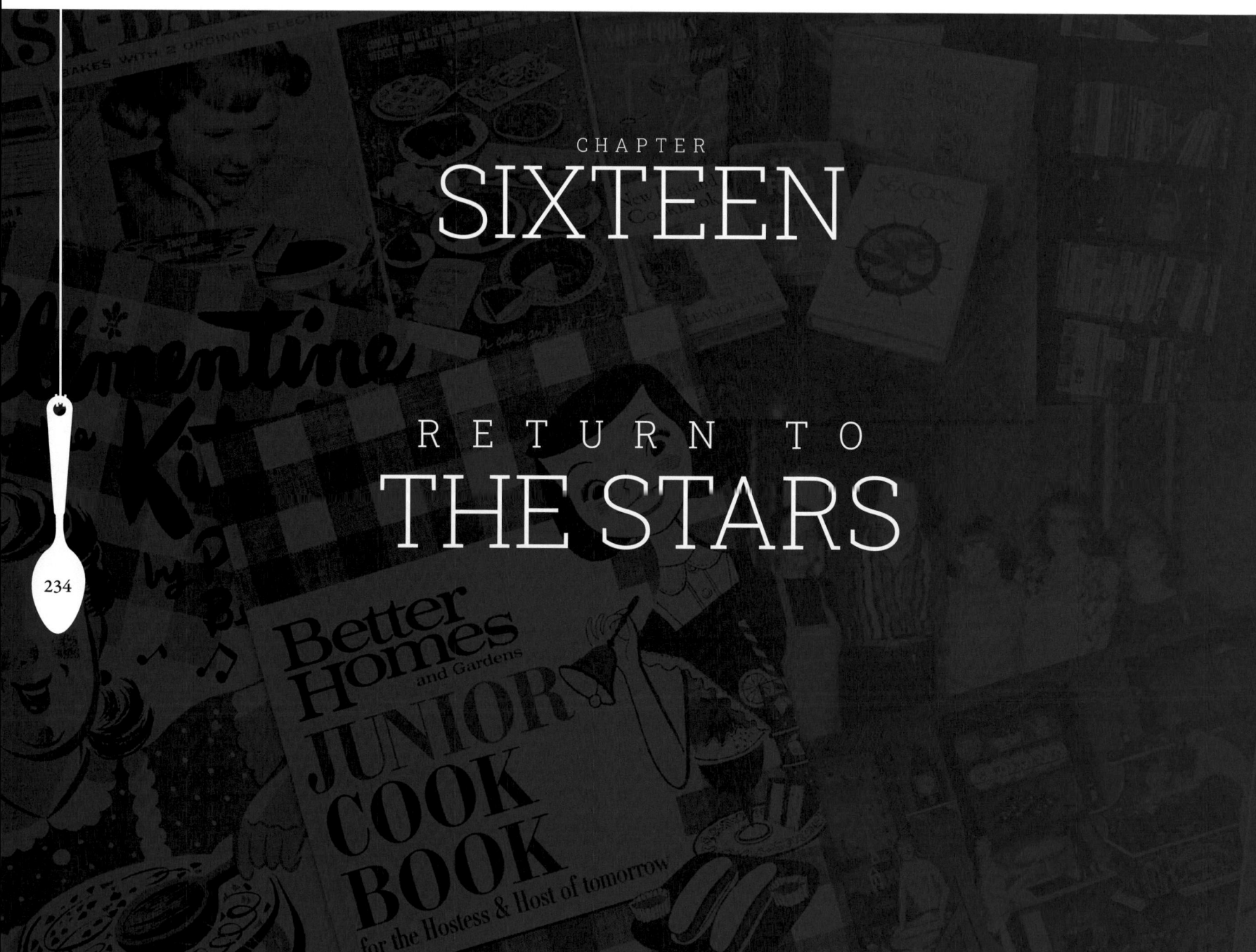

CHAPTER
SIXTEEN

RETURN TO
THE STARS

234

PAMELA KURE GROGAN

CHAPTER SIXTEEN
Return to the stars

***'Priced'* Right For Your Library**
"A Treasury of Great Recipes" by Mary and Vincent Price.

The horror film actor lived as a connoisseur of the finer things in life, not only with cuisine, but in art, a Yale graduate in Fine Art. "Treasury" is like fine art, gilded, faux leather, gold ribbon markers, and to the connoisseur Mary and Vincent cull the best by featuring the top world restaurants of the early 1960's, including France's La Reserve, Tour d'Argent and Italy's Passetto and Harry's Bar in Venice. U.S. examples: Gage and Tollners, The Four Seasons, Sardi's West and Luchow's. You can understand the passion when you learn Vincent was the son of a candy manufacturer and the grandson of the inventor of baking powder. Near book end, the authors add, "Specialties of Our House" with modern technology of that era leading to a chapter on "Blender Magic." This is a workbook, with blank pages for favorite guests, wine, and your own recipes. I have created and tasted from these pages with pleasure. One of my favorites is *Gazpacho Andaluz* (Andalusian Cold Soup).

Vincent Price tasting the best Gazpacho originated in Andalusia, the colorful southern section of Spain. From Sobrino De Botin restaurant in Madrid (a favorite hangout for bull fighters). For the best recipe, you must be sure to use very ripe tomatoes, otherwise the taste falls flat.

MY COOKBOOK PASSION

CHAPTER SIXTEEN
Return to the stars

GAZPACHO ANDALUZ
Into a mixing bowl put: **6 thin slices bread, diced, 3 very ripe tomatoes, chopped, 1 cucumber, chopped, 3 tablespoons olive oil,** and **1 quart water.** Let soak for 1 hour, then puree in food mill or blend, half at a time, on a high speed in an electric blender for 8 seconds. Strain through a coarse sieve into a large soup bowl.

Add: 2 **cloves garlic, minced, 2 tablespoons wine vinegar, 2 teaspoons salt, 1 teaspoon ground cumin,** and **4 ice cubes.** Chill in refrigerator for al least half an hour.

PRESENTATION
In separate small dishes put: **1 red or green pepper, diced, 1 large ripe tomato, diced, 1 small cucumber, diced, and 2 slices bread, diced.** If desired, the bread cubes may be browned in **butter**. Serve the gazpacho in well chilled bowls. Let each person help himself to the diced garnishes in the small dishes, sprinkling some of each into his soup bowl. Serves 4 to 6.

"The National Treasury of Cookery" by Mary and Vincent Price is five volumes in slipcase. Recipes of Early America; of the Young Republic; of Ante Bellum America; of the Westward Empire; and recipes of Victorian America. "Come into the Kitchen" ('A collector's treasury of American's great recipes'). Followed the theme of 'Treasury of Cookery from colonial but adds a chapter on "Modern America" and several sections, the historic "Wines in America" and "Wine Making in the Home". Less hands-on by the Prices still a strong expertise editorial team assisted them in showcasing Americana eras, featuring chapters like before 'Young Republic' (Chicken and Okra Soup) or 'Victorian America' (Parker House Rolls). If you like early Americana foods that are edible today and don't want to try to decipher archaic colonial dialect this is the short-cut. The artwork drawings and illustrations by Charles Wysocki and Nicholas Amorosi make me feel like I'm back in history class.

Collector's Corner:
Myrna Donato of Amber Unicorn Books tells the story when friends of Vincent Price contacted her. They discovered Mr. Price did not have a first edition of his own book, *Treasury of Great Recipes,* and they asked her to send him a letter and quote him a price. She did and received a handwritten postcard back from the actor. "I would never pay $30 for a cookbook! And don't intend to do so even for this one!"

Treasury of Great Recipes is a classic in haute cuisine, an epicurean's delight. Abundant copies reside in the market place and priced quite reasonable. Since this book shows like a museum *piece d'resistance* please acquire the best quality. Reality check: Mary and Vincent's cooking collaboration would end by their divorce in 1973.

Editor's Note: The National Treasury of Cookery volume set [left] is well-worth having, but photos were not included because books are small to reproduce and displaying them would not have presented quality views. Instead we present [next page] **Come into the Kitchen** which captures same early Americana flavor. Author has **A Treasury of Great Recipes** signed.

PAMELA KURE GROGAN

CHAPTER SIXTEEN
Return to the stars

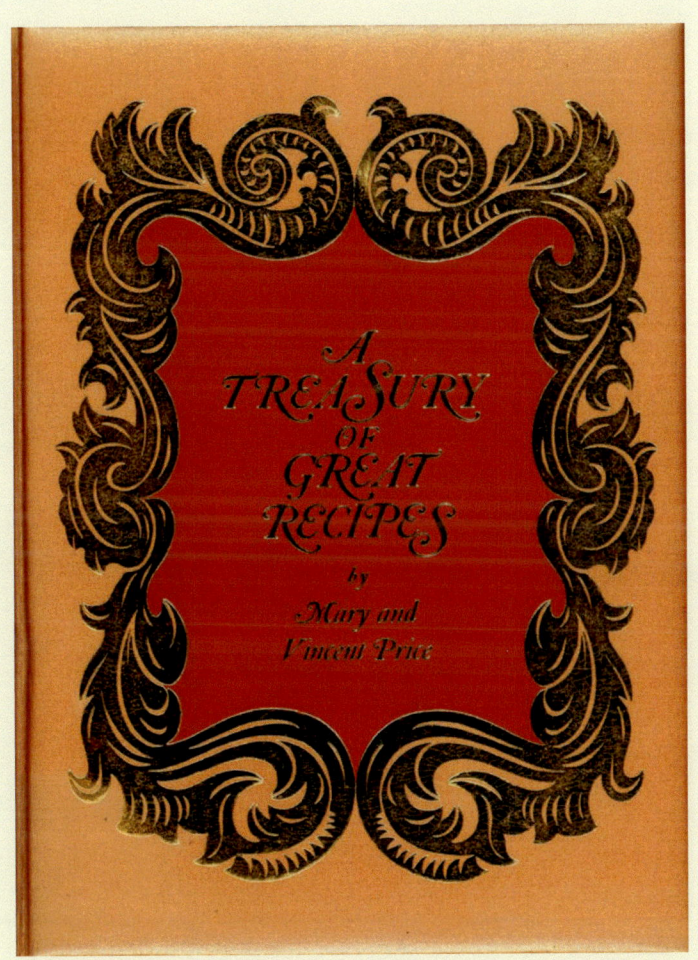

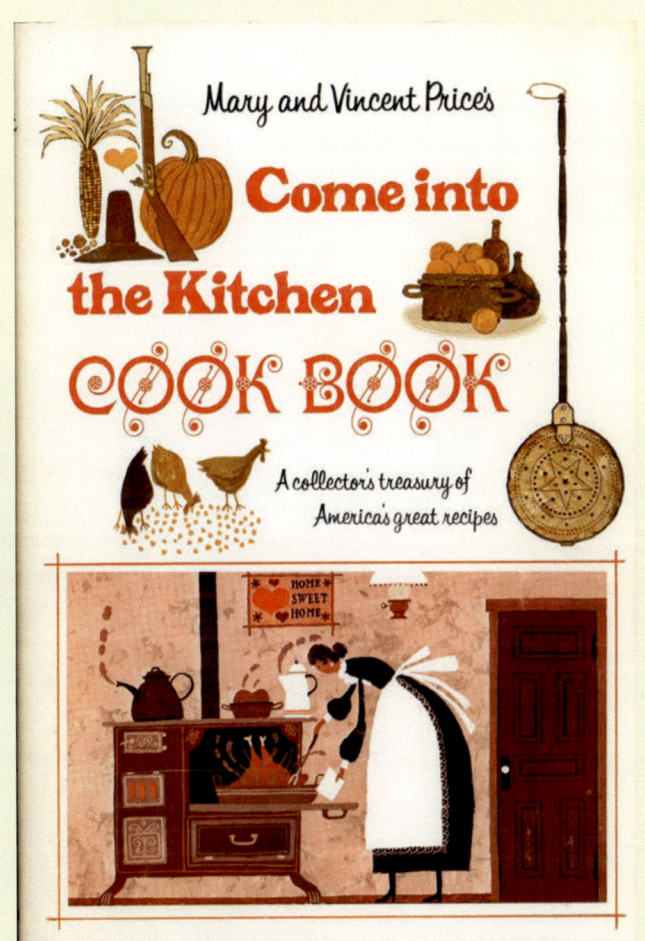

"A Treasury of Great Recipes" by Mary and Vincent Price (Edited by Darlene Geis, Illustrated by Fritz Kredel. Published by Ampersand Press, 1965. 456+ pages.

Artwork in book is by famous illustrator Charles M Wysocki (1928-2002) portrayer of what we envision of an idealized Americana, the primitivism of horse & buggy days.

MY COOKBOOK PASSION

CHAPTER SIXTEEN
Return to the stars

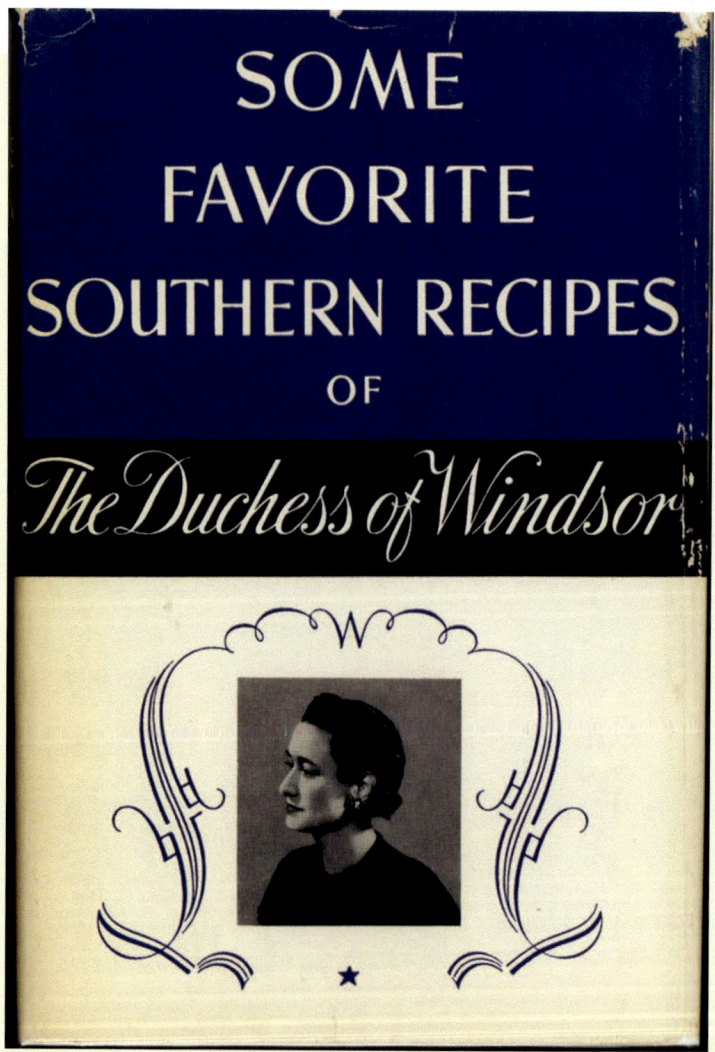

The Mystery Chef's Own Cookbook, First Edition, Inscribed. (1936, Longmans, Green & Co., 366 pages) Smart marketing line--"The Book a Million Women Asked for."

The U.S. Southern-born Duchess (Wallis Simpson) and her husband were considered Nazi sympathizers and exiled during WW II by the Duke being appointed as Governor of the Bahamas

PAMELA KURE GROGAN

CHAPTER SIXTEEN
Return to the stars

Some Favorite Southern Recipes of The Duchess of Windsor. Published by Charles Scribner's Sons, 1942. Rare. Note: *She did not write the book, just the Forward, introduction by Mrs. Franklin Delano Roosevelt. Shows the use of a 'celebrity's name'. During the war, proceeds went to the British War Relief Society. 140 recipes tested by the Home Institute of the New York Herald Tribune.*

What's Cookin' by Jack Bailey. (1907-1980) The World Publishing Company, 1949. 187 pages. Note: *Bailey was emcee of radio's "Queen for a Day" program. Includes humorous kitchen-food photos.1954-1955, emcee of 'Truth or Consequences'. After Ralph Edwards before Bob Barker.*

Elsie's Cook Book by Elsie the Cow (with the aid of Harry Botsford). The Bond Wheelwright Company, Publishers, 1952. 374 pages. Note: *Of course, Elsie's a star, one of the most recognized advertising characters in the U.S. and Canada, first created to advertise the fresh milk products of the Borden Company. Mr. Borden succeeded as the first to condense milk. Elsie's husband, Elmer, went on to his own endorsement fame, Elmer's Glue.*

The Dark Shadows Cookbook, compiled by Jody Cameron Malis. Ace Publishing Company, 1970. Paperback. 175 pages. Note: *Vampires have to eat! This campy book from the television hit show features Barnabas's Beastly Beverages and Quentin's Ghoulish Goulash. I don't really want to try Magda's Underground Meats. Small world. The back cover advertises the 75 cent paperback of* **Egg's I have Known** *by Corinne Griffith.* Collector's Corner: **Dark Shadows** signed by two cast members. Difficult to find in good condition; expect yellowing pages.

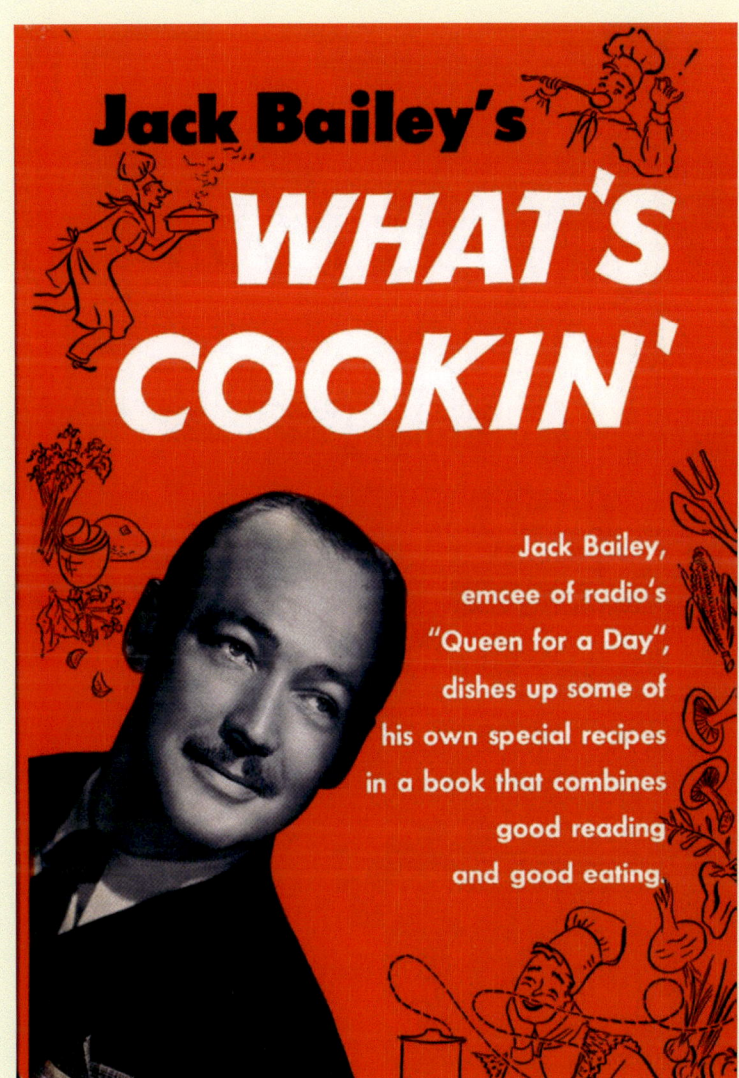

Jack Bailey's What's Cooking, 1949

MY COOKBOOK PASSION

CHAPTER SIXTEEN
Return to the stars

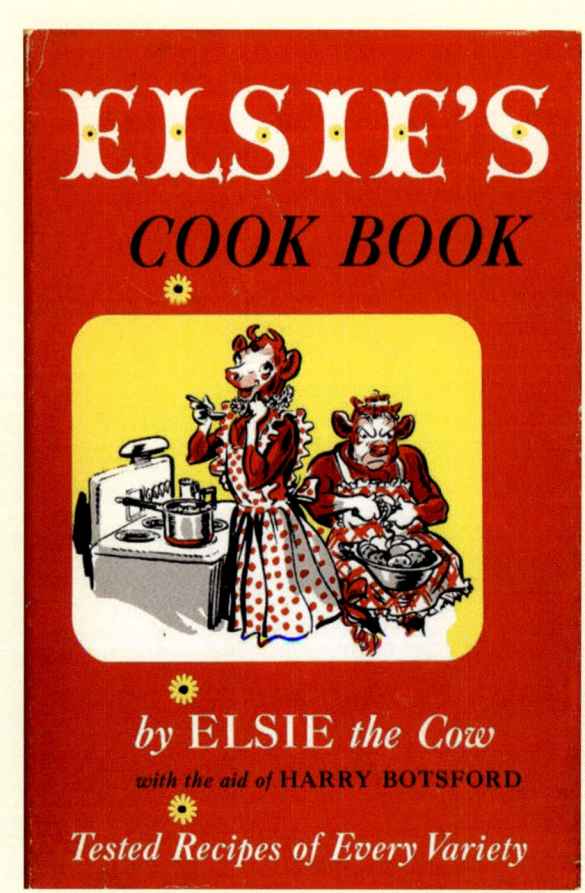

Elsie's Cook Book, 1952

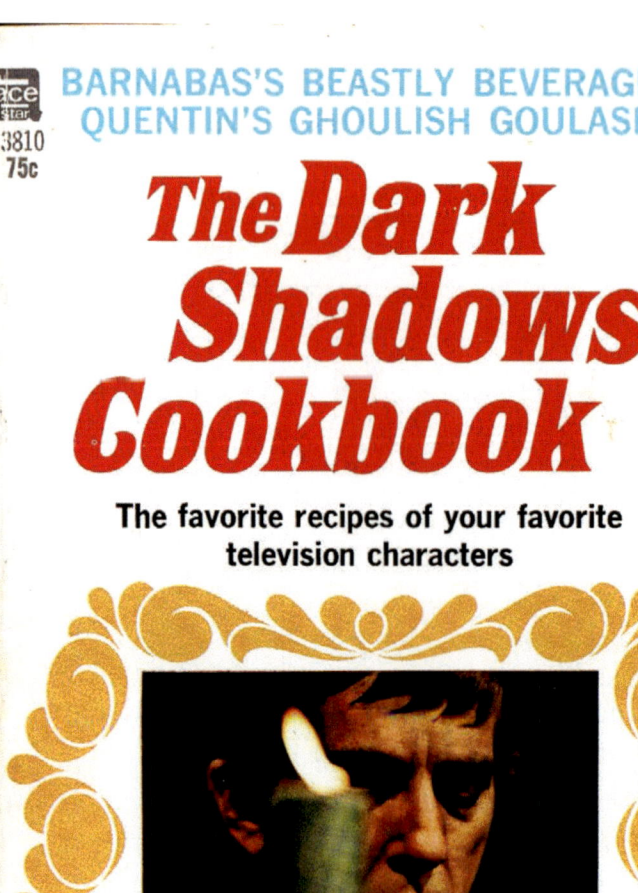

PAMELA KURE GROGAN

CHAPTER SIXTEEN
Return to the stars

Minnie Pearl Cooks by Minnie Pearl (1912-1996). Aurora Publishers, Nashville. 1970. 185 pages. Note: *Real name: Sarah Ophelia Colley Cannon. Outside of being a comedic fixture at the Grand Ole Opry and later TV's 'Hee Haw' show, she survived devastating breast cancer and went on to be a cancer survivor spokeswoman under her real name. Several Tennessee hospital cancer research centers are named after her.*

Someone's in the Kitchen with Dinah (her personal cookbook), Double Day and Company, 1971. 179 pages. Signed. Note: *Dinah Shore (1916-1994) sums it up best: "I've been collecting and trying recipes ever since I can remember." She says she even hid a few 'diet' recipes in the pages but likes the 'fat fun' ones better. Other recipes: "You'll find a Ratatouille that cleans out the vegetable bin."* Signed.

MY COOKBOOK PASSION

CHAPTER SIXTEEN
Return to the stars

In the Kitchen With Love by Sophia Loren (born 1934). Doubleday & Company, 1972. 250 pages. Signed. Note: More personal than most cookbooks, after two miscarriages, she is with child, required rest and lying-in, she's looking for something to do, so begins writing out her past reminiscences of cooking. Therapy of writing was the right medicine: her son is born healthy. **Collector's Corner:** First published in Italy as "In Cucina con Amore", 1971, the U.S. version is highly sought after and more valuable. **Trivia:** Her famous quip when people comment about her voluptuous curves: *"Everything you see, I owe to spaghetti."*

FONDUTA *This is an equally famous dish and so simple that I have often had to fall back on it in emergencies.*

For each person, pour two tablespoons of milk and 2 ½ ounces of soft cheese (the classic cheese is Fontina) into The top of a double boiler. Cook over boiling water until the cheese is melted, then mix in one egg yolk per person. The eggs are already beaten and diluted with half a spoonful of warm milk and a large pat of butter. You mix it all until it blends with a shining surface. When the fondue is ready I prefer to serve it in individual cups over toast points, according to the old die-hard habit in Piedmont. And what could be more splendid than to top it with a good handful of grated truffle?

PAMELA KURE GROGAN

CHAPTER SIXTEEN
Return to the stars

Bless The Bountiful

We could say singer Kate Smith (1907-1986) enjoyed what she ate, weighing above 235 pounds at various points in her career, sadly the brunt of many brutal jokes by her fellow stars. In the 1960's she got hold of her weight, dropped 90 pounds, and became a blonde. Later she let it slide, going back, as she said, "to real chocolate fudge sundaes." Published in 1958 **"Company's Coming"** appealed to her many radio and television fans, and even had sections for 'Teen-Age Cooks' and 'Fan Fare' where she recognized recipes of her many fans. I have seen no other cooking star give credit to those who made them popular. Go, girl.

Did you know?

She recorded over 3,000 songs, 1,000 she introduced and of those 600 made the Hit Parade. Her most famous song

introduced in 1938 was "God Bless America", written by Irving Berlin for his Broadway show in 1918. This has become "The Second National Anthem". Neither Smith nor Berlin took any royalties but donated proceeds to the Boy and Girl Scouts of America. The Kate Smith **"Company's Company"** Cookbook, published 1958 by Prentice-Hall. Illustrated by H.W. Doremus. 312 pages.

Collector's Corner

What's a star's cookbook worth? When collecting memorabilia of the stars, including cookbooks, sometimes the values are based on fan emotion and not what a store owner would pay for a used book. Those that want everything about a famous person, star, author, or historic figure are called 'completists'. They must have everything, including perhaps a lock of hair.

MY COOKBOOK PASSION

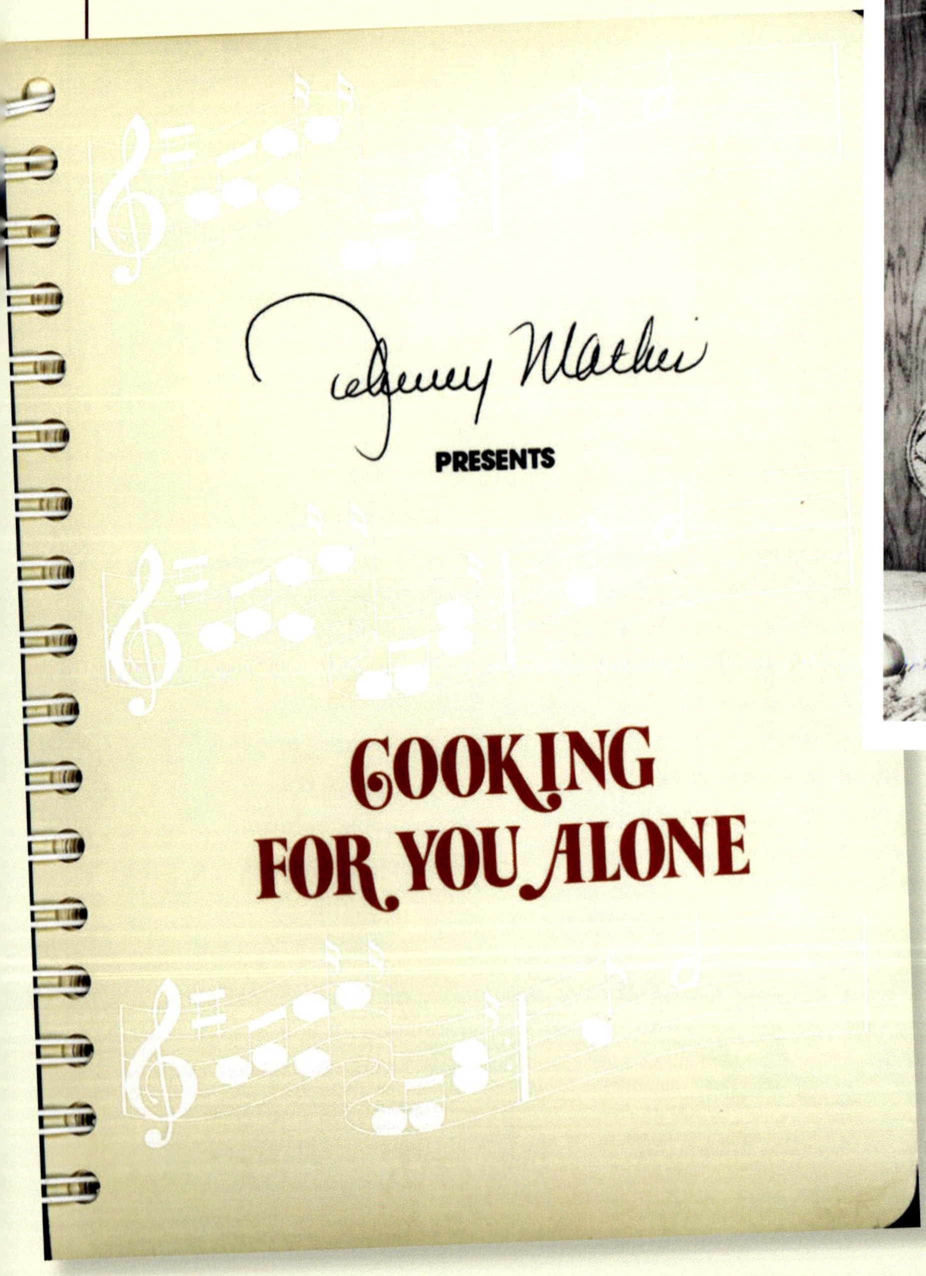

CHAPTER SIXTEEN
Return to the stars

Johnny Mathis presents **"Cooking For You Alone"**. The publishers tout that 40,000 copies were run off in the first print run but I have my doubts as this has become one of the rare collectibles among culinary bibliophiles. Here's the behind-the-scene story. My husband Stephen knew I was looking for this Holy Grail. He ran across Johnny's book by chance at this on-line auction site (you know which one I'm referring to) and it was priced "Buy It Now" at $125. He immediately bought it only to have the lady contact him apologetically saying that she had listed it for a friend and

PAMELA KURE GROGAN

CHAPTER SIXTEEN
Return to the stars

made a mistake and the item should have been for open bidding. Graciously, he allowed her to re-list and told me how he lost acquiring this treasure. I was devastated. At Christmas time there was an envelope in my holiday stocking hung on the fireplace: a treasure hunt of clues, going one place to find another clue that led me to a hidden Christmas box in a closet. Inside, a signed Johnny Mathis record album as a consolation price, but surprise! Under the record album was the Johnny Mathis cookbook...and it was autographed by the singer himself. and dated! Stephen came out on top in the bidding; what he paid he won't tell me to this day...just to make me happy...great guys, both Johnny and Stephen.

The book is spiral bound, a grey durable plastic recipe folder (9x6½ inches) where you can tripod the book sideways to see each recipe page (coated to be washable). Color food photo at the start of the six separate food chapters. Someone wrote, whether true or no, Johnny thought the book was a hassle because each recipe had to be verified. Recipes seem a basic variety, nothing outstanding, but so what, I am still glad I'm holding the book in my hands.

"Cooking For You Alone" by Johnny Mathis (with Peter & Marge Birch, TEC Publishers, First Printing, November 1982) 190 page

Did you know?
As his book states Johnny learned cooking from his Mom, Mildred, and to this day enjoys cooking when his large family of brothers and sisters gathers. In 1958, *Johnny's Greatest Hits* was released and was the first ever Greatest Hits album in the music industry. It began the Greatest Hits tradition copied by every record company. *Johnny's Greatest Hits* spent an unprecedented 490 consecutive weeks (nine and a half years) on the Billboard Album Chart; a feat unmatched by any other recording artist in history, earning him a place in the Guinness Book Of World Records. He has had five of his albums on the Billboard charts simultaneously, an achievement equaled by only two other singers, Frank Sinatra and Barry Manilow.

Autographed Mathis record cover.
Part of my holiday treasure hunt.

MY COOKBOOK PASSION

CHAPTER SEVENTEEN

FINAL MUSINGS

PART I
FOOD WRITERS

PART II
MY CULINARY WORLD

PART III
FINIS

PAMELA KURE GROGAN

CHAPTER SEVENTEEN
Final musings

My library is a friend of a thousand years
Kyo-Sya

Part I.
A Tribute to *Literature of the Edible*

I cannot make a quality exit off these pages without acknowledging the four-legged kitchen throne of food glory, three of those supportive legs being: ingredients combined, the artistry of the cook to deliver, the ambiance of setting (whether restaurant, picnic, dining room table, etc.) and the final critical balanced leg? The extoller of the all encompassing culinary experience who provides the *immortality:* The Food Writer.

Of many to choose from I have selected two that I feel embody the essence of a maturing/evolving industry: *André Simon* and *M.F.K. Fisher*

CHAPTER SEVENTEEN
Final musings

André Simon

André Simon's love of life (1877-1970) was wine. In his early career he was a wine merchant but better known for founding the Wine & Food Society in 1933, with the inaugural dinner at the Savoy, 1934, and later the New York branch would become the International Wine & Food Society. Like James Beard an award was named in his honor, André Simon Book Awards for food and drink books, and you can understand why as he has penned: The History of the Champagne Trade, **The History of the Wine Trade in England, A Concise Encyclopedia of Gastronomy,** among the 104 books he wrote during six decades. He was to have said: "A man dies too young if he leaves any wine in his cellar".

Crosby Gaige: "I first made M. Simon's acquaintance when I became associated with him and other mutual friends in organizing *The Wine and Food Society of New York*." The following recipe is found in **André Simon's French Cookbook.**

Gasconnade of Lamb

Twenty-four hours before you intend to cook it, set a nice tender leg of spring lamb to marinate in ½ cup of olive oil, 2 cups of white wine and 1 cup of vinegar, with a couple of bay leaves, a big pinch of thyme, 12 peppercorns, 2 cloves, a stalk of celery, a couple of stalks of parsley, a clove of

PAMELA KURE GROGAN

CHAPTER SEVENTEEN
Final musings

garlic, 2 sliced onions, 2 shallots and 2 sliced carrots. Add enough water so that the liquid covers the lamb. When you are ready to roast, drain and dry it and set it in a 350° F. oven, allowing maybe 30 minutes to the pound. Meantime, boil and reduce the marinade liquor to 1 ½ cups. Add to it ½ pound mushrooms, sliced, a small tomato cut in dice, and ¼ pound of chicken livers sautéed in butter, and 2 chopped gherkins. Let all this stew together for 10 to 15 minutes, and serve it as sauce for the lamb, which should come to the table sprinkled with chopped pistachios.

AUBERGINES Á LA ARISIENNE
The eggplants are cut longways and their two halves are served filled with their flesh, which has been finely chopped up and mixed with some dry duxelle and some finely pounded pork sausage meat; pepper and salt, of course, and chopped parsley. The halves of the *aubergines,* thus filled, are ranged side by side in a well-buttered dish, sprinkled with bread crumbs, refreshed with melted butter, and gently *gratinées* in a moderate ovendish.

Art from Simon's French Cook Book

CHAPTER SEVENTEEN
Final musings

Within my library the one most obvious and who deserves our homage is: Mary Frances Kennedy Fisher (1908-1992) better known as **M.F. K. Fisher.** She wrote over 25 books nearly all on gastronomical personal views. I was fortunate enough in my book detecting travels to run across a private collector in California and acquired first editions of most of her works.

Of her early life M.F. K dealt with harsh near-poverty and exhaustive circumstances of lengthy close family care-giving. To offset these tribulations, reading was one form of escapism, and as she matured happier times were gained as she learned disparate cuisines with stays in France and California. This led to her first serious work published by Harper in 1937, **Serve It Forth**. Within all her writings there is intelligence, wit and optimism.

Of her, they wrote:

John Updike – [She is] "Poet of the appetites."

W.H. Auden—"I do not know of anyone in the United States who writes better prose."

PAMELA KURE GROGAN

CHAPTER SEVENTEEN
Final musings

Clifton Fadiman—"She writes about food as others do about love, but rather better."

To catch a brief glimpse of M.F.K.'s charm and bookish output, I suggest **The Measure of Her Powers, an M.F.K. Fisher Reader**, *Edited by Dominique Gioia, With an Introduction by Ruth Reichl* (Counterpoint, 1999) and also, **A Welcoming Life, the M.F.K. Fisher Scrapbook** (1997).

From her pen:

"Probably one of the most private things in the world is an egg before it is broken."

"No yoga exercise, no meditation in a chapel filled with music will rid you of your blues better than the humble task of making your own bread."

"First we eat, then we do everything else."

"And with our gastronomical growth will come, inevitably, knowledge and perception of a hundred other things, but mainly of ourselves."

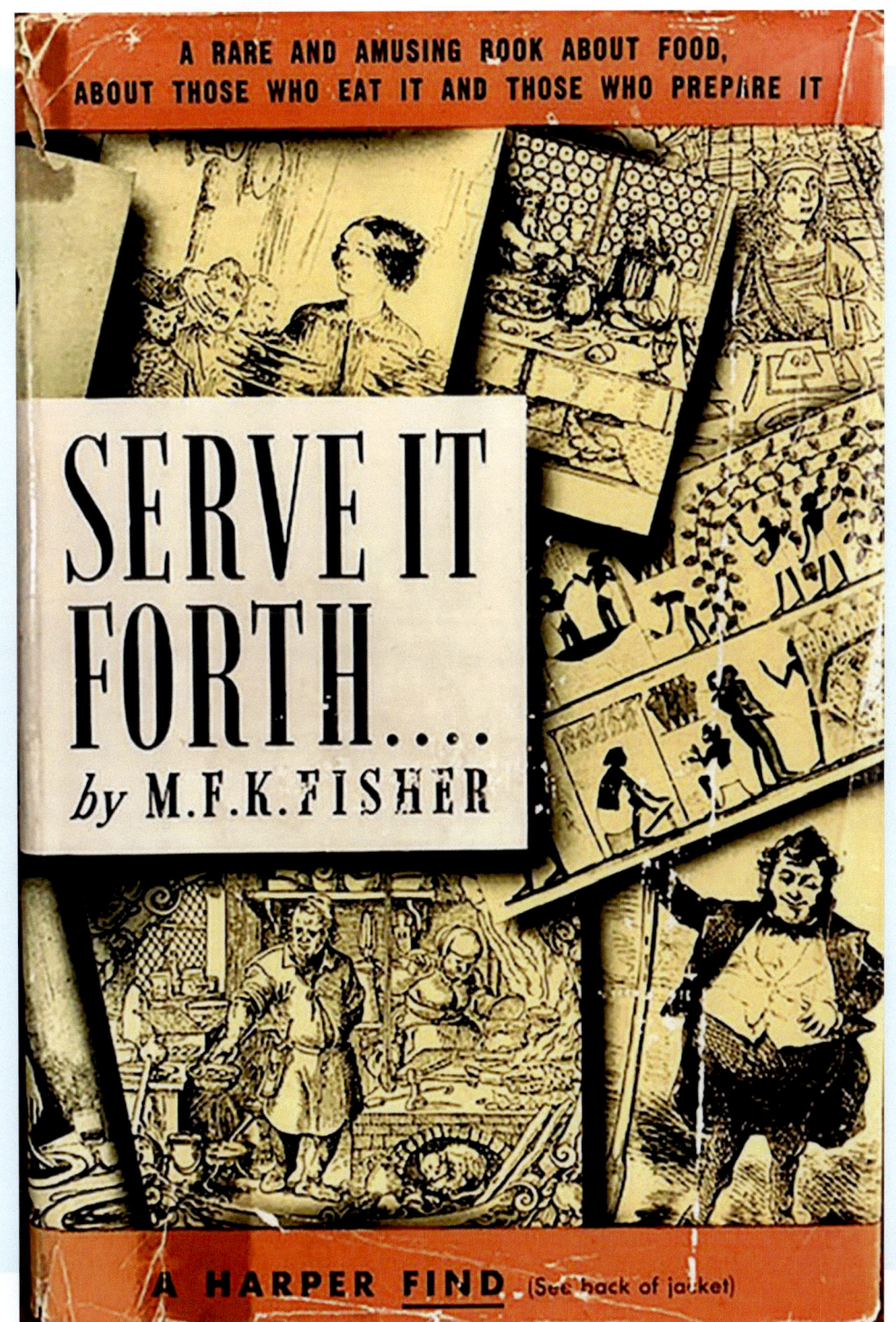

CHAPTER SEVENTEEN
Final musings

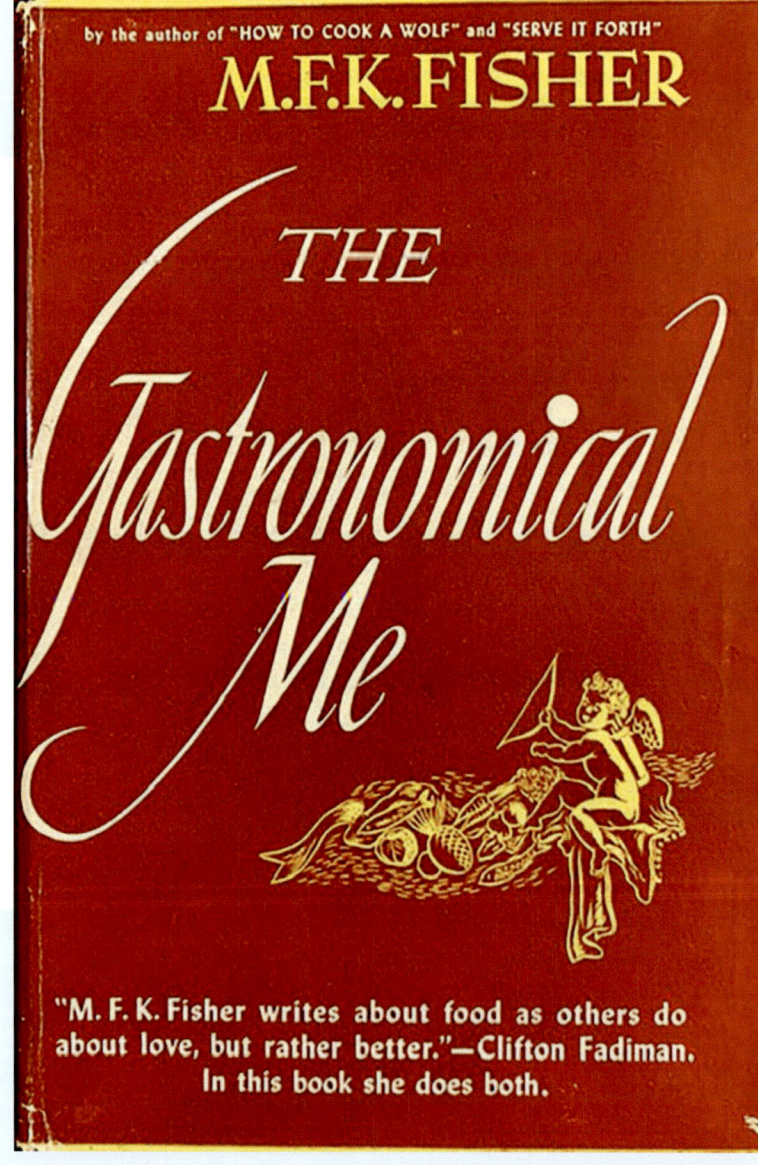
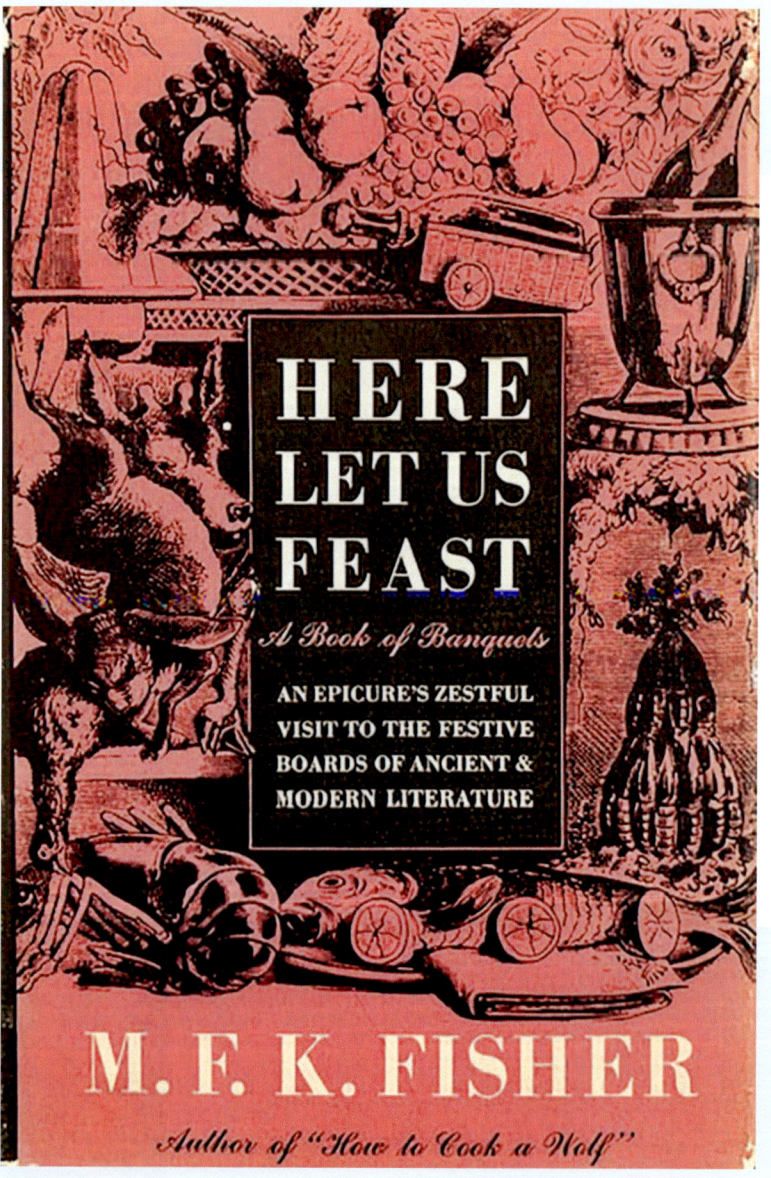

PAMELA KURE GROGAN

CHAPTER SEVENTEEN
Final musings

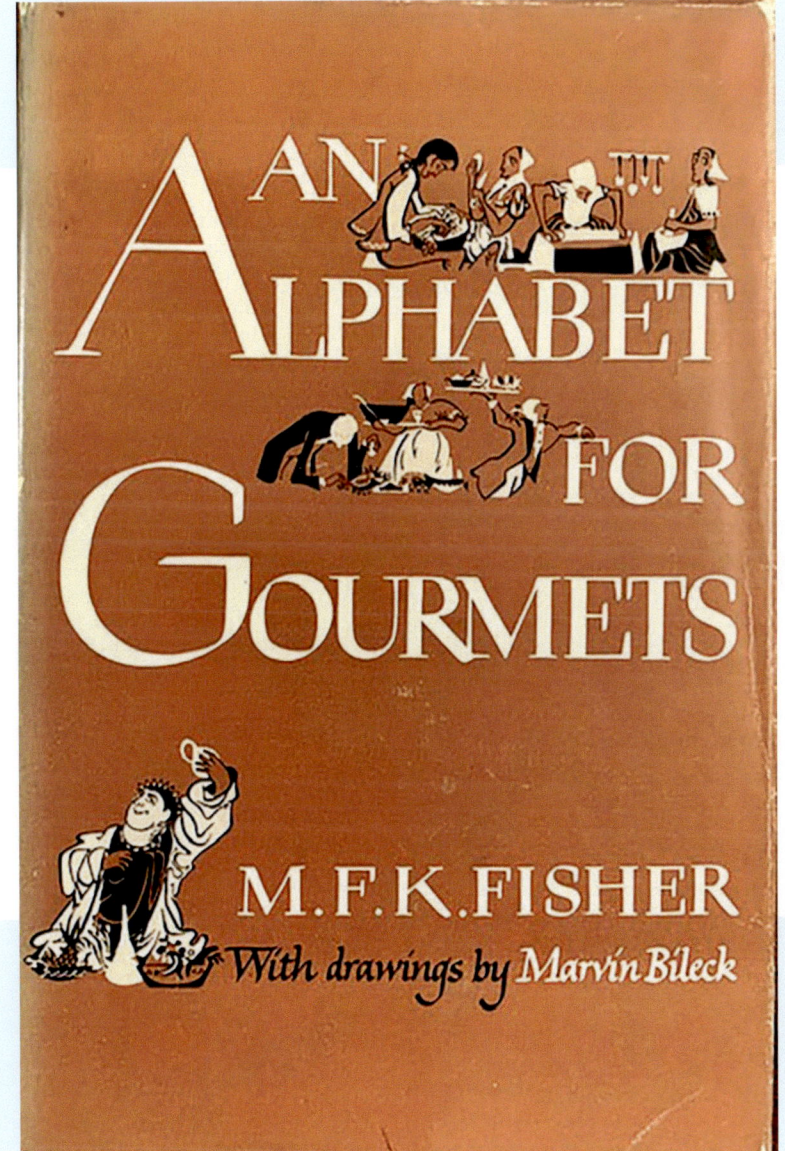

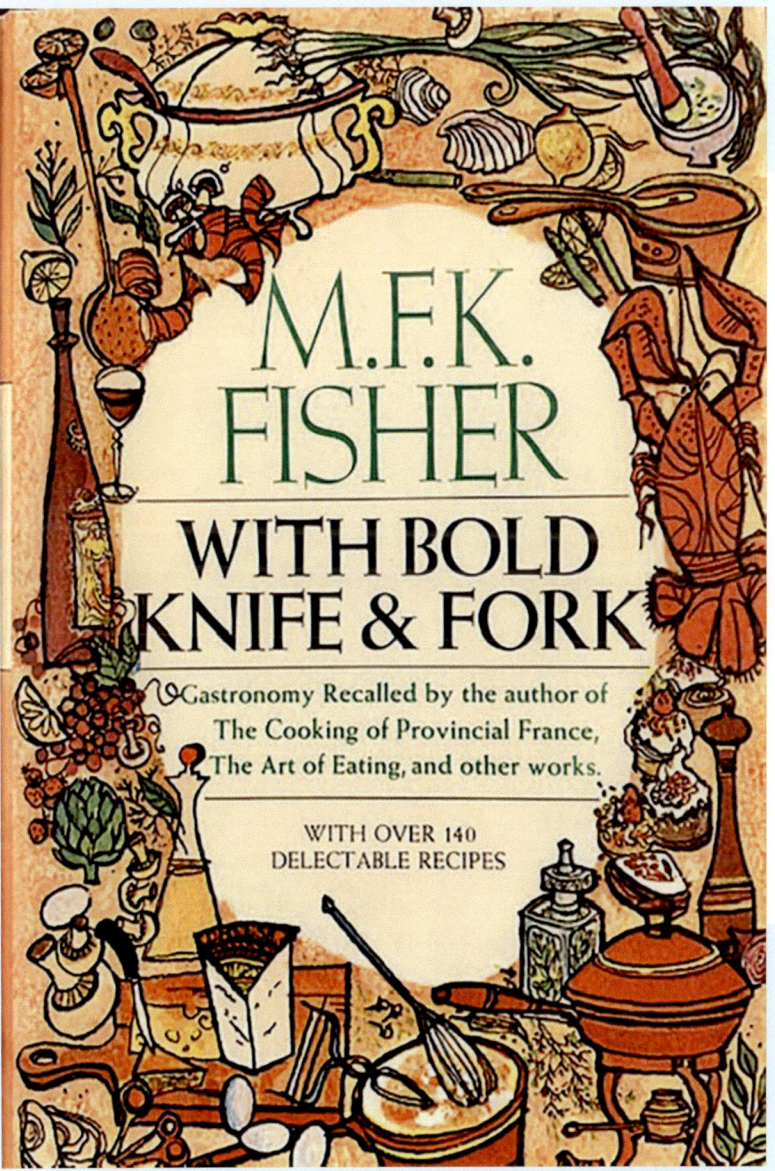

MY COOKBOOK PASSION

CHAPTER SEVENTEEN
Final musings

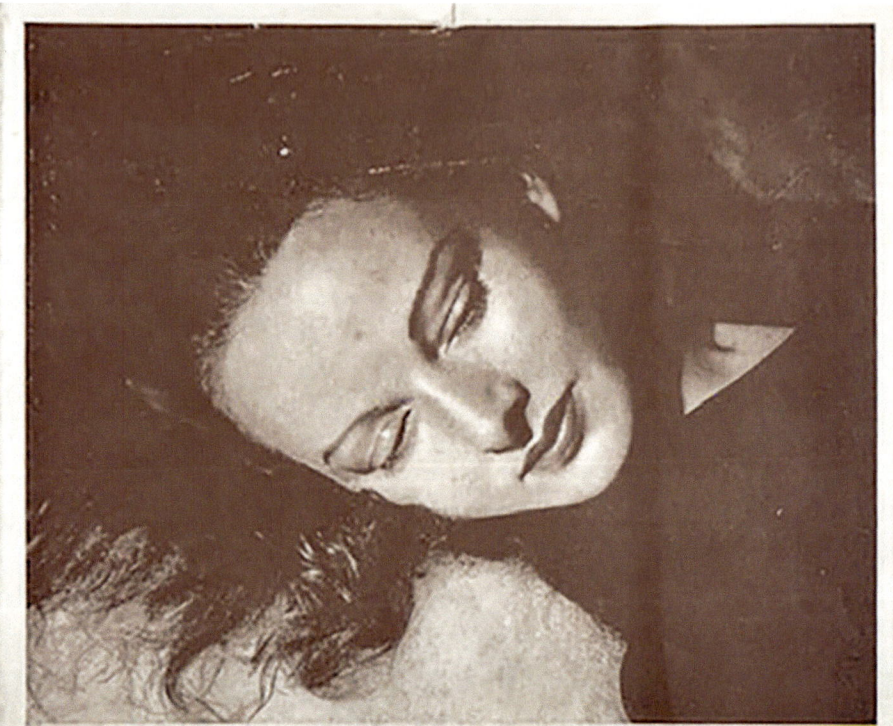

Quote from poet-philosopher Santayana on title page of M.F.K. Fisher's **The Gastronomical Me** (Duell, Sloan & Pearce, 1943)

"To be happy you must have taken the measure of your power, tasted the fruits of your passion, and learned your place in the world."

Sidenote: M.F.K. in 1991 interview with Ruth Reichl in LA Times: "I show Fisher the book [**The Gastronomical Me**]. She looks at the photo on the jacket—a head shot with eyes almost closed and long hair thrown back—and says, 'That's rare, you know. They pulled the jacket after the first edition. The picture was considered too sexy.' No wonder, I say, and read her the passage underneath...'Oh pooh,' she snorts, 'that's not sexy.' She says it as if there must be some unfathomable generational divide between us, if I could find sexiness in a passage such as this." [Dust jacket left].

M.F.K. Fisher in her writing did not create her own tested recipes for print but rather wrote of the entirety of tasteful creations and how they fit

PAMELA KURE GROGAN

CHAPTER SEVENTEEN
Final musings

snug into the world, many times extolling the dish from other cookbooks. Thus, in her **Consider the Oyster** (1941) a paen to the 'flavors of the incomparable mollusk', she extols other cookbooks that I have in my collection, including **Fit for a King** by Merle Armitage. In the Chapter "A Lusty Bit of Nourishment" she provides us with the New Orleans's *Antoine's* Restaurant and the Alciatore Family's 1889 secret recipe *'Sauce for Oyster Rockefeller'*; then jumps to *Gourmet* Magazine and an excerpted recipe from New York's Pierre Hotel Head Chef Georges Gonneau with his *"French Creamed Oysters"*; why not try the Chinese recipe *"Ho Tsee Soong"* (Dried Oysters with Vegetables); and with an extended highlight— to discover in the 1873 edition of Marion Harland's **Common Sense in the Household**, the makings of *'Oyster Castup'*.

Notice I am teasing that I can't supply all recipes herein but it is now you who must embark upon your own adventure of discovery, creating, and tasting.

M.F.K. writes: "Firm chilled oysters rolled quickly in crumbs and dipped into good fat for almost no time at all, and then served quickly on hot plates with an honest tartar sauce or lemon slices, can be one of the best dishes anywhere, and it is perhaps a proof that optimism is inherently human and that after several hideous experiences with restaurant-fried oysters, I still say that." [See Consider Oyster recipe next page]

MY COOKBOOK PASSION

CHAPTER SEVENTEEN
Final musings

II. My Culinary World
THE COLLECTIBLE

The ancient Egyptians might have been right in trying to take all their treasures to the after-life, but I have made decisions not to buy *all things cookery* and continually tweak my collection to upgrade and/or cull those cook books and peripherals. Here are a few sub-categories where I started down the path and then said 'whoa'.

TARTAR SAUCE*

1 cup mayonnaise – 1 teaspoon chopped Chives – 1 teaspoon Tarragon – 1 teaspoon Chervil – 1 chopped gherkin – 1 teaspoon capers – Dash of cayenne Prepared mustard to taste (optional) – 1 chopped olive – Wine vinegar to taste

Mix all ingredients except vinegar, then put that in slowly until proper tartness is obtained. Approx. 1 tblsp will be necessary.

*Recipe from Herbs for the Kitchen, Irma Goodrich Mazza, (Little Brown & Co. 1940)

I love kitchen utensils from my kitchen store management days but one should go only so far. These European rolling pins are unique and great designs -- for baking but I'm not going to start a wall collection of hundreds.

I have over 500 advertising pamphlets. In 24 binders in plastic sleeves by subject. Love the 1900's art

PAMELA KU

CHAPTER SEVENTEEN
musings

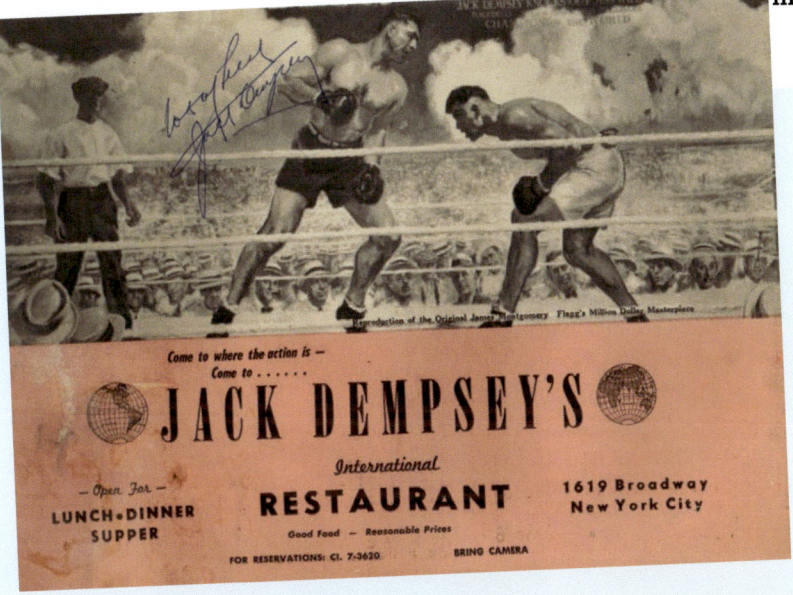

menu is signed. The artwork on the menu is of a famous Dempsey fight by artist James Montgomery Flagg ('Uncle Sam') who also had an illustration in our 'Bottoms Up' drink book. Dempsey's was famous for their cheesecake. The establishment closed in 1974.

Romance and Melodies. Saturday night, August 14th, 1937. The Starlight Roof at the Waldorf-Astoria. The menu is autographed by orchestra leader Guy Lombardo (remembered for his Auld Lang Syne song of New Year's fame) Author's collection.

Menus make great framed art plus conversation pieces like these. Owned by world heavy weight boxing champion Jack Dempsey (1895-1983), Jack Dempsey's Restaurant opened in 1935 near the third Madison Square Garden and later moved location.

Dempsey spent a lot of time as host and signing photos. This

MY COOKBOOK PASSION

CHAPTER SEVENTEEN
Final musings

I have complete collection In Gourmet Magazines beginning 1941 – 1960s again for the artwork Jan.'42 not printed because of Pearl Harbor. I have limited my magazine buying. Many modern recipes are `repeats' of what I have in the 'original' cookbook.

PAMELA KURE GROGAN

"To eat good food is to be close to God." Primo (actor Tony Shalhoub) in "Big Night" 1996

My Favorite Top Food-related Movies

To choose from, there are certainly a minimum of 150 food-related movies (fiction). At one time I had over 500 general movies collected but went through technology downsizing, like everyone else, going from Blockbuster, to CDs to streaming. In my food related movies I am down to about 23 movies which I would watch again without being bored. I turn them on under two standards: (a) background while I am baking and (b) exhaustion mode from baking. I tend to stray away from highbrow artsy; nothing depressing even though well filmed/acted; No cannibal horror films; and no weak plots with one meal cooked. Food /cooking must encompass the plot. I need to be entertained in the realm of what I enjoy doing most. Here are my selections (not ranked):

Big Night (1996) After this movie came out, I had friends over and made a major production in creating the Italian pasta dish known as Timpano (my effort seen above).

Mostly Martha (*Bella Martha*, 2001, German)
Babette's Feast

Like Water For Chocolate

Chocolat * The Mistress of Spices, 2005 (a fan of India's star Aishwarya Rai) * **Woman on Top**

What's Cooking?
Tortilla Soup * No Reservations * Dinner With Friends

Julie & Julia (probably played this over 100 times, my go-to background noise

Eat, Drink, Man, Woman (1994)

The Hundred-foot Journey * Tampopo * Chef

Ratatouille

Sideways and **Bottle Shock** (my wine selections)

The Founder (McDonald's story)   **Jiro Dreams of Sushi**
This is Not What I Expected (2017)

Love's Kitchen (2011)

On Television, there is a lot to choose from: the Masters Class Programs; actor Stanley Tucci in Italy, and 'Somebody Feed Phil' (Philip Rosenthal) traveling everywhere. Certainly, miss watching Anthony Bourdain. *What are your favorite movies, television shows, podcasts?*

MY COOKBOOK PASSION

CHAPTER SEVENTEEN
Final musings

One Thing Leads To Another

In 1986, a long time ago, I was in some restaurant where I was served a Dutch Baby pancake. The waitress told me how to eat it, slather with butter, squeeze fresh lemon juice, and dust with powdered sugar, then roll up and devour. I fell hungrily in love with Dutch Baby pancakes, weak in the knees even, and I wanted to bake it. So my stomach leading the way I went to Kroch and Bretanno's Bookstore in Oakbrook, Illinois looking for this particular recipe and found **"The Great Pancake Cookbook"** by George A. Zabriskie and Sherry LaFollette (Contemporary Books, Chicago, 1985, soft cover).

I bought the book, then went in search of the special 'French' pan they said was best to make it in. Where did I go? Williams-Sonoma, and this was my first time in the store because up until that moment I had never been exposed to a specialty kitchen store. Fascinated, I signed up for the catalogue and after numerous return trips where they had cookbooks as well as a wide selection of everything kitchen , and I guess my constant voicing admiration of the store caught someone's attention and I was hired. Thus, a hunger urge led to a cookbook leading to kitchen utensils, to more cookbooks that led to a job and a career!

BAKED PANCAKES DUTCH BABY

1/3 stick margarine or butter – 1 cup all purpose flour – 1 cup milk – 4 eggs

1. Preheat oven to 450° F

2. When oven is hot, put margarine in a 10-inch all-metal skillet and place in oven.

3. When margarine has melted and begins to bubble, place all remaining ingredients In blender and blend thoroughly at high speed, about a minute.

4. Open the oven just enough to pour the batter quickly into the skillet. Close and bake

About 20 minutes, or until the 'Baby' has popped up over the edge of the pan and is delicious golden brown. Serve at once with a topping of your choice. *Makes 1 10-inch pancake*

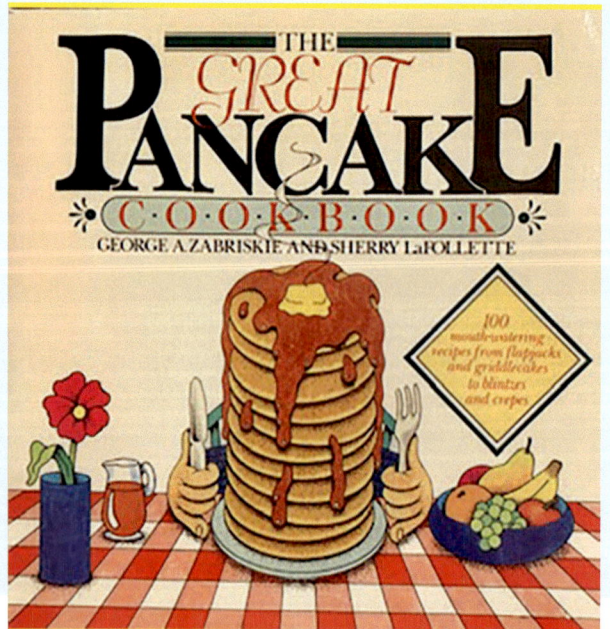

PAMELA KURE GROGAN

CHAPTER SEVENTEEN
Final musings

For My Own Satisfaction

Baking I have 25 binders filled with plastic-sleeve protected recipes that I have selected over the years from food magazines and deem as my favorites. Yet, for my own private pleasure I have moved into the world of baking, and though exploring all sorts of new cookbooks and recipes, have specialized in baking an Eastern European pastry known in Slovenia as 'potica' ('po-teet-sa'), in Croatia it's 'povitica', 'Makowiec' in Poland, 'kalács' in Hungary and 'banitsa' in Bulgaria. Last year, for the holidays, for friends and family, I made close to 700 potica rolls, walnut and poppy seed. My recent new cookbook purchases have been baking oriented. See my creative attempts at our website, www.CookbookPassion.com or at www.Facebook.com/kitchenastir/

Ingredients Ready

From the Oven

Taste Test Time

MY COOKBOOK PASSION

CHAPTER SEVENTEEN
Final musings

Food Travel

The world-wide epidemic and the writing of this book has put into hiatus my international epicurean adventures. Surprisingly, I am discovering new neighborhood and city-wide restaurant experiences.

The bags are packed and the hungry road beckons for tasty regional cuisines, untried recipes, and a cookbook purchase here or there.

Window shopping is so-oooo hard! And dangerous!

Need to get back soon—Here, I'm on a cheese tour in Paris

PAMELA KURE GROGAN

CHAPTER SEVENTEEN
Final musings

More Cookbook Passion?

Hopefully, if you spread the word and book sales do well, who knows, on the horizon might be the 'more' from my collection.

Maybe 'More' Early Historic.

Cooking In Old Creole Days (1903) By Celestine Eustis Illustrated by Harper Pennington P.F. Collier & Son, New York

Written in English and French-Creole patois *La Cuisine Créole à l'usage des Petits Ménages* – Creole cuisine for use in small households.

CHAPTER SEVENTEEN

More Cookbook Passion? Perhaps more of Chefs & Restaurants.

Between 1901 and 1910 Philadelphia publishers George W. Jacobs & Co. produced a colorful '365' cookbook series with recipes by the culinary gods of the days. The books aimed towards the elites had such titles as 365 Foreign Dishes (1908), 365 Luncheon Dishes, 365 Tasty Dishes, among several others.

My book here in excellent shape is 365 Orange Recipes (1909).

From *The Mary Frances Cook Book -- Adventures Among the Kitchen People* (1912) by Jane Eayre Fryer

PAMELA KURE GROGAN

CHAPTER SEVENTEEN
Final musings

More Cookbook Passion? Perhaps more of children cooking.

Kitchen Fun (1932) by Louise Price Bell Cover illustrations by Jesse Wilcox Smith Harter Publishing First Edition

MY COOKBOOK PASSION

CHAPTER SEVENTEEN
Final musings

Scrapbook Memories

SOUP COMMITTEE FUNCTIONS—It's 10 a.m. and the soup committee is on time. Only a few potatoes remain to be prepared for the dish, and these six second-year pupils at Adams Elementary School will soon have them ready. In the foreground may be seen the ingredients from which the tuna salad sandwiches will be prepared by the sandwich committee. It was part of a lesson on health in Mrs. Thelma Friesen's class. Left to right, the soup committee members are Roberta Walters, Malinda McCoy, Joe Kreie, Judy Wilder, Sharla Oliver and Stephan Grogan.—(Eagle Staff Photo.)

What a surprise to learn he always was a 'chef-at-heart'.
[The Editor, in kitchen class photo, far right]

PAMELA KURE GROGAN

Scrapbook Memories

Being noticed years ago--the kitchen store manager and future author: "As you have learned, I do have the culinary and Cookbook Passion!"

Pam Kure is a child in a toy store where she works.

Cook learns a thing or two from books, patrons

Mary Jo Bergland
Cook of the week

Pam Kure of Naperville was one of six children who grew up in a family with a mom who made everyone help out. She grew up never being afraid to try recipes such as strudel dough and poppy seed potica.

Several years ago, Kure ate Dutch Baby Miniature Pancakes at a restaurant. It was love at first bite. She searched cookbooks until she found the recipe and then she went shopping for the skillet. Her search for the French-made iron skillet took her to the Williams-Sonoma store in Oak Brook. Besides purchasing the iron skillet, she also landed a part-time sales job which became full time 2½ years ago. In March of this year she was made the store manager.

"Coming to work here is a hobby and a pleasure," she said. "I'm constantly learning things. I learn from cookbooks and I learn from the customers."

She cooks in a style that favors comfort foods — in other words, hearty food where you have to take a nap after eating. Kure was in her kitchen from 8:30 a.m. to 1:30 p.m. Easter day cooking breakfast. Her 17 guests left and returned for dinner at 4 p.m. (with two additional guests) for 22 pounds of Easter ham, 15 pounds of mashed potatoes, leek casserole and cream pies. "I get great satisfaction out of doing this for my family."

Kure purchased the 22-pound bone-in ham at Mitchell's Meat Market in Lockport. She glazed it with a paste of Dijon mustard and merara (a crystalized brown sugar) followed by a final paste of apricot jam and merara.

"My sister and I plan all the holidays and we start the month before. My mother really enjoys it and is flattered by the way we do things," Kure explained.

Kure said she recently moved into a Naperville house built in 1850. Imagine the combination: A kitchen with no cupboards or cabinets and a cook/owner with every dish and gadget for every kind of ethnic food. But Kure found the solution: "The closets have been converted to china cabinets and I've lots of open racks in the kitchen," she said.

Besides cookware and a collection of serving dishes, Kure also has a substantial cookbook collection of about 400 volumes. "Sometimes customers ask me about recipes: I was able to find the original red devils velvet cake recipe for a special customer."

"My favorite cookbook is Noteworthy, also Junior League cookbooks because a lot of the recipes are geared to comfort," Kure explained. The simple, hearty cooking of the Amish also appeals to Kure and she's begun collecting information about their simple and basic good food.

Polynesian Steak Kabobs is Kure's favorite back-yard grill recipe. She makes it three or four times each summer for friends and family. Powder Horn Potatoes is a hearty side dish to serve with it.

"Anybody would like this food whereas gourmet food appeals not to all people," this gourmet cooking store manager concluded.

DUTCH BABY MINIATURES
- 2 eggs
- ½ cup milk
- ½ cup flour
- 1 teaspoon vanilla
- 3 tablespoons butter

Preheat oven to 425 degrees. Blend eggs, milk, flour and vanilla with whisk to mix. Place butter in 5-inch iron skillet. Set skillet in oven and heat until butter is melted and sizzling. Pour batter into hot skillet. Bake 15 to 20 minutes. (It will puff up.) Serve with maple syrup, powdered sugar and fresh lemon juice squeezed over the top. Serves one or two.

POLYNESIAN STEAK KABOBS
- ¾ cup pineapple juice
- ¼ cup vegetable oil
- 3 tablespoons soy sauce
- 3 tablespoons brown sugar
- ¾ teaspoon ground ginger
- 1 clove garlic, fine chopped
- 2 pounds beef tenderloin, cut into 1-inch pieces
- 2 medium green peppers, cut into 1-inch square
- 18 mushroom caps
- 18 pearl onions
- 18 cherry tomatoes

Combine first six ingredients in glass dish; add beef cubes, turning to coat well. Cover; marinate overnight. Thread meat cubes onto 6 skewers alternately with peppers, mushroom, onions and tomatoes. Grill over hot coals 10 to 15 minutes. Baste frequently with remaining marinade. Serves six.

POWDER HORN POTATOES
- 10 potatoes
- ¼ cup melted butter
- 8 ounces mild Cheddar cheese, shredded
- 2 tablespoons chopped green onions or chives
- 2 cups sour cream
- Salt and pepper to taste

Preheat oven to 400 degrees. Bake potatoes in skins 40 minutes. Cool overnight.

Preheat oven to 350 degrees. Peel and grate baked potatoes. Mix butter with shredded cheese, onions, sour cream, and salt and pepper; stir into grated potatoes. Spoon into greased 2½ quart casserole. Bake 30 to 40 minutes or until lightly browned. Serves eight to 10.

For Southwestern flavor, stir in 1 small can of diced green chilies.

Enjoyment in discovering a vintage postcard to frame

Part III
A book shelf – half empty or half full?
So many books on the shelves, so few pages in this book.

The time has come. My publisher says I have run out of pages and all the books piled up haphazardly from my perusing will have to wait, my plaintive cries to no avail—"They need to see this one, no, this one, and that one, and that one."

Now, I'd be fascinated to discover what your favorite cookbooks are, nostalgic or current. How many cookbooks do you own? Is there a recipe with a special fond memory? What would you like to hear about next?

With this 'autobio-gastronomical-anthology' now available to the public you will see me increasing my social media presence, especially in hosting my active site at **Facebook.com/kitchenastir.** My brand name is kitchen a' stir defining me as a person 'in the state of excited movement'. Ask my friends--that's me! It is with this brand I intend to reach out and provide content on cooking/baking/ingredients, kitchen tools and practices, in doing so continuing to improve my own culinary skills.

As it comes to cookbooks I am still scouting for old and new ones. My primary focus in gaining new cookbooks are seeking those about baking. I am excited when I discover a well known bakery has published their cookbook. As to improving my cookbook collection I have created an associated website (www.CookbookPassion.com) for those of us with similar interest in cookbooks, vintage and present day. At both websites I offer my personal preference on what I would seek out within a book store or online sourcing. With over 2,500 cookbooks published world-wide each year, we will have a lot to talk about.

As I say good-bye for now I wish you much enjoyment for all the cookbooks you will acquire and cherish.

Savor Your Passion!
Pamela Kure Grogan

COOKING
GOOD MAINE FOOD
Clementine in the Kitchen
Blueberry Hill COOKBOOK
MEN IN APRONS
THE GUN CLUB COOK BOOK
EAT DRINK AND BE MERRY IN MARYLAND
TOASTS AND TRIBUTES
TAPAS
PENELOPE CASAS
KNOPF
THE FOODS & WINES OF SPAIN
MARGE POORE
1000 MEXICAN Recipes
A TASTE OF CUBA
AUTHENTIC MEXICAN
COOKING CARIBE
MEXICAN COOKERY
From TAPAS to MEZE
WEIR
FEASTS OF LIFE
QUINTANA
Barbara Hansen
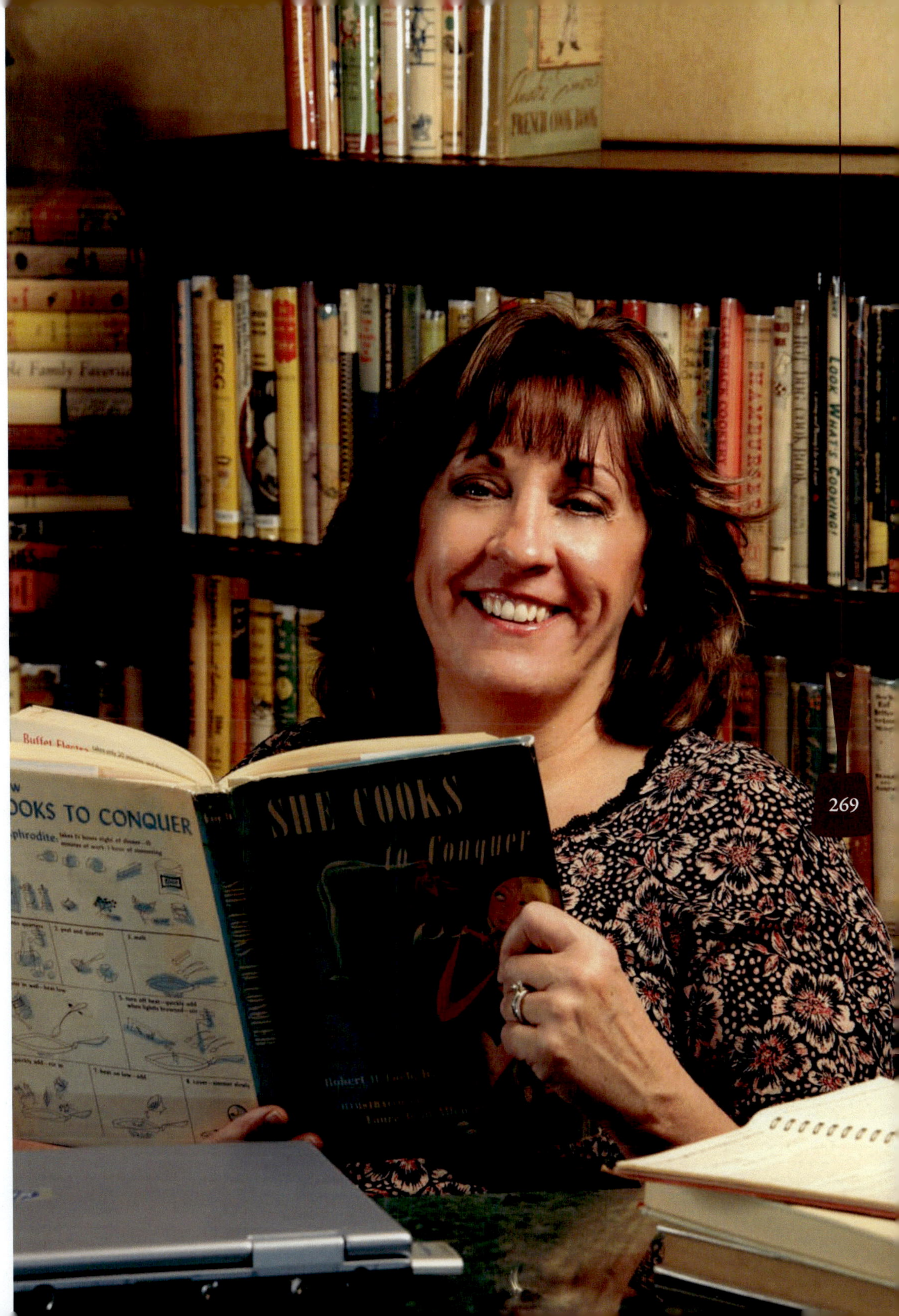
FRENCH COOK BOOK
LOOK WHAT'S COOKING!
SHE COOKS to Conquer
COOKS TO CONQUER

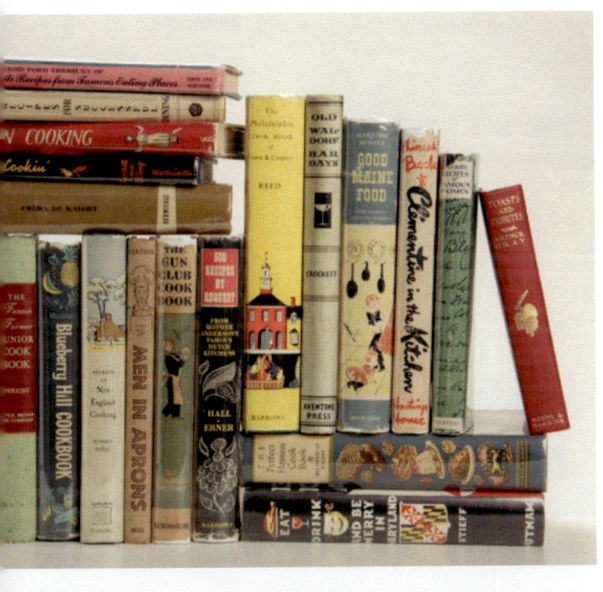

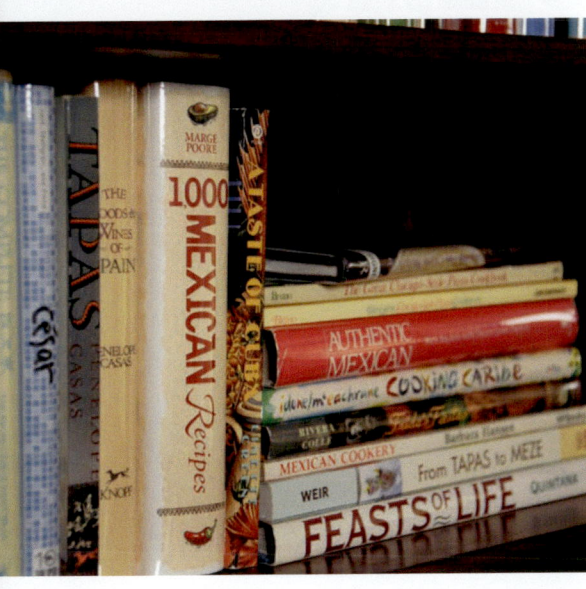

RECIPES - INDEX

PAMELA KURE GROGAN

Recipes - index

Even in our own dining room. Signed menu by Hawaiian artist John Kelly (1878-1962) from the Princess Kaiulani Hotel back when the entrée, Blue Pacific Mahimahi in Ti Leaves, was only $3.75.

MY COOKBOOK PASSION

Recipes - index

Actor-Epicurean Vincent Price autograph
Author's collection. See Pages 225-227

Central heating, French rubber goods and cookbooks are three amazing proofs of humankind's ingenuity in transforming necessity into art, and, of these, cookbooks are perhaps most lastingly delightful... M.F.K. Fisher

* Photos unless otherwise noted
by Barrett's Photography, Las Vegas

* Book Design Layout
by Silvio Sequera

Beef
Veal Carbonade page 101
Filet De Boeuf Wellington 125
Calf Liver on Skewer 140
Pot Roast with Potato Dumplings 144
Swedish Meat Balls (beef, veal, pork) 203

Chicken/Turkey/Pheasant
Liberace Breakfast (eggs) 22
Old One Hundred Chicken Pie 60
Chicken Tortola 74
Chicken Pie, Lady Baltimore 86
Chicken Cacciatora 159
Le Faisan Sovaroff (pheasant) 195
Roast Turkey with Peanut Butter 210
Paprika Chicken 226

Pork
Welsh Rabbit (bacon & cheese) 67
Baked Ham Steak Hawaiian 136

Lamb
Bolsagan Kufté (lamb stew) 153
Roast Leg of Lamb—Turkish Style 156
Gasconnade of Lamb 248

Fish & Shellfish
New Shrimp Wiggle 34
Brook Trout Gourmet 43
Pickled Opihi 64
Lobster 'Paul' 81
Clam Fritters 89
Crabmeat Monza 94
Coquille St. Jacques Parisiene (scallops) 101
Crabes Moux a la Meuniere (soft shell crabs) 126
Lobster Thermidor 137
Curried Shrimp with Bananas 138
Poached Salmon in Champagne 155
Frog Legs, Poulette 191
Billibilli 198
Rice with Shrimps 216
Lightly Fried Oysters 255

Breads
Virginia Fruit Muffins 29
Baking Powder Biscuits 61
Cherry Bread 69
Dilly Rolls 88
French Pancakes 94
Elsie's Biscuits 98
Beignets Souffles 133 (see Sauce Sabayon)
Marbury Rolls 194

PAMELA KURE GROGAN

Recipes - index

**Signed Julia Child.
Author's Collection**

Pasta & Dumplings
Fettucini Alfredo 26
Macaroni À La Chef Lugot 34
Franconia Baked Strawberry Dumplings 59 (see 'Sauce')
Potato Dumplings 145
Strukllji (rolled dumplings) 225
Cheese rolled dumplings 226

Vegetables
Apples & Onions 61
Pineapple Beets 109
French Onions & Rice 109
Southwestern Corn Scallop 110
Favorite Green Beans 115
Wilted Cucumbers 190
Pea Timbale Ring 191
Brussel Sprouts 211 with Paprika Sour Cream
Cucumbers with Sour Cream 227
Aubergines á la Arisienne 249 (eggplants)

Potatoes
Potatoes 'Anna' 80
Banana-Sweet Potato Bake 108
Potato-Macadamia Nut Puffs 110
Special Stuffed Baked Potatoes 115
Sweet Potatoes with Carmel Sauce 197

Soups
Bogie's Manhattan Clam Chowder 27
Lobster Bisque 123
Old Fashion Cream of Chicken 146
Summer Soup 200
Crab and Tomato Bisque 210
Cold Curry Soup 231
Gazpacho Andaluz 236

Salads
Special Salad 95
Oscar's Waldorf Salad 120
Cobb Salad 135
Oyster Salad 220

Appetizers/Snacks
Antipasto: Mozzarello in Carrozza 158
Hot Crabmeat Canapes 185
Ham & Mushroom 187
Cabbage for a King 187
Fonduta 242

Fruit
Hawaiian Pineapple Pickle 48
Banana Poi 65
Two in one Prune Rule 211

Jams
Oven Apple Butter 106
My Granma's Beet Jam 160

MY COOKBOOK PASSION

Recipes - index

Sauces & Dressings
- Strawberry Butter Sauce 59 (see Pasta/Dumplings)
- Green Goddess Dressing 63
- Sauce II (for fish) 72
- Barbecue Sauce #1 82
- Basic French Dressing 90
- Maintenon Sauce 120
- Sauce Sabayon 133
- Mornay Sauce 138
- Caramel Sauce 197 (with Sweet Potatoes)
- Wine Froth Sauce 203
- Tartar Sauce 256

Desserts— Cookies, Pies, Ice Cream Cakes, Candies
- Grandma Taskay's Roczki Cookies 14
- ZuSu's Chocolate Fudg 20
- Almond Marron Mousse 30
- Toll House Chocolate Cookies 57
- Pink Popcorn Balls 66
- Fresh Strawberry Mousse 69
- Cherries Jubilee 83
- Marshmallow Date Pudding 91
- Crunch Drops 91
- Mama's Rice Pudding 97
- Date Nut Bars 110
- Creamy Lime Sherbert 111
- Pioneer Potato Candy 112
- Oklahoma Brown Candy 113
- Coconut Snack Cake 116
- Salzburger Nockerl 140
- Gramma Kure's Cottage Cheese Strudel 228
- Rebecca Pudding 208
- Katish's Cheese Cake 229
- Peach Foam 233

Drinks, Cocktails, Punch
- Zombie 53
- Champagne Punch 53
- Tom & Jerry 164
- Strawberry Grape Float 165 (non-alcoholic)
- Imitation Old Tom London Gin 166
- Jersey Flashlight 167
- Charlie Chaplin 167
- Leap Year Cocktail 168
- Bees' Knees 170
- SS Manhattan 171
- Sibby's Special 172
- An Absinthe Cocktail 172
- Okolehao Punch 174
- Dowager Duchess Punch 174
- Cape Cod Collins 175
- Rosalind Russell 176
- Baltimore Eggnog 176
- Alexander the Great 176
- Crum Bum 178
- Kentucky Mint Julep 179
- The Johnson Delight 180
- Bottoms Up 182
- Rum Jubilee 181
- Fish House Punch 183
- Sorbets au Champagne 216
- Peach Foam (non alcoholic) 233

Home-made 'Rosky' before going into oven

PAMELA KURE GROGAN

Creating Steak Tartare at Chef's Demonstration, Mon Ami Gabi, Paris Hotel and Casino, Las Vegas — Here I am, always learning